Also Published

The Diary of Dr. Thomas Flint. California to Maine and Return, 1851-1855. Waterville: pagesofpages.com, 2021. 109 pages. ISBN 979-8709343993.

This diary recounts the day-to-day experiences of Thomas Flint, a young doctor from Maine, who made two trips to California between 1851 and 1854. He travelled via Panama twice (including a return to Maine with 30-some pounds of gold), and finally returning to California overland, driving 2,000 head of sheep, cattle, horses and oxen.

The main part of the diary covers the second trip to California, in 1853, overland and driving a herd of livestock though the Illinois - Nebraska - Wyoming - Utah route to California. The detailed day by day entries describe distance, difficulties with the herds, crossing rivers, encounters with American Indians, Mormons, and other groups heading west on the same trail. It is full of very specific detail - daily logs of mileage, people they encounter, expenditures, income from trading along the way, and so on. Flint wrote "my pistol, whether awake or asleep was always at my right hand."

This is a reprint of the original edition published by the Historical Society of Southern California and edited by Waldemar Westergaard. The text has been reset, and there are additional introductory materials and notes by Gary Menchen.

The Trial
Of Dr. Valorus P. Coolidge
And its Aftermath

A portrait of Coolidge, printed in Dr. James A. Spalding's "The Case of Dr. Coolidge, of Waterville, Me., 1847-1849", *Journal of the Maine Medical Association*, Vol. VIII No, 8, March, 1918. No source for the image was provided.

THE TRIAL
OF
DR. VALORUS P. COOLIDGE

AND ITS AFTERMATH

EDITED BY GARY MENCHEN

2023
pagesofpages.com
Waterville, Maine

ISBN: 979-8-9855566-6-7 (Paperback)

Copyright ©2023 by Gary Menchen

pagesofpages.com
Waterville, Maine

Contact: editor@pagesofpages.com

The image on the cover is a section of a map of Waterville, Maine published by Presdee and Edwards in 1853, and hanging in Waterville's City Hall.

Table of Contents

Foreword

The trial of Dr. Valorus P. Coolidge for the murder of Edward Mathews generated enormous interest when it was held in March of 1848. Newspapers throughout the northeastern United States sent reporters to cover the trial. The trial was relocated from the courthouse in Augusta, Maine to "Dr. Tappan's Meeting House", with seating for 1500 people. The meeting house was packed throughout the eight-day trial. It was reported that only those sitting near the front could really follow the trial. For the rest it was apparently a kind of carnival. There are numerous complaints of drunkenness and lewd behavior. The gallery of the meeting house was reserved for ladies, whose behavior was shocking to the male newspaper editors.

This story is told here via the newspaper reports of the time, but a brief summary will be useful. Edward Mathews was a young man from a well-to-do family with branches settled in Waterville and the surrounding area, and who had recently gone into business with a man from Clinton, Maine. In early September they had driven a herd of cattle down to market in Brighton, Massachusetts[1]. Mathews had come back and spent a few days in either Clinton or Waterville. On September 30th of 1847 he arranged to withdraw $1500 from the Ticonic Bank. Family members co-signed the note at the bank. After the withdrawal he went to his cousin's bookshop, took a book of legal forms, and wrote out a mortgage for personal property, telling his cousin, Charles Mathews, that he was loaning money to Dr. Coolidge, with the doctor's books as security; by "books" is meant the doctor's accounts receivable.

That evening he went to a social event at the Parker House accompanied by his cousin, Charles; he left around 8 PM, telling his cousin that he was going to Dr. Coolidge's office. He came back in a few minutes, and then again left, in the direction of the doctor's office.

The next morning, in the back of the building that housed Dr. Coolidge's office (which was on an upper floor), as well as a tailor's establishment, and other offices, Mathew's body was found - one foot visible though a partially open bulkhead door.

---

[1] Such cattle drives from Maine to Massachusetts were a common occurrence at the time, and continued even after the railroads reached central Maine. Clinton was a central collecting point for cattle to be sent to market, and raising beef cattle was a major cash industry.

1

Various wounds were visible on the body; he was recognized after someone wiped a frothy discharge off his face.

Coolidge was immediately suspected since Mathews's relatives knew of his planned meeting with Coolidge. "Committees of vigilance" were formed to search the town, but there is no mention of any action they took that did not involve either Coolidge or the immediate area of the town, which was the area where Main, Silver, Front and Water Streets came together.

On that Friday an autopsy was held in Williams's Hotel. Attending the autopsy were Drs. Coolidge, Thayer, Plaisted, Professor Loomis of Waterville (now Colby) College, and medical student Thomas Flint. There were numerous other people in the room. Coolidge was asked to conduct the autopsy, as either the most skilled at dissection, or the youngest physician (different sources give different reasons). The doctors all agreed that wounds on the skull were sufficient to cause death. In the course of the autopsy, Coolidge removed the stomach, which was placed in a basin - it smelled strongly of brandy, and Coolidge suggested it be taken from the room so as to not "scent the place." Williams, the owner of the establishment, took the basin out, and put it behind a barrel at the back side of an outbuilding. Early next morning he placed it in an empty outbuilding which he locked. Later in the morning he gave it to Prof. Loomis, who would conduct tests on it that revealed the presence of prussic acid, a deadly poison.

A coroner's jury had been immediately convened in Waterville. There Coolidge testified to Mathews borrowing money from him rather than the other way around. Thomas Flint testified that he had been in Coolidge's office, with Coolidge, late in the evening, looking up cases in medical books. He had not seen Mathews and knew nothing about his death. Coolidge's testimony was recorded for his signature; early reports indicted that Flint's "merely negative" testimony was not recorded, but counsel for the defense did introduce it towards the end of testimony.

At a grand jury convened in Augusta on October 7th, Thomas Flint changed his story - he now said that on the evening of the 30th, Dr. Coolidge came over to the Williams's Hotel, where he (and Coolidge) boarded, and asked him to go back with him to the office. There he showed Flint Mathews body, told him that Mathews had grabbed the wrong flask, taken a drink of prussic acid, and fallen down dead. He had thumped him a few times on the head to make it look like an assault. After considering various ways to dispose of the body they carried it downstairs into the basement and put it on top of a woodpile. By changing his story Flint was in effect admitting to perjury before the Coroner's jury, and to assisting in the coverup of a crime, although he could plausibly say that at the time he was before the Coroner's jury he had believed Coolidge's story and did not think it murder.

The trial, from jury selection to its final statements, lasted 8 days. The prosecution endeavored to show that Coolidge was an active borrower of money, and in financial difficulties. They go to extraordinary lengths on this, calling not just witnesses who were owed money by Coolidge, but also apparently anyone who had ever loaned him money, even if long ago repaid. They even had testimony from a Professor at Waterville (now Colby) College who had called on Coolidge to ask for a donation to the school and been put off. Certainly Coolidge was an active "hirer" of money, but he also had a very successful and growing medical practice. It seems generally agreed that the prosecution failed to show that financial difficulties were a motive. They proved he owed a few thousand dollars, howev er the defense was able to show that Coolidge carried on his books as due to him significantly more than that, and in fact there was testimony that in just a single day his agents had collected $1600 from those of his patients in the immediate vicinity of Waterville who had ready access to cash.

As far as prussic acid was concerned, the prosecution showed that Coolidge had it, that he had recently placed two orders for more of it, one from Hallowell and another from Boston, asking for it in its strongest form. And that no other physicians in Waterville seemed to make much or any use of it. The defense's reply to that was that Coolidge kept more medicines than other physicians, and that he was a progressive physician. A witness for the government testified that all the best physicians in Boston made use of it. There was some testimony that the very strong kind of prussic acid could be used to treat eye disease, but that was never really developed. The defense, however, had another answer to this issue, which was that the stomach contents were stored in a basin, unprotected, outdoors over night, and who could say what might have happened to those contents during that period of time. And why was the very distinctive odor of the acid not noticed by the physicians present during the autopsy?

The government also provided minute testimony of witnesses who saw Coolidge or Flint walking up or down the street in the afternoon or evening - but those sightings might have been made on any date when they were in town. A witness for the prosecution was called to testify that, at about the time of the murder, he was on the street opposite the doctor's office, and his dog howled strangely. Defense had some fun with that.

In general, the evidence as to financial difficulties was inadequate. The reports that Mathews had said he was going to Coolidge's office were important, but the real basis of the prosecution was the testimony of Flint, the former medical student. Flint, who is probably the most interesting person involved with the trial, held up to a long cross examination[2], and presented believable testimony. He was, however, a confessed perjurer, and if he had been tried and convicted of perjury his testimony could not have been allowed.

At the trial, Coolidge was found guilty, and sentenced to one year of solitary confinement at Thomaston State Prison, after which he was to be hung - if the Governor signed a warrant for the execution. There was strong sentiment throughout much of the country against capital punishment and the prosecutor more or less insinuated that any execution would not be carried out. The Governor did eventually commute Coolidge's sentence to life imprisonment

After that commutation, the oddest part of the whole story commenced. In May of 1849, the Warden of the prison announced that it had been discovered that Coolidge had been in communication with the outside world, and that a plot had been discovered to have Flint murdered and framed for Mathew's murder by leaving a forged letter of confession next to the body. This murder was to be done by another prisoner who was soon to be released. When confronted with the evidence of his plot, Coolidge collapsed, and died a day later. The prison physician, with another physician who was an overseer of the prison[3], held an autopsy, and found that he had "died in a fit, brought on by extreme mental depression, and the general prostration of the

---

[2] 2 hours direct examination, 3 hours cross examination. The press made much of his self-possession.

[3] Benjamin Buxton, later a president of the Maine Medical Association.

4

whole nervous system, caused by the sudden frustration of his long fostered hope."

This plot was absurd in the extreme. There are very long and detailed instructions ("Proceed direct to Bangor, buy a pair of green specs".) The prisoner is to become acquainted with Flint. He is to learn Flint's handwriting so that he can forge a very long letter of confession, that is to be supposed to be by Flint. He is to give his name as "Cathew E.I. Moolidge", and get Flint to write it, so that he will have most of Mathews's and Coolidge's names in Flint's handwriting.

The "letter of confession" to be written in Flint's hand is two thousand words long. One would expect forgers to attempt some concision. And it reads like a parody. Flint, in the supposed letter, is made to write of Coolidge's

> beauty of person · his *lovely countenance* and his *sweet voice* · his *noble* heart · his amiable *disposition* · his superior skill, and the fair prospect [...]

The plot and the letters were reportedly discovered because Coolidge had needlessly shared them with another prisoner, not the confederate, but a young prisoner confined to his cell due to illness. If this is true · and taking into consideration the original murder of Mathews · then Coolidge had to have been the most incompetent plotter in the world.

Both the letter and the instructions · an additional 2500 words · were printed in full in newspapers throughout the country, and are included in this volume. The level of literacy is not high. When it was first published, the editor of the primary report, published in the Lime Rock Gazette, noted "he was sadly deficient in language and orthography, and seemed entirely ignorant of the philosophy of condensation.[4]" To take the plot, the instructions and the "letter of confession" at face value is to believe that they were written by the same person who had, a year earlier, published a succinct and technical article in the Boston Medical and Surgical Journal.

After the death there were immediate suspicions that Coolidge had not really died, and that a body had been substituted for his. A physician, Amos Mann (not a "regular" physician), who had a long history of controversies with the

---

[4] A very curious or perhaps ironic use of the term. "Philosophy of Condensation" comes from a pre-socratic philosopher's attempts to describe the origin of the physical world.

medical establishment, and with his own newspaper to promote his theories, was the main proponent of the charge that Coolidge had actually escaped. Coolidge's remains were dug up several times, sometimes affirming that it was Coolidge, sometimes that it was not. Coolidge's father signed a deposition that his son had one thumb that was much shorter than the other, and that the corpse had two thumbs the same size. One thing is clear, this question was of intense interest, and large crowds came to view a weeks-old, unembalmed, corpse.

And finally, after the reports of death, there were sightings of Coolidge in various parts of the country, by people who had "known him well" in Waterville. First in Anson, Maine, a report that no one seems to have paid attention to. In late 1849 he was reported to have been seen in California, with two companions, looking very "rough", a story carried by newspapers throughout the country. In 1879 as the leader of a gang that robbed trains in Iowa; then 1892 a woman in California reported that she had nursed Coolidge in an illness, and that he had died of small pox in 1852. There are other stories with other dates.

Many of these stories are given here as they were printed in contemporary newspapers.

When considering a trial that was held more than 150 years ago, one can form an opinion about whether the person tried was guilty or not, but such an opinion is simply conjecture. Unless entirely new evidence is discovered, all that can be really known today is how events were reported and published at the time they occurred. There are several mysteries about this case that stimulate speculation, though - and they did at the time as well.

First: Coolidge was a very successful physician; he had graduated from Dartmouth Medical School in 1844, purchased a practice in Waterville, and was very popular. He was of good character; that was testified to over and over in the court, and was not contested by the government. All innuendos about gambling and women were made after the trial, and with no details. They look very like a combination of jealousy and after-the-fact reaching for a motive. For example, the Boston Medical and Surgical Journal had published an article written by Coolidge himself, describing an autopsy he performed, in the company of Prof. Loomis, doctors Thayer and Boutelle, and a medical student. Subsequently the journal published very brief notices of the trial and conviction, all of which are included here in an appendix. The last notice was undoubtedly supplied by a local physician and looks very like jealousy.

He has not the look of a murderer, neither has the appearance of much genius or talent. His face and form look as if he might have been a ladies man. And this quality, no doubt, carried him along in his profession more successfully than any deep science or great skill.

The second mystery is the letter of confession that was to be forged in the name of Thomas Flint, and the instructions to an unnamed confederate. Both are absurd in the extreme. To me they read like a parody.

A related mystery is the way Coolidge's death was reported by the warden, Benjamin Carr. Papers revealing a plot to murder the chief witness against him, Thomas Flint, were said to have been handed in to authorities by a young prisoner to whom Coolidge had given them "to read". This prisoner is never identified. The supposed confederate is also not identified, until many years later, and then is said to be a prisoner who was not due for release for another four or five months, and who was also the source of the letters. No one other than the unidentified writer of the "Only Full and Authentic Account Published" ever seems to have seen these documents. A leading sceptic of the time, Dr. Amos Mann, offered a $500[5] reward for the identification of either of the prisoners, or for the original documents. There were no takers. There is never a subsequent mention of the "young prisoner" who had revealed the plot.

Related to the way the report of the death was handled is the autopsy on Coolidge, which concluded that he died from a fit brought on by depression. This received several severe criticisms from contemporary physicians, including one from a classmate of the physician who performed the autopsy, who wrote that it was so grossly incompetent that he was now convinced that Coolidge was still alive. To further muddy the waters, a visitor to the prison in 1851 who visited Coolidge's cell, was told that Coolidge had been hung. And then, more than forty years later, two men who had been employed at the prison while Coolidge was there (one of whom, many years later and after a distinguished career, became warden himself) said Coolidge was undoubtedly poisoned, and that the papers were received directly from the proposed confederate, with no mention of any "young prisoner".

---

[5] Nearly $20,000 in 2023 dollars.

Next is the question of Coolidge's body. After burial it was dug up at least three times. Coolidge's father signed a deposition that the body in the grave could not have been his son, because one of his son's thumbs was missing a joint, and the corpse had two normal thumbs - as well as other significant physical differences. Other near neighbors who had known him all his life signed similar statements. This was convincing even to contemporary skeptics, such as the editor of the Gospel Banner, who remained certain Coolidge had died in prison - his conclusion was that the body had been switched.

As for the sightings of Coolidge in after years - any possibility that they were real is dependent upon one's view of the earlier issues described above. If there had been no absurd plot - or if the papers in Coolidge's handwriting had ever been viewed by any third party - if there had been a sound autopsy and cause of death reported - if his father had been able to identify his son's body based on known marks on the body - then any possibility that Coolidge was seen in California or Iowa or anyplace else would never have been considered.

Most of the contents that follow are taken directly from newspapers of the time. The report of the trial itself is a merger of various reports, including those published in pamphlet form by the Boston Daily Advertiser and the Northern Tribune, as well as the reports in the weekly newspapers the Portland Advertiser, the Eastern Mail, and the Maine Farmer. All the accounts varied from sections that appear to be literal transcripts to paraphrases and briefer summaries; sometimes first person, sometimes third person. One can imagine the labor involved in trying to capture all the speeches and testimony without the use of shorthand, and to complete the reports in time to meet the newspapers' submission deadlines. The reporter for the Eastern Mail, fifty years later, gave a brief interview to an Augusta paper describing some of the difficulties he encountered, which is included here. In general I try to select the most detailed accounts. In most cases the Northern Tribune, of Bath Maine, which was a daily newspaper, had the fullest accounts.

For the events from before and after the trial itself, each source is identified where it appears, and is printed as it originally appeared.

A Murder Is Discovered

On October 7th, 1847, the *Eastern Mail*, a weekly newspaper published in Waterville, and edited by Ephraim Maxham, printed, in the middle of page two, among its usual mixture of stories, poetry, brief news items copied from other newspapers, updates on the Mexican War, and the occasional bit of local news, the following.

The following, in substance, was issued on a slip[1] from this office on Monday:

Shocking Murder in Waterville

Between seven and eight o'clock on Friday morning last, the dead body of Mr. Edward Mathews was found in the rear of Mr. Shorey's Clothing Store, Pray's Building, Main street, under circumstances which indicated beyond question that he had been murdered and robbed. There were several severe wounds on the head, some marks of violence on the throat, and a cut across the thigh near the groin, apparently made in cutting open the pantaloons pocket.

The body was found lying just within the door of a bulk-head entrance to the store-cellar, where it had probably been thrown by the murderer, as there was no indication that the deed was committed where the body was found.

On inquiry it was ascertained that Mr. Mathews had on his person, at nine o'clock the evening previous, fifteen or eighteen hundred dollars, and a gold watch, for which, no doubt, the murder was committed.

A jury of inquest was summoned as soon as a coroner could be obtained from a neighboring town, which has continued in session to the present time, and may sit for some days.

We forbear, for the present, giving any of the thousand stories and surmises which are afloat, or anything that has been developed, so far as has been made public, before the jury. Strange facts are said to have been disclosed, but under present circumstances we can rely upon nothing so far as to make it public. No arrest has yet been made, though it need not be concealed that suspicion is very decided in its direction.

---

[1] The O.E.D. defines "slip" as an obsolete newspaper term meaning "A newspaper (or part of one) printed in the form of a long slip of paper". Maxham uses the term repeatedly in subsequent articles on the case. Different newspapers shared information by sending each other "slips".

The stomach of the deceased was taken out and its contents committed to scientific gentlemen for examination, upon suspicion that he has[sic] been drugged. Of their testimony we know nothing, except by report, which says that is contents gave symptoms of prussic acid.

The deceased was a son of the late Simeon Mathews of this place, and brother of William Mathews of Boston, editor of the Yankee Blade, with whom he was recently associated in the publication of that paper. His mother, sisters, a brother, and extensive family relatives, reside here. He was a young man of enterprise, and highly esteemed, and was in partnership with Mr. Soule, of Clinton, in a store at that place. He came from Clinton to Waterville on Thursday morning, for the purpose of completing certain negotiations relative to the money of which he was robbed; $1,500 of which he took from the bank during that day. He was seen by numerous individuals, and at various places, between 7 and 9 o'clock, on Thursday evening.

The funeral took place yesterday afternoon, at the Universalist church, and was attended by a very large assembly.

This dreadful affair has thrown a gloom over our village, which it is feared will only be increased by further developments.

About ten o'clock Monday morning, a part of the money - report says about $150 - and the watch, were found in the shed of Mr. Williams's Hotel, a few rods from where the body was found.

The verdict of the jury was rendered last evening - that the deceased came to his death by poison, or by blows inflicted on the head, or by both - by person or persons unknown. Further investigation, as we learn, was to be had before the Grand Jury yesterday, at Augusta, the result of which is not yet known.

The poison detected in the stomach was prussic acid, which appeared to have been administered with brandy, a quantity of which was also found in the stomach. This poison, it is known, produces almost instantaneous convulsions, terminating in death sometimes in four or five minutes. Circumstances indicated that the blows were inflicted after death - perhaps to conceal the agency of poison.

That the murder was not committed in the street, or on the ground, was indicated by the absence of mud or dirt on the boots or clothes. There was no appearance of the body having lain or been dragged on the ground, or any scuffle or struggle in the vicinity of the place where it was deposited. There was strong evidence of strangling by the grapple of a hand upon the throat and the clothes doubt the waist were drawn upward, as if it has been lifted by passing an arm or a rope around it.

We do not learn that there is any evidence to direct suspicion upon any one out of Waterville, or any good reason to think that the murderer is not among our own citizens. Suspicion - it need not be concealed, · rests upon a single individual, heretofore held in high esteem: but in the opinion of those best qualified to judge, there is not sufficient grounds to warrant any very decided opinion.

The Jury of Inquest was composed of the following individuals, summoned by coroner Shaw of China: Col. E. H. Scribner, Joseph Marston 2d, Oliver Paine, Wm. Goulder, S. Percival, D. Moor, Jr.

This announcement, sandwiched between the by-laws of a proposed agricultural fair and a report on the nominations of the Democratic and Whig parties in Massachusetts for Governor, was the first local notice of an affair that would eventually be reported on in newspapers across the country, inspire bad poetry, provide fodder for controversary continuing for decades, reach the pages of the *Journal of the Maine Medical Association* in 1917, and to this day spark an occasional paragraph in local publications. Full reports of the trial were published by a multitude of newspapers, the trial was reportedly attended by reporters from as far away as New York City and Philadelphia, it became a staple of surveys of notable American criminal trials, and provides a glimpse, narrow but in depth, of life in a Maine town a few years prior to the arrival of the railroad.

Preparing for the Trial

Suspicion immediately fell on Dr. Valorus P. Coolidge, and that continued over the next few weeks. Thomas Flint, one of Coolidge's three medical students at that time, who had testified before the coroner's jury to knowing nothing of Mathews's death, changed his story.

Eastern Mail Oct 14 1847.

Since our last number was issued, disclosures have been made, which put to rest all question as to the real murderer of young Mathews. · Strong suspicion had previously rested on Dr. V. P. Coolidge, of Waterville, from the following circumstances, developed before the jury of inquest. It was shown that Mathews had told his partner in Clinton that he had an opportunity to realize a very large profit on $1500 for a few days, if he could raise the money for a friend; and finally gave the name of Dr. Coolidge; adding that he proposed getting his uncle, John Mathews, to sign a note to the bank for that sum. On the following day he asked his uncle to sign the note, who declined, unless informed of the circumstances. He told him privately that the money was for Dr. Coolidge, who offered notes and accounts for security, and a bonus of $400 for the use of the money ten days · adding the strongest injunction of secrecy, as the same had been enjoined on him by Coolidge.

As Mathews had been last seen entering Coolidge's office, inquiry was made of him in regard to the negotiation about the money, when he denied all knowledge of it, and protested that he had loaned Mathews $200 the previous evening, for some private purpose.

The fact that the money was raised for Coolidge was so fully established, that this denial immediately fixed suspicion on him as the murderer. The result of the analyzation of the contents of the stomach tended to strengthen this suspicion.

Immediately after the verdict of the jury of inquest, the subject was carried before the Grand Jury, at Augusta, and the testimony, as far as previously obtained, was in process of examination, when a development of the whole matter was announced from another source, which leaves no room for further doubt, that Dr. Coolidge is the author of the dreadful murder.

For nearly two years past Mr. Thomas Flint, a son of Hon. W. R. Flint, of Somerset Co., has been a student of medicine in Dr. C.'s office. He had admitted being in the office in the evening, after young Mathews was known to enter it, and though he denied all knowledge of the murder, in his examination before the inquest, there was a suspicion, that regard for his friend and teacher had prevented his disclosing what he knew on the subject.

Young Flint had three times sent for his father, after the murder, but the message was repeatedly intercepted, and Senator Flint received the information only in time to arrive in Waterville on Thursday morning, and after consulting his friends in regard to all the circumstances, took his son to a private room at Williams's Hotel, and requested a full disclosure of whatever he might know relative to the murder. The father's course was successful. A full disclosure was made, and on the following morning Senator Flint proceeded to Augusta, and took measures for bringing his son's testimony before the grand jury. A 3 o'clock P. M. on Friday, officers Norris, Nudd, and Miller arrived in Waterville, took Dr. Coolidge into custody, and proceeded to Augusta, where he was committed to prison the same night.

The following is the testimony of young Flint; which we have taken pains to obtain from the most reliable source:

About 9 o'clock, on the evening of the murder, Dr. Coolidge came to the door of the room in which young Flint was sitting, at Williams's Hotel, and asked him to accompany him to the office, which was but a few steps distant. They went together into the office, which consisted of two large rooms, front and rear, on the second floor. After entering the front room, Coolidge locked the door, and immediately told Flint that he was going to reveal to him a mystery in which his life was involved; - he then proceeded to say, that Mathews came in a short time before - that he gave him a glass of brandy to drink, and he immediately fell in an apoplectic fit, and was lying in the other room. He said the affair would ruin them if the body was found in the office, and he had called him in to aid in disposing of it.

Various plans were then suggested for secreting the body. It was proposed to leave it in the street, and also to cast it into the river. It was thought the night was not dark enough to venture being seen in taking it to the river, and it was deposited where it was found. Coolidge was occupied a considerable portion of the night in secreting the money, and removing evidences of the deed. At four o'clock in the morning he started for Winslow to visit a patient.

Flint knew nothing of this money till after the return of Coolidge, when he was told he obtained $1800, which had been secreted under the carpet, beneath an iron safe. Flint, afterwards, at the persuasion of Coolidge, removed it, and deposited a part of it where it was found, in Williams's shed, and another part in another place; but ultimately put the whole · except the roll found · into a small jug in the office. Coolidge at last insisted the whole should be burnt, and Flint broke the jug, and burnt the money. He had not at any time counted it, and knew not whether the whole $1800 was burnt, but he thinks it was.

In regard to the real nature of young Flint's connection with this tragedy, there is no diversity of opinion among those who have carefully and candidly weighed all the circumstances. No one presumes he had the least suspicion of the murder till after it was committed. His error was in yielding to help conceal it. · His desire was to save life rather than be made an instrument in destroying it. Till he learnt the fact in regard to the money, he doubtless believed the death of Mathews had occurred as Coolidge had stated. He had then proceeded so far, that the constant solicitation of Coolidge for aid, added to his strong anxiety to save the life of his friend prevented his breaking away from the wrong course he was pursuing. When he first entered the room, he was both ignorant and innocent of any wrong. All he did afterwards proceeded from too strong attachment to a teacher whom he had long known and loved.

Coolidge was doubtless fearful he would relent and disclose the truth, and resorted to every artifice to involve him as deeply as possible in the affair, in order to prevent his doing so. It is easy to imagine how an artful and wicked man might affect such a purpose. He even endeavored to persuade him to secrete the money in his own trunk! · and repeatedly told him that in the event of detection, they were both implicated in the murder beyond any hope. After the first wrong step, where was the point on which to turn? A refusal to take that step, as there is strong reason to suspect, would have cost him his life? · He who had so coolly committed one murder would not have hesitated to commit another to prevent an exposure of his crime.

Young Flint proceeded from step to step, till the prompt and honorable course of his father snatched him from the most imminent danger. His error was a great one, and involved a great wrong to community but it is easier to suggest a different course, than to pursue it, under all the circumstances of this case.

The public will judge for themselves, · but we cannot forbear suggesting a close regard to extenuating circumstances. Very imprudent we admit he was, but guilty only of too great zeal to save his friend. His error came rather from an over kind than a wicked heart. Those who judge him in so important a matter, should do it with the candor due to one who has up to this time, exhibited an amiable disposition and lovely character, and who has had a very high place in the esteem of those who knew him best.

There are probably few instances in which the murder of a single individual has involved so many in deep and enduring distress, as in this case. The immediate relatives of Mr. Mathews are numerous; and to his widowed mother, especially, the affliction is overwhelming. Dr. Coolidge has a father and other relatives residing in the State, to whom his growing reputation and prospects were justly a subject of pride. The father arrived in Waterville shortly after his son departed on his way to prison. He proceeded to Augusta, and had an interview with his son in prison. We are told by one who saw him, that he seemed completely prostrated by the blow. And through the error - it is hard to say crime - of young Flint, a large and lovely family are deeply afflicted. Though they may readily acquit him of guilt, they must anticipate that a rigid public will be less generous - it always is. This community, notwithstanding the excitement against the criminal, have a deep sympathy with those who have been involved in undeserved suffering.

____

The analyzation of the contents of the stomach of the murdered Mathews was very successfully and satisfactorily effected by Professor Loomis, of Waterville College. The presence of prussic acid was established beyond question, by four distinct, independent tests. It has been reported that a portion of the contents were sent to Brunswick to be analyzed. This is not correct. There was no necessity for doing so. Probably no man could conduct such an experiment with more certainty than Prof. Loomis.

There is clearly some special pleading on the behalf of "young" Flint. Flint was not that young - he was 22 years of age, just a few years younger than Coolidge, and he had perjured himself before the coroner's inquest, a serious crime. His testimony, however, was going to be vital for the prosecution, providing the only direct evidence against Coolidge.

Flint's testimony in court is quite close to the testimony above, from before the grand jury in Augusta. The report of three letters sent to his father having been intercepted is not corroborated anywhere else, and seems to imply that Coolidge or his allies somehow were able to prevent the letters from reaching his father. The idea of letters being intercepted seems doubtful.

Trial of Dr. Valorus P. Coolidge

Morning Star (Limerick, Maine) Oct 20, 1847.This newspaper was reprinting from the Bath Tribune; published on Friday Oct 20, we can assume that "Friday last" refers to October 13th.

THE WATERVILLE MURDER · ARREST OF DR. COOLIDGE.

Dr. Coolidge, the individual on whom suspicions of the murder of Mr. Mathews have rested ever since the body was found, was arrested at Waterville on Friday, by an officer despatched by Attorney-General Moore, with a warrant for that purpose, having understood that Flint, the Doctor's student, was about to disclose, and fearing that Coolidge might learn the fact and escape before an indictment could be found. The Grand Jury found a bill against the Doctor that afternoon.

Flint's story, we understand from several sources, is as follows: · That Coolidge came to him at Williams's tavern, on the evening of the murder, and requested him to go and find a certain book which he had been using. On entering the office he found Mathews dead. Coolidge said he had drank a glass of brandy and died in a fit, and he must help get him out of the office. Flint at first refused, but Coolidge said if he was found there, folks would think he had been murdered by them that they must carry him out, and they would think he had been murdered by others; that he had given him two blows on the head, to carry on the deception. Flint assisted in carrying him down the back stairs to the rear of the building where he was found, and then left. After the search for the money, the Doctor gave him $1500 of it, and ordered him to burn it, which he did. It had previously been concealed under the carpet, directly under the Doctor's safe. This, we believe, is the amount of Flint's testimony, as we gather it from hearsay. We may be incorrect in some particulars.

It seems that Coolidge had requested Mathews to get him $1500 to $2000 for a short time, and promised him a bonus of $400 for the use of it, with a bill of sale of his books and accounts for security, but requested him not to tell any one of it. Mathews did, however, inform his uncle and cousin, who signed the note at the bank with him for the money, that he was going to let it to Coolidge. The money was drawn from the bank on Thursday, the day of the murder. On Thursday evening, Mathews was at a party, composed of young people, at Doer's tavern[1], and left, saying that he was going to the doctor's office to transact some business with him. He was afterwards seen conversing with two students on the sidewalk, and nothing more seen of him until he was found murdered in the morning.

The body was not so bruised and mangled as our first report represented, although the statement of the deep cuts and blows on

---

[1] Also referred to as the Parker House.

16

the head were correct. The fact that the wounds did not have the appearance of having bled, led to the belief that he was dead before they were given. Suspicions of poison were thereby excited, which led to the examination of the stomach and an analyzation of its contents, which, it is understood, confirmed those suspicions - rendered it certain that he came to his death by prussic acid.

Dr. Coolidge has heretofore born a good character, was enjoying an extensive practice, and is said to have seven or eight thousand dollars on his books. He is somewhere about twenty-six years old, we believe, and unmarried. It is thought his trial will be deferred until the excitement has somewhat abated. - Bath Tribune.

Over the following weeks there were just occasional references to the murder. On October 28th there was the report of a discovery of an order for prussic acid that the doctor had sent to Boston, and which was made much of during the trial.

Oct 28th, 1847 -The Waterville Murder, Again. On the 13th inst., Wyman B. S. Moor, Attorney General of Maine, wrote a letter to Marshall Tukey, of this city, in which, after stating that Dr. V. P. Coolidge had been indicted for the murder of Edward Mathews, of Waterville, and that there was amongst his papers, a bill from Joseph Burnett, of Boston, for one ounce of Concentrated Hydrocianic Acid, and it being supposed that the Doctor had written a special order for it, he requested that it be procured if possible. Accordingly a search was ordered, which resulted in finding a latter from Dr Coolidge to Mr. Burnett, in which among other things ordered was 'one ounce of Hydrocianic Acid, *strong as it can be.*' The letter was dated Waterville, Sept. 19th, and directed to Joseph Burnett, 33 Tremont street, Boston. — *Boston Traveller.*

On November 14th they reprinted from the Yankee Blade (a publication edited by Edward Mathews's brother) a letter relating to Coolidge's explanations for why he wanted money.

Nov. 18, 1847. - It will be remembered that in the first account published respecting the murder of Mr. Mathews, at Waterville, a statement of Dr. Coolidge was embodied to the effect that he wanted money to send to Dr. J. F. Potter, at Cincinnati, to enable him to prosecute certain speculations of his to advantage. This assertion has subsequently been proved to be false, and the following letter, written by Dr. Potter, contains an emphatic denial of the statement. Through probably not intended for publication, we have thought it best to lay it before our readers, as an act of justice to the party interested. · *Yankee Blade.*

Mr. Mathews, · Dear Sir: The account of the murder of your brother, as given in the Blade of the 16th, and copied into the papers of this city, places my name in an unfavorable position in a community of strangers, and appears to be a subject of some comment among my new acquaintances. With regard to the statement made by Dr. C. in reference by myself, I have only to say it does not contain the first syllable of truth. As the correspondence of that unfortunate young man must now be in your possession, you can easily satisfy yourself as to the falsity of his statement. I hope you will find it convenient to place the affair before your readers in its true light.

There is much sympathy and pain expressed here by your acquaintances and friends.

I am, dear, sir, very respectfully,

J. F. Potter

While there was reference to Coolidge's having told people he wanted money for speculation with Dr. Potter, Potter's refutation above was never mentioned during the trial · probably such a letter was simply not eligible to be put into evidence.

On December 23rd, there is a report of someone going around the county canvassing opinions about the Coolidge case.

Caution. It is understood that an individual is traveling about this county, and is probably now in this town, making certain enquiries in regard to the case of Dr. V. P. Coolidge, and apparently with the purpose of ascertaining the opinions of Jurors drawn for the trial of that case. Such an interference with the course of public justice it is believed is unjustifiable. A conversation, conducted as it might be by such an agent, might lead to the formation or declaration of opinions in regard to the matter to be tried on the part of the jurors drawn, which would give an unwarrantable advantage to the accused, and greatly embarrass the proceedings at the trial. Persons drawn as jurors, and all others would do well to avoid holding any conversation with that agent, (whose name we are told is Greenleaf,) which would in any way indicate opinions in regard to capital punishment generally, or in regard to the guilt or innocency of Dr. Coolidge, who it is well known is soon to be tried on an indictment found against him at the late session of the Court in this County.

It is notable that none of the jurors questioned from the jury pool were from Waterville or adjacent towns.

The *Eastern Mail* had the most complete coverage of the first attempt to hold the trial, in January.

January 27ᵗʰ, 1848 · Trial of Dr. Coolidge. The Supreme Court commenced a special session at Augusta on Tuesday last, of the trial of Dr. V. P. Coolidge for the murder of Edward Mathews.

The Court met at the court-house at 10 o'clock, but immediately adjourned to Dr. Tappan's church which had been fitted up for the occasion.

At 20 minutes before eleven the prisoner was conducted into the court by Dept. Sheriffs Nudd and Stinchfield. His dress was very similar to that in which he appeared among us a few months ago. In fact there was nothing in dress or appearance to distinguish him, unless it be the rich fur cap by which he was known in Waterville, last winter. He seemed perhaps rather dejected, though perfectly calm. He entered the prisoner's box without any apparent emotion · laid his cap upon a small table before him · took off his overcoat, placed it upon the back of his chair, and sat down. He very composedly rested his head upon his hand, and sat most of the time in that position, not gazing around the room, yet so situated that he could see all that was transpiring.

An appropriate prayer was then offered by Dr. Tappan, during which the prisoner with the rest of the audience stood. During this exercise we could perceive no indication emotion in the prisoner, even while direct allusion was made to him. He seems to have power of absolute control over those movements of expression in the face, which in most persons are completely involuntary.

In the course of the prayer, Dr. Tappan alluded to the blessings of civil government · to the rights which it protects · to the healthful restraints which it imposes · and to the wanton disregard of these rights and restraints in the act for which the prisoner was arraigned. He then implored the Divine blessings upon the judges, the witnesses, the jury, and finally upon the prisoner.

The counsel for the Government then stated to the court that everything had been done on their part which could have been done to be in readiness for the trial · but that an important · an all important witness was not present on account of sickness, and that a competent Physician had been dispatched to ascertain the facts. The government requested that time might be allowed for the Physician to return, before moving for a *copias* to compel the witnesses' attendance.

In the meantime the clerk called the roll of the jurors, and all answered to their names · one hundred having been drawn.

Dr. Hill then entered the court, and stated under oath, that in his opinion the illness of Cyrus Williams, of Waterville, was such that he could not safely be removed to Augusta, and he declined to fix upon any day when in his opinion he would be so far recovered that he could be present to give his testimony. The government then proposed to the defense to agree to certain points to which it was understood that the witness in question would testify. The Defense, however declined, and the Government thereupon moved an adjournment. After some further deliberation the court consented to an adjournment, dismissed the jurors, with a strict charge to avoid conversation on the subject of the guilt or innocence of the prisoner, expressing an opinion in the case, or allowing themselves to come to the knowledge of any facts which would tend to establish an opinion, and finally appointed the 2nd Tuesday of March next for the Trial.

Excerpts from the Portland Transcript provide additional detail.

Portland Transcript Jan 29, 1849, excerpted.
Mr. Paine[2], addressing the court, said that a vacancy having occurred in the office of Attorney General, the responsibility for prosecuting this trial had devolved upon him; and in order to be better able to discharge the unusual duties thus imported upon him, he had associated with him Lot M. Morrell, Esq., a member of this bar. He said that Subpoenas had been served upon all persons who should attend as witnesses. Among those subpoenaed, was *Cyrus Williams*, of Waterville. The proper return had been made, showing that regular notice had been served. But last night information was received, that the witness was indisposed, and had been so for several days, so much so, that it was not deemed safe for him to incur the exposure of appearing here this day; and perhaps he would not be able to attend during the week. The prosecuting Attorney immediately despatched a competent physician to examine the condition of the witness, with directions to report today upon the practicability of obtaining his attendance. – The physician had not yet returned. The testimony of this witness was important – indeed it was of a highly indispensable character, and the Government did not deem it safe to proceed with the trial until it was known whether this witness could be present. It was barely possible that this information could be had this forenoon – perhaps not till the afternoon, He did not now feel at liberty to move for a copias to compel the attendance of the witness.
Chief Justice. Has the Counsel for the defendant any thing to offer?

---

[2] Attorney-General of Kennebec County.

Mr. Evans. The prosecuting officer has submitted no motion – we have therefore nothing to say.

Mr. Paine. The Court cannot fail to perceive that my object was to obtain a postponement of the trial till the afternoon, when information relative to the condition of the witness will have been obtained.

Mr. Evans. We offer no objection to adjournment till afternoon.

C.J. Was the physician directed to return immediately?

Paine. He was.

C.J. We will wait awhile – perhaps he may return soon.

At eleven o'clock, Dr. H. H. Hill (the physician sent to examine the condition of the witness) appeared, and stated that it would be dangerous to the life of the witness to attempt to get him here.

Dr. Hill was then sworn. He saw Williams two and a half or three hours ago. Examined him critically and carefully. He is suffering from an acute catarrhal affection of the lungs – accompanied by a head ache, and hard cough. There is some congestion at the base of the lungs. It would be hazardous to expose him to cold air. It would not be safe to have him brought down upon a bed. Was sure his life would be jeoparded by the exposure. Judging from the history of the case an improvement in the patient was beginning. It was impossible to say, definitely, at what time the witness could, with propriety be brought here. The physician in attendance and the patient himself were of opinion that he might be able to ride out by the last of the week.

Cross examined by Evans. Williams has been unwell about six weeks, and was most indisposed during the last fortnight. Is confined to his room and to his bed most of the time under medical treatment. Learned this fact from his physician and his own statement, During the last two weeks he has not been so well as during several weeks preceding. My impression is that it will not be proper to get Williams here during this week, unless the weather shall be very pleasant. Convalescence has commenced. His cough has been very dry and hard, but is now beginning to be free – indicating a return to health. It will be some time before it will be safe for him to be exposed. Could not define how long. A slight cold would reduce the patient and renew the disease. The cold air and fatigue incident to a journey to Augusta, would tend to produce an inflammation of the lungs.

Mr. Paine said that the circumstances were such that he felt compelled to submit a motion, which he was very loth to do, as it might cause the Court very great personal inconvenience. But duty to the government required him to move for an adjournment. The witness detained by sickness was an important one – an all important one. No affidavit had been prepared to the expected testimony, because it was apparent, that no counsel, in a case of this magnitude, involving the liberty and perhaps the life of the prisoner, would proceed to trial by admitting the statement of another as to what an important witness would say. Without this testimony it would be unjust to proceed. We are now, of course, precluded from issuing a capias.

Some conversation here occurred between the Court and council, (inaudible to the reporters) which resulted in a postponement of the trial till the second Tuesday (11th day) of March.

The Chief Justice cautioned the gentlemen summed as jurymen, relative to their deportment during the intervening time. After which the prisoner was remanded to jail, and the Court adjourned to the Court House to attend to civil matters.

The postponement of the trial was no small thing considering that reportedly 1500 people, including reporters from throughout the northeastern parts of the United States, had traveled to Augusta for the trial. Cyrus Williams was the proprietor of the Williams's Hotel or Tavern - as it is variously called - where Flint was the evening of the murder before being called for by Dr. Coolidge. And more importantly, Williams was the person who took the stomach contents from the room where the autopsy was being performed.

This delay of the trial, after the jury pool had been chosen and identified, was viewed as an advantage for the defense; they would have several months to attempt to learn the character of the members of that pool. There was a common belief that, because of this, the jury would never come to an agreement.

The Reporters Gather

On March 14th the Northern Tribune, of Bath, Maine, which was a daily newspaper, made the following announcement.

Augusta will be the source of news matters for the coming week, and perhaps longer. The additional Counsel engaged for the defence will increase the before strong desire to see or read the doings of the trial. We are in hopes to lay before our readers the earliest intelligence, even in advance of any other paper. We have engaged the services of a reporter of many years' experience, and feel confident of giving our readers a thorough and correct report of the trial.

We shall issue a large edition in order to be able to meet the demand; and send them to the neighboring towns.

The trial began on March 14th, and the Tribune began their report of the trial the next day, March 15th – they were able to report on the trial a far as the completion of jury selection. They had extensive coverage each day through to sentencing; on several days the trial filled the first two pages completely, and spilled over onto the third page, replacing space usually filled with advertising.

The Portland Advertiser, a weekly, first ran coverage of the trial in their March 21st issue (they may have had daily specials as well). They printed a letter from their reporter on the front page of the same issue, describing his trip to Augusta, the other reporters he encountered, and the state of feelings in Augusta.

Augusta, March 13, 1848
Friend Edwards,
I arrived here Saturday evening, after a long and tedious passage by way of the Back Route. – After we left Lewiston and in passing through Greene and Monmouth the roads were filled with drifts of snow, so that it seemed like passing along on the high grading of a Railroad. We upset only three times, however, on account of the narrowness of the beaten track and the depth of snow outside; and it would be hardly worth while, according to our friend Barnes's

ideas of sketching, to trouble your readers with the incidents connected, although they were at the time to us somewhat amusing. Suffice it to say, that owing to a careful driver, soft beds of snow, and *very* careful, kind horses, no one experienced any injury; and when the horses waited so quietly and patiently for us to crawl out and right up the stage, we felt reproved for the anathemas we had previous poured out upon them as lazy, good for nothing beasts. A Reporter for two of the Boston Penny papers was on board, and at our first mishap, he was in extacies of delight at the great good fortune which had thus furnished him with so exciting an incident as a subject for a letter. At the second, however, he thought we were getting a little too much of a good thing · and I soon found him in serious doubt as to the propriety of condensing both incidents into one article, or devoting an article to each. The third, I believe, settled the question in favor of at least two articles.

I have had pleasant interviews with several of the editorial fraternity, and, among others, with that "fellow traitor" and "Mexican Whig" Luther Severance[1], and Mr. Matthews of the Yankee Blade, and brother of him whose murder is to be the subject of the trial which is to commence tomorrow. Brother Willey[2] I have not seen yet, and I fear from the tenor of his last paper, I shall not have the pleasure of making his personal acquaintance at present. I trust, however, that when he has successfully "animated a worn-out man", and upon a further editorial acquaintance, he will become a little more amiable, and we shall jog along together harmoniously – for it does look so ridiculous for editors, and especially old veteran editors, covered over with scars, to say nothing of the "raw spots", to get cross and sulky every little while.

"Editors should never let
Their angry passions rise."

Tomorrow commences the interesting trial of Dr. Coolidge, of which I shall endeavor to give you a full and early report. There has been some doubt in the public mind whether Attorney General Blake would assume the management of the case. I saw him yesterday, however, and he will attend to the case, assisted, I presume, by Mr. Paine, County Attorney of Kennebec. Mr. Evans, assisted by Mr. Noyes of Waterville, son-in-law of Mr. Boutelle, is to conduct the defence. The Reporters of the Boston Mail Bee, Times and Herald

---

[1] Founder of the Kennebec Journal, just completed his second term as a Whig representative to the US Congress from Maine

[2] Maine editor, crusader against slavery, 1806-1896

24

are here, and hoping not to be again prevented from giving their readers the particulars of this interesting trial by any vexatious adjournment. One of the Boston Reporters, I am informed, was highly incensed at the former adjournment, considering it a high misdemeanor in a "down east" Court thus to disappoint the "gentlemen of the press." The approaching trial does not yet appear to create so much excitement as was manifested at the former session of the Court. Many were then anxious to *see* the prisoner, and having gratified in that their curiosity has somewhat abated. This decrease of excitement and the opportunity which the postponement has given the prisoner's counsel to learn all the particulars in relation to the character, habits and mind of each juror summoned, are thought to be circumstances very favorable to the accused. There is a vast change too in public feeling since the time of this arrest. Men who were then almost ready to hang him without judge or jury, now state, apparently without feeing or regret, that he will probably be acquitted. Such is human nature ever. When a murder is committed, and strong grounds of suspicion against any individual are discovered, men naturally turn from the horrid crime and its unhappy victim, with exasperated feelings towards the accused, and too frequently, amid the surging tide of popular feeling, look upon him, not as a fellow creature, but as some wild beast who should be shut out from all human rights and sympathies. Time, however, produces a reaction. Men think less of the deed of blood and its victim, and they begin to feel that the accused is a human being, a fellow creature of like sympathies and affections with themselves, and not unfrequently become as much too ready to acquit as they were formerly to condemn, and visit with condign punishment, when they find the accused about to endure the terrible ordeal through which he must pass – to have the suspicious and searching glances of thousands concentrated upon him, at once seeking to read his every thought. If he is cool, collected and self possessed, some will say he appears like a brazen faced, hardened villain; if his bearing is the reverse, those same persons will say that he betrays, in his timidity and down cast looks, the confusion of a guilty culprit. On the other hand, others will read in the interesting and almost fascinating expression of countenance which I am told he possesses, an almost certain evidence of innocence. But these speculations are all idle, and fortunately those who freely indulge in them are not to judge him. An able Court and I hope and trust an impartial and intelligent jury, are to pass upon his guilt or innocence, after hearing all the testimony. If innocent he can triumphantly pass through all that awaits him. If guilty he must have a yet more severe ordeal to endure than that to which we have alluded – the doubt, suspense and fear during the process of the trial, and the awful reflections which must be suggested by his own conscience while communing with himself in his lonely cell and in the silent watches of the night.

Yours, truly, C.

More than fifty years later the Kennebec Journal published a brief interview with a visiting physician who had, as a student, reported on the trial for the Eastern Mail. The reporter got the name of the chief justice wrong; it was not Mitchell but Whitman. Ezekiel Whitman was Edward Mitchell's maternal grandfather.

Daily Kennebec Journal. July 1, 1899, page 4

Dr. Edward C. Mitchell of New Orleans, of the class of 1849 at Colby, one of the visiting alumni this year, in conversation with a Waterville Mail reporter said that when he was a junior in college he was detailed by the publishers of The Mail to report the famous Coolidge murder trial at Augusta. Dr. Mitchell's grandfather, Judge Mitchell, was Maine's chief justice at that time and presided over the Coolidge trial. There were no shorthand reporters in those days and Dr. Mitchell said he never worked harder in his life than he did trying to get a good report of his grandfather's charge to the jury, which was entirely offhand. There were reporters present from Boston and New York papers, the case being perhaps the most celebrated that had yet engaged the attention of any court in New England, and Dr. Mitchell felt greatly pleased when the judge told him that The Mail had a better report of his charge than any other paper got. Dr. Mitchell came from the same fitting school[3] as did Flint, who was implicated with Coolidge in the murder, and frequently called at Dr. Coolidge's office to talk over school days with Flint. On one of those visits Flint pointed out to Dr. Mitchell a bottle of poison that Dr. Coolidge had recently purchased and explained its deadly qualities. This was the bottle from which the fatal dose was poured for Mathews a little later.

The onset of the trial was announced throughout the country.

The Public Ledger (Philadelphia, PA) March 17, 1848

TRIAL OF DR. COOLIDGE – The trial of Dr Coolidge, for the murder of Mathews, commenced at Augusta, Me, on Tuesday morning. This will probably be one of the most interesting trials that has been had in this country. A jury was empanelled the first day, and the trial is now progressing.

---

[3] Probably North Yarmouth Academy.

The Trial Begins

The trial of Valorus P. Coolidge began on Tuesday, March 14, 1847, and completed in its tenth day, Friday, March 24th.

Most of the trial report that follows is taken from the following sources. See the section on Sources at the end for more details.

The pamphlet published by the *Boston Daily Times.*
The pamphlet published by the *Northern Tribune*, Bath, Maine.
Issues of the *Maine Farmer,* including a special issue that contains a report of the entire trial.
Issues of the *Portland Advertiser*
Issues of the *Eastern Mail*

There is considerable variation in what each published; this was in the days before the use of shorthand, so each reporter had to follow the trial on their own and get down what they could. Sometimes there is what appears to be a faithful transcript; sometimes there is paraphrase; sometime summary. See Appendix V for an example.

Most of the individual testimonies are taken from either the Boston Daily Times or the Northern Tribune, The other sources were also consulted in an attempt to provide the most complete report of the trial. The *Maine Farmer* had the most complete coverage of the jury selection process; the *Boston Daily Times* the most complete report on Lot M. Morrell's introductory address to the jury; The *Eastern Mail* the most detailed report on the last minute maneuvers on the day of sentencing and of Chief Justice Whitman's instructions to the jury – the *Eastern's* reporter was the Chief Justice's grandson; the *Maine Farmer* was very good on both ending arguments; the *Portland Advertiser* was sometimes better on general testimony and so on. The *Northern Tribune* reports more objections than the other sources, and provides the fullest single account.

Additional commentary on the trial from other sources is occasionally inserted at appropriate places in the text; the sources of such insertions are identified on the page. Any editorial comments are limited to footnotes.

The Judges

Three judges of the Maine Supreme Judicial Court presided at the trial.

Ezekiel Whitman (March 9, 1776 - August 1, 1866) was the chief justice of the Maine Supreme Judicial Court from 1841 to 1848. He practiced law in New Gloucester and Portland Maine. Whitman was a Federalist representative to congress when Maine was a part of Massachusetts, a delegate to the convention that formed Maine's first constitution, and a judge of the court of common pleas from 1822 to 1841.

Ether Shepley (November 2, 1789 – January 15, 1877) was admitted to the bar in 1814, and practiced in Saco, Maine. He was a delegate to the Maine constitutional convention, U.S. Attorney for the District of Maine from 1821 to 1833, elected to the United States Senate in 1833, resigning in 1836, when he became a justice in the Maine Supreme Judicial Court. He replaced Ezekiel Whitman as chief justice later in 1848.

Samuel Wells (August 15, 1801 - July 15, 1868) practiced in Maine, first in Waterville, then Hallowell and Portland. He was elected to the Maine House of Representatives from 1836 to 1840, and was an associate justice of the Maine Supreme Judicial Court from 1847 to 1854. He became Governor of Maine in 1856, chosen by the legislature when none of the candidates in a three-way race received a majority of the popular vote. He lost a subsequent bid for the governorship. He later moved to Boston and resumed the practice of law.

The Attorneys

Two attorneys each appeared for the prosecution, referred to variously as the Government or the State, and for the defense. All were, or became, prominent men.

Samuel H. Blake (1807 - 1887) had recently become Attorney General of Maine - he was not counsel for the Government when the trial had first convened in January. He settled in Bangor and practiced law there, was elected to several terms in the Maine Senate, as a Democrat, was elected Attorney General of Maine (by the legislature) in 1848. He ran for U.S. Congress in 1854, losing to Israel Washburn who ran representing the new Republican Party, the key issue being the extension of slavery to the territories. In later life he managed the Merchants National Bank in Bangor.

Lot M. Morrell (May 3, 1813 - January 10, 1883) assisted in the prosecution. He practiced law in Readfield and Augusta and was a popular speaker for the cause of temperance. A Democrat, the leader of the Maine Democratic Party for a period, he switched his allegiance to the Republican Party over the issue of slavery in the territories. He was elected to the Maine House of Representatives in 1854 as a Democrat, and the Maine Senate in 1856 as a Republican. He was elected Governor of Maine in 1858, a United States Senator in 1861, and later became a highly respected Secretary of the Treasury at the end of Grant's administration.

George Evans (January 12, 1797 - April 6, 1867) led Coolidge's defense. He graduated from Bowdoin College in 1815, and settled in Gardiner, Maine to practice law. He was a Whig, and as such was elected to the Maine House of Representatives from 1826 to 1830, becoming Speaker of the Maine House. He was elected to the U.S. House of Representatives in 1829, serving as chairman of the Committee on Expenditures. In 1841 he moved to the U.S. Senate where he became Chair of the Finance Committee. He lost his seat in the election of 1847, when he returned to Portland to practice law. In the 1850's he became Maine Attorney General.

Edwin Noyes (February 21, 1812 - March 23, 1888) assisted in the defense. He graduated from Brown University, was a Tutor at Waterville College for a few years, studied law with a prominent Waterville attorney, Timothy Boutelle, marrying his daughter. He was heavily involved in politics and in the development of the railroads in Maine, and was a controversial superintendent of Maine Central Railroad - at one time ordered to be arrested by the railroad's directors (for reportedly selling thousands of cords of wood that were harvested for the railroad for his own benefit though his wood yard in Lewiston). The New York Times for September 20, 1863 has an article describing how he was arrested at the Astor House in the city just before he was to leave on a steamer for Europe after city detectives received a telegram from the railroad's directors in Maine. But a few years later he was again Superintendent of the Maine Central.

The Leading Players

Valorus Perry Coolidge (January 19, 1820 - May 18, 1849). Born in Jay (or Canton) Maine, where his grandfather, a veteran of the revolutionary war, had received a land grant. After graduating from the local school he taught in the local school for a year or two, and studied medicine with his physician uncle, Cyrus Hamlin Coolidge. He then attended Dartmouth Medical School to complete the requirements for a medical degree, graduating with the class of 1844. Decades later a woman who had been his student in Canton remembered him as "a good teacher, kind to children, very handsome and exceedingly well dressed.[1]" All sources agree he had a very successful medical practice in Waterville and the surrounding towns. He began in Waterville by purchasing the practice of Dr. Potter (whose name was frequently mentioned during the trial) who had moved to Ohio. Coolidge's name was often spelled "Valorous" by the newspapers.

Edward Mathews (July 26, 1822 - September 30, 1848. His brother, William Mathews, was editor of a publication, *The Yankee Blade.* It had been published in Gardiner, Maine through March 1847, but then was moved to Boston. Edward had been assisting with the publication, but apparently decided not to make the move to Boston. At the time of the murder he was just returned from driving a herd of cattle to the market in Brighton (Massachusetts, west of Cambridge) - this was before the railroad had reached Waterville, and so was a actual cattle drive as was common though the 1850's. Maine newspapers regularly reported on prices and activity at the Brighton Market. Typically drovers moved herds of several hundred cattle at a time; Clinton,

---

[1] Spalding. "The Case of Dr. Coolidge".

Maine was the main collection point for cattle to be driven to Brighton. It would be normal for a drover such as Edward Mathews, just returned from the Brighton market, to have access to large amounts of cash.

Thomas Flint (May 13, 1824 - June 19, 1904). He grew up in Anson Maine; his father was three times in the Maine Senate; his grandfather a physician in the early days of Farmington Maine. He was a medical student of Dr Coolidge's, and became embroiled in the case. A good deal of effort was made to clear him of suspicion; see Appendix V and Sources for more information on his remarkable later career.

All three of these men were within four years of age with each other; in September of 1847 Dr. Coolidge was 27 years of age, graduating from Dartmouth Medical School at the age of 24 a few years before. Edward Mathews was 25 years old, and beginning to go into business. Thomas Flint was 23 years of age, and perhaps a year away from getting his medical degree.

The Indictment[1]

At the Supreme Judicial Court of said State, begun and holden at Augusta, within and for said county of Kennebec, on the first Tuesday of October, in the year of our Lord eighteen hundred and forty-seven -

The jurors for said State upon their oath present, that Valorus P. Coolidge, of Waterville, in the county of Kennebec, aforesaid, Physician, at Waterville, aforesaid, in the county of Kennebec, aforesaid, on the thirtieth day of September, in the year of our Lord one thousand eight hundred and forty-seven, with force and arms, in and upon the body of Edward Mathews, then and there in the peace of said State being, feloniously, wilfully, and of his malice aforethought, did make an assault, and that he the said Valorus P. Coolidge, with a certain stick of wood, which the said Valorus P. Coolidge then and there in his right hand had and held, the aforesaid Edward Mathews in and upon the head of him the said Edward Mathews, and near the top thereof, then and there feloniously, willfully, and of his malice aforethought, did strike, penetrate, wound, and fracture, giving to the said Edward Mathews then and there with the stick of wood aforesaid, in and upon the head of him the said Edward Mathews, and near the top thereof, one mortal wound, bruise and fracture, of the length of three inches, of the width of two inches, and of the depth of one inch, of which said mortal wound, bruise, wound and fracture, he the said Edward Mathews, then and there instantly died; and so the jurors aforesaid upon there oath aforesaid do say, that he the said Valorus P. Coolidge, then and there, him the said Edward Mathews, in manner and form aforesaid, feloniously, willfully, and of this malice aforethought, did kill and murder, against the peace of said State of Maine, and contrary to the peace of the statue in such cases made and provided."

---

[1] From here through to the end of the trial, all text other than the occasional footnote comes directly from one or more of the published reports of the trial. The only amendments made are corrections of obvious spelling errors, and minor adjustments to smooth some of the stylistic variations in the way different reporters recorded the events.

Three other counts in the indictment, and those on which it is supposed the government will mainly rely, charge that Valorus P. Coolidge, administered Prussic Acid to Edward Mathews, from the effects of which he died; the second count that Coolidge mixed the Prussic acid in a glass of brandy, and presented it to Mathews to drink; the third that Coolidge persuaded Mathews to drink the poisoned brandy, and the fourth that Coolidge put poison into the brandy, which he knew Mathews was about to drink.

As will be observed the indictment is framed in the usual form, and covers all the possible modes of killing which could have been imagined by the Attorney who drew it up. There is a very general impression here, that the accused will be convicted, and from what I can learn, there seems to be a prejudice in the public mind against him · a prejudice which too often exists where the real facts of a case are unknown, and where rumor's thousand tongues find as much employment as in country towns and villages.

The Judges of the Supreme Court will sit on the trial, with the exception of Hon Mr. Tenny, who, it is supposed, will not be present. Hon Samuel H Blake, of Bangor, lately appointed Attorney General, will conduct the case in person, and be assisted by Lot M Morrill, Esq. of this town, a gentleman of much reputation hereabouts as a skillful Attorney. That the accused will be ably defended, there can be no doubt, as Hon Geo Evans has the management of the defense, and is to be assisted by Edwin Noyes, Esq., of Waterville, a gentleman who, it is said, has been quite successful in the practice of the law.

Ezekiel Whitman, Chief Justice of the Maine Supreme Judicial Court, 1841-1848. He presided, with two colleagues, at Coolidge's trial.   He also presided at the previous conviction for murder in Maine, the trial of Thomas Thorne in 1843.

Day One: Tuesday, March 14, 1848

The Court was opened at 10 o'clock at the Court House, and immediately adjourned to the Meeting House of the Rev. Dr. Tappan. The prisoner was brought into Court, being neatly plainly dressed, and bearing himself with remarkable calmness and propriety. He is about 27 years of age, and has a very quiet, intelligent and pleasant expression of countenance ·The most fastidious could not complain of the bearing and whole appearance of the prisoner, or argue from it either guilt or innocence, although it certainly shew him to possess great self-possession, and a nice sense of the situation in which he is placed. His head is rather small and narrow, perceptive faculties large, with keen deep set eyes and heavy eyebrows, giving to his countenance a sharp, penetrating although quiet expression.

The Clerk then proceeded to call over the names of the Jurors, and ninety-nine answered to their names. He then proceeded to empannel the jury.

Joseph B. Allen. · Called, and sworn to make true answers. Stated that he had neither formed nor expressed any opinion, and had no bias · no conscientious scruples in convicting a man when the punishment was death. He was sworn as a Juror.

Theodore C. Allen. · Being sworn, stated that he had formed no opinion · had expressed none. The Counsel for the prisoner proposed to enquire whether the juror had read any report on the evidence, and referred to a case in New York, in conformity with his view of the case; also a case from the 17th Pickering's Reports. But the Court refused to allow the questions to be put, because it would seem to cast an imputation upon the juror, who had already stated that he had neither formed nor expressed any opinion. The juror was challenged peremptorily. The Counsel for the Government said it was too late, because they had seen fit to examine him previously; that a juror having stated that he had formed no opinion, could not afterwards be challenged peremptorily, but only for some good cause shown. The Counsel for the prisoner controverted this opinion. The Court decided that the peremptory challenge might be allowed, and the juror was accordingly rejected.

Otis Andrews. · Have formed and expressed an opinion prior to being drawn as a juror. Upon being interrogated by the

Attorney General, he stated that he was not sensible of any present bias upon his mind; but in reply to a question put by Mr. Evans, he said that his opinion remained, founded upon the reports he had heard, provided those reports were true. The Court decided that an opinion so formed would not exclude the juror. The juror was then challenged peremptorily.

Hiram Averill. - Have formed no opinion - have expressed none. He was sworn as a juror.

Brown Baker. - Have formed no opinion - have expressed none. Sworn as a juror.

Samuel Baldwin. - Have formed no opinion - expressed none. Challenged peremptorily.

Albert Berry. Have expressed an opinion frequently, about the time the affair took place - sensible of no bias, or prejudice, in this case - made up a deliberate and full opinion - seen nothing to change it. He was rejected.

John Berry, Junior. Formed an opinion, and expressed one at the time the affair took place - have seen nothing since to change that opinion. He was rejected.

James A. Bicknell. - Have fixed no opinion - have expressed none - no bias. Challenged peremptorily.

David Bowman. - Have formed no opinion - expressed none. Challenged peremptorily.

William Bridge. - Have neither formed no expressed an opinion - no bias - no conscientious scruples. Challenged peremptorily.

Enoch Brown. Have neither formed nor expressed an opinion - no bias nor prejudice. Challenged peremptorily.

Eleasor Burbank. - Have not formed or expressed an opinion, except upon the condition that what I have heard was true - have conscientious scruples. He was rejected.

Joshua Carr. - Have formed and expressed an unqualified opinion - no bias - entertain an opinion now. Rejected.

Abel Chadwick. - Have formed an opinion, if reports were true - have expressed none - sensible of no bias - no conscientious scruples. Challenged peremptorily.

Jonathan Clark. - Have formed no opinion - expressed none - no bias - no conscientious scruples. Sworn as a juror.

Levi Cochran - Have formed no opinion - expressed none - no bias - have conscientious scruples. Rejected.

Hiram B. Colcord. - Have formed no opinion - expressed none, but this: if what I have heard was true, this must be the man - no bias - no conscientious scruples. Challenged peremptorily.

Robert Cornforth. - Have neither formed, nor expressed an opinion - no bias - no conscientious scruples. - Challenged peremptorily.

Daniel Cunningham. - Don't know that I have formed or expressed any opinion - no bias - no conscientious scruples. Sworn.

Alfred Davenport. - Have formed no opinion, expressed none, no bias - conscientious scruples. Rejected.

Lewis Dexter. - Form formed no opinion, expressed none, no bias - conscientious scruples. Rejected.

Oren Dowst. - Have formed no opinion, expressed none; no conscientious scruples. Sworn.

Russell Eaton. - Have formed an opinion and expressed one, made up from the reports in circulation - not absolute, but predicated from the reports I have heard. No bias - not formed a very decided opinion, only from the reports. He was rejected, for cause shown.

James Drummond, - Have not formed nor expressed any opinion - no bias - no conscientious scruples. - Challenged peremptorily.

David Elliott. - Have formed no opinion, expressed none; no bias, no conscientious scruples. Sworn.

Isaac Fairfield. - Can't tell whether I have formed an opinion or not - can't say I am not sensible of a bias. Rejected.

Isaac Farr. - Have formed no opinion, expressed none - no bias, no conscientious scruples in deciding according to the law and evidence. Sworn.

Eliphalet Flagg. - Have formed and expressed an opinion - sensible of a bias. Rejected.

John Freeman. - Have formed no opinion, expressed none - no bias, no conscientious scruples. Challenged peremptorily.

William Frost. - Have formed an opinion in some measure, expressed none - no bias -mind not altogether free, as if I had heard nothing about the case. Rejected.

Daniel Fuller. - Have formed an opinion; don't recollect having expressed one. Rejected.

Jonathan Furber. - Have formed and expressed an opinion in some respect - rather a bias upon my mind - don't seem to feel free to judge. He was rejected.

Harrison Gould. - Have formed no opinion - expressed none - no bias - no prejudice - no conscientious scruples. Sworn.

Caleb Gray. - Have formed no opinion - expressed none - no bias - no conscientious scruples. Challenged peremptorily.

Wm. Greene. - Have formed no opinion - expressed none - no bias - no conscientious scruples. Sworn.

Cyrus Judd, Jr. - Have formed no opinion - expressed none - no bias - no conscientious scrolls. - Challenged peremptorily.

Francis F. Haines. - Have formed no opinion - expressed none - no bias - no conscientious scrolls. - Sworn.

Harrison Ham. - Have formed no opinion - expressed none - no bias - no conscientious scrolls. - Sworn.

The following individuals compose the Jury:

Joseph B. Allen, Monmouth; Hiram Avery, Pittston; Brown Baker, Gardiner; Jonathan Clark, China; Daniel Cunningham, Windsor; Oren Dowst, Vienna; David Elliott, Readfield; Isaac Farr, Gardiner; Harrison Gould, Leeds; Wm. Greene, Pittston; Francis F. Haines, East Livermore; Harrison Ham, Wales.

Mr. Haines was appointed Foreman by the Court.

The Clerk then read the indictment.

A motion was here made by the Counsel for the prisoner, that the witnesses on the part of the government should be examined apart, and not in the hearing of each other. The counsel for the government stated that they had no objection, if the same rule could be applied to the examination of the witnesses for the prisoner. It was then proposed by the Court, and assented to on the part of Counsel, that a list of such witnesses on either side, as they should wish to have examined apart, should be made up. It was accordingly done.

Mr. Noyes, Counsel for the prisoner, suggested the propriety of the Court ordering that all publication, in newspaper of the proceedings, testimony, &c., be suspended until after the verdict. The Attorney General said the Government had no wish about the matter - of course all publications of the trial would be kept from the jury, but suggested that the Court could not resent the publication in Boston papers circulating in this State. Judge Whitman stated that having no control over papers out of State, such publications would of course be made in them and they would monopolize the publication if the newspapers of our State were deprived of the privilege by any such order. This matter was urged no further, and Mr. Morrell proceeded to open the case on the part of the government.

Day One: Tuesday, March 14, 1848

Mr. Morrell's Opening Argument for the Government

May it please the Court and Gentlemen of the Jury:
The offense with which the prisoner at the bar stands charged, is one of the most important known to the laws. In approaching an examination and enquiring into it, your duties and responsibilities are corresponding to the magnitude of the crime charged. I need not press upon your attention the solemnity, dignity and importance of your office. You are selected to maintain the public laws by convicting the guilty or acquitting the innocent. The oath that has been administered to you contains an epitome of the duty required of you, - at once the guardians of the public peace, and of the rights of the prisoner. You are to try the issue presented to you unaffected by any motives but those which should influence conscientious and rational minds. You are to examine the question of the innocence or guilt of the prisoner without fear, favor, affection or hope of reward, on the one hand, and without the prejudices arising from hated envy or malice on the other.

The crime of which the prisoner is indicted, is murder of the first degree. The statute of your State, in concise and appropriate language, defines the crime of murder (Rev. Stat. Ch 151, sec 6) "Whoever shall unlawfully kill any human being with malice aforethought either expressed or implied." Sec 2d defines what constitutes murder in the first degree. "Whoever shall commit murder with express malice aforethought, or in perpetrating or attempting to perpetrate any crime punishable with death or imprisonment in the State Prison for life, or for an unlimited term of years, shall be deemed guilty of murder in the first degree" By section 4th it is made the duty of the jury "Upon the trial of an indictment for murder, if they find the defendant guilty, to inquire and by their verdict ascertain whether he be guilty of murder of the first or second degree."

I have said the prisoner is charged with murder of the first degree, and you will perceive according to the statute I have read to you, in order to sustain this charge, the government must satisfy you that the murder was committed, "Either with express malice aforethought, or in perpetrating or attempting to perpetrate," &c (see sec 4th) The Government assume that the murder was committed "with express malice aforethought."

To render more intelligible to you the statute definition of the crime of murder, it may not be improper that I should explain to you the legal import of the term employed in the statute, "Express malice aforethought."

Whenever the law makes use of the term "malice aforethought," as descriptive of the crime of murder, it means simply this: a settled purpose or formed design to do the act. "Malice aforethought" is deliberate premeditation, (2nd Chst Cr Law, 785 - 4 Bl Com 199) - and the length of time during which the thought of committing the deed is immaterial, provided that in fact he had entertained such a thought.

When therefore, murder has been committed, according to a formed design or purpose, and such formed design is indicated by external circumstances, showing an intent to do the act, it is said to be done with express malice. (Russell on Crime, 421)

You are then in inquire and by your verdict ascertain whether the prisoner murdered the deceased, and if so, whether he committed the act in accordance to a settled purpose or design to do it. If you shall so find, he is then guilty of murder with malice aforethought, which is murder in the first degree. The principles of evidence applicable to this prosecution are equally plain.

In entering upon the introduction of evidence on the part of the government, it is admitted to be a settled principle of law that in proportion to the magnitude of the crime charged, is to be the care and caution of the jury, with respect to the nature and amount of testimony necessary to procure conviction. But while you regard this as a pertinent rule of evidence, you must remember that your oaths require you to listen and judge impartially, uninfluenced by sympathy or prejudice. The burden of proof is on the government. Before you can be called upon to convict, all reasonable doubts of the guilt of the prisoner must be removed from your minds. The presumption of law is, that you have formed no opinion as to the guilt or innocence of the prisoner, who is entitled to the presumption of innocence until found guilty. But while you will faithfully regard these cardinal maxims of the law, you will also bear in mind that it is a provision of these maxims, if from compassion, sympathy, weakness or other improper influences you allow the prisoner to escape because he *may possibly* be innocent, when by the law and the proof, the *probabilities* of his guilt are certain.

You are to expect and demand satisfactory proof, and what in law is considered full proof, is that measure of evidence which satisfies the mind of the jury of the truth of the matter charged, to the exclusion of all fair and reasonable doubts. You are not to expect absolute mathematical or physical certainty. This in all judicial investigations is utterly unattainable, and is not required.

When the proof is full and clear, for the jury to acquit upon light, trivial and fanciful suppositions and remote conjectures, is a virtual violation of their oath of office, and is no trifling offense against the best interests of society, to the hindrance of public justice and the encouragement of offenders.

In this, as in all like prosecutions, a portion of the testimony will be that denominated in law circumstantial, that is, although the government may not be able to produce and put upon the stand a witness who saw the prisoner administer the fatal poison; we shall prove other distinct facts, and which facts shall be so connected with the fatal fact that by their own natural force, they will irresistibly produce conviction upon your minds that the individual connected with these latter facts must have been the guilty agent.

The secrecy with which crimes of a flagrant character are generally committed, is such as renders detection and proof of the overt act impossible; and yet there is such an intimate coincidence in events, that no eventing *moment* can possibly happen without evolving circumstances of such conclusive tendency to force conviction and to exclude all reasonable doubts.

The vestiges which the commission of crime always afford, form a chain of circumstances which lead unerringly to the offender, and by which he may be traced and ascertained.

With this statement of general principles I will proceed to detail to you the evidence, which I doubt not will satisfy you of the guilt of the prisoner, and under circumstances exhibiting a cool depravity unparalleled in the history of crimes.

The first inquiry most naturally suggested is, was the deceased in fact murdered? This is denominated in law "the body of the offense," and is often a point of great nicety and difficulty. Such were the circumstances under which the body of the deceased was found, and such the marks of violence upon it, that you will have no difficulty in concluding that the crime of murder had been committed.

The deceased left the Parker House at about 8 o'clock P.M. in health, and in the morning was found dead in a cellar, the body resting on a pile of wood, the head bearing marks of repeated violent blows, and the pockets rifled of money and a watch he was known to have had on the evening previous.

The indictment charges the murder to have been committed by administering to the deceased a certain deadly poison, - and also that he was murdered by the infliction of blows upon the head by a stick of wood. These charges must be proved in substance as alleged, and it is in compliance with this principle of law, if in the charge of murder by a certain kind of poison, the proof is of death by certain other poison, or by a compound of poisons ; and so if death by blows with a stick or club of wood, or if the proof of death by blows inflicted with a broad sword or hatchet, the opposite enquiry then will be whether the deceased fell by the hand of violence by blows inflicted on the head, or by secret poison, or both.

Was the death caused by poison? We shall show to you, gentlemen, that a large quantity of the most deadly poison, of the kind charged in the indictment, hydrocyanic or prussic acid, was found in the stomach of the deceased - a quantity sufficiently large to have produced death - that the presence of such poison was found in the brain of the deceased, as well as in other parts of the system, as would be natural to expect from the subtle and diffusive nature of the poison if death had been produced by taking it into the stomach in any considerable quantity - that at the *post mortem* examination, effects of poison, and of the peculiar character charged to have been employed, were apparent in various parts of the system, as indicated by the morbid appearance of the coatings of the stomach, the discoloration of the blood, and other indications peculiar to death by this kind of poison.

From these facts and the peculiarly deadly nature of the poison it is probable that death resulted almost instantaneously with the introduction into its stomach. So destructive is this poison to animal life, that the smallest quantity proves almost instantaneously fatal.

Was death in any way caused by blows upon the head?

We shall show you that there were deep gashes upon the head, the scalp lacerated and the skull fractured, as if blows had been inflicted with the edge of a stick of wood. The blows were in reality probably inflicted by the edge of an unground hatchet, and were supposed to have been sufficiently violent to produce death, but probably not sudden death. These wounds, however, gave indications of having been inflicted after death. There were

42

also marks of violence upon the throat, as if it had been clutched severely by a man's hand. From these facts it may be assumed that death was produced by the poison, and that the wounds upon the head were inflicted after death, probably to avert suspicion from the deceased having died of poison, and to raise a suspicion that he fell by the hand of violence in the street. The facts however may be inconsistent with the hypothesis that the poison was relied upon as the principal agency. The blows may have been inflicted the more readily to despatch him, and the marks upon the throat the effect of clutches there to prevent any scratches in the struggles of death.

Having shown that the deceased was murdered, and the *manner*, the next important inquiry is: -

Did the prisoner commit the act?

When the act of murder has been proved, the *motive* which the accused may be supposed to have had to commit the deed, whether of intent of otherwise, is proper to be considered by the jury. The law supposes an intimate connection to exist between a man's motives and conduct; and in judicial investigations it confides to the experience of the jury to infer the *motives* of the accused from his *acts*, also to infer what his conduct would be likely to be from the motives by which he was known to be influenced.

We shall show such acts and conduct on the part of the accused as to indicate a most pressing want of money, and he *evinced great embarrassment in his monetary affairs;* shall also prove such *shifts and extravagant offers by which to raise money as would naturally lead to most extraordinary and desperate measures to procure it.* That he offered one man, on the day before the murder, $500 for the use of $2000 four or five months - to another man a short time before the murder he tried to obtain $1000, and offered for its use six months, $500. That he negotiated with deceased on the day of the murder and the day before, the sum of $1500, and was to pay $400 for its use ten days. We shall show various other unsuccessful attempts to obtain money all under enormous offers of usury, and also that for the last year to two he had borrowed of numerous individuals in various sums large and small, as he was able to obtain it, and upon terms indicating most pressing need - and that latterly all these offers were made under injunctions of profound secrecy. That he was indebted and involved for borrowed money not less in amount than $3000, and that his various applications and offers seemed to show a necessity for two or three thousand more.

Whether thus involved from extravagant and improvident expenditures or from speculations with Dr Potter, as he often declared, or from other speculations which he was not willing to disclose, may not perhaps, be particularly important, but it will be your province to enquire into them.

If the prisoner was incited by the powerful motive, by which I have supposed him to have been governed, and by which he was urged on, how was this desire to be gratified by the murder of the deceased?

The deceased had what the prisoner desired, what he had tried to negotiate for. He had $1500 and a gold watch - had them that afternoon - had procured it from the bank on an agreement to let the prisoner have it, and he the prisoner, knew all this. If he had the motive, and that motive was avowed by the knowledge of the fact that deceased had the money, the enquiry then is.

Had the prisoner the means to accomplish his desire. Had he the poison?

We shall show you that on the 17th day of September, 17 days prior to the commission of the deed, he sent to Hallowell for one ounce of Prussic acid, and the order read to have it "as strong as it can be made." This was received the next day. On the 19th he sent to Boston for one ounce of the same acid, "as strong as it could be made," and between the 21st and the 25th he received that, with a letter describing it as the "strongest kind," and containing a caution as to its use. Hydrocyanic acid is little used in medicine and the prisoner had when he sent these orders, a large amount already on hand, of a diluted quality fit for medical uses, and prepared in the only proper manner for such uses - a quantity quite sufficient to have lasted him a life time. He sent for and received such as is not used for medical purposes, and could not have been needed or intended for such uses. It is not usually found in the concentrated form he desired, in the apothecarie's shops.

The hatchet also with which the blows were given will be produced here.

Having the means, the motive and the object, had he the opportunity?

Deceased was known to have been under an agreement to meet the prisoner at his office that evening at about 8 o'clock.

We shall show that he was known to go in the direction of the office, with the expressed intention of going there - that he did in fact go there between 8 and 9; that the situation of the office is such, that the prisoner was secure in his purposes, being in the second story; that the tailor's ship under the office was closed and vacated before 8 o'clock; that the adjoining tenements are so situated that he was free from interruption from that quarter, and that noise could not be heard from one tenement to the other; that he would not be interrupted by his students - one of them, Mr. Dingley, and the office boy living across the river, at considerable distance, and had gone home for the night at about 8 o'clock, at the request of the prisoner, who said he had a private engagement with a man at the office to arrange about procuring a subject for dissection; that the body could be readily conveyed from the office to the place where it was found; that in the back room where his medicines were compounded, he kept brandy, of which deceased drank on the day of his death at 3 o'clock in the afternoon; that on the same shelf from which the bottle of brandy was taken, was an *empty* phial, which had contained prussic acid, and another which had a portion of the acid still remaining, Here was the phial which contained the prussic acid for medical purposes, as was also the unground hatchet.

We shall show you also that this was a scene with which the deceased had been made familiar by former invitations, and to which he had been specially invited that evening under injunctions of profound secrecy. He would approach it with an *incautiousness* induced by former visits.

Thus artfully had all things been arrayed; nothing there would could excite suspicion, and yet the *opportunity*, in time, place, means, and other favorable circumstances, were complete. There sat the brandy bottle out of which the deceased had drank in the afternoon, inviting him now as then; but the contents of that phial, *then full*, now *empty*, had been commingled with it. In the language of the prisoner, "he went to take a glass of brandy, and fell down dead." Thus fatal and sudden was the effects of this compound.

In connection with this we shall show that a few minutes before 10 o'clock, probably after the fatal deed had been performed, the prisoner was seen on a back street in the rear of the building, probably calculating the difficulties of getting the body to the river. That about this time he was seen coming from the direction of his office and passing up the platform in front of the sitting room in Williams's tavern, turned, looked in, saw Flint (his student) with other members of the family, then retraced his steps without going in. That after this he came into the front entry, met Flint there on his way to his bed chamber, and requested him to go with him to the office. Flint did go and returned a little after 10 o'clock, but the prisoner came in late. That he arose the next morning by 4 o'clock, and was seen coming from the direction of the stable, where afterwards was found the watch which belong to the deceased.

Having shown you the opportunity, I shall now show you that he sought the opportunity, and planned and arranged for it.

The deceased was known to the prisoner to be in Brighton with a drove of cattle. He is known to have made special and repeated enquiries, as to how much money deceased's drove would sell for - how much he paid for it - when he was expected back, and made arrangements with the bar keeper of the house where he boarded, and where the stages with passengers from the west always stopped, to let him know when the deceased arrived, for he was anxious to see him before he went to Clinton, where he had a partner. Deceased arrived on Saturday, but was not seen by the prisoner until the following Wednesday. He then met him in the street and invited him to his office. He went there secretly, and the prisoner was overheard to enjoin secrecy on him. Prior to this the deceased had put his money in the bank. We shall show that the prisoner proposed a negotiation with deceased by which it was arranged that the deceased should obtain for him from the bank $1500, on the security of his books. All of the being arranged, deceased, on Thursday, received a note from the prisoner to meet him at his office at 8 o'clock in the evening, for the purpose of closing up the agreement.

Having detailed to you the proof that a murder has been committed, the manner in which it was done, and the prisoner's motives, objects, money and the opportunity of doing it, and his seeing the measures and opportunities, there is another specie of proof to which I propose to turn your attention, and to which the law attaches the utmost importance, viz: the conduct and declarations of the accused after the murder, and when it is known to him that he is suspected. The law scrutinizes the conduct of the accused so critically that it is made a presumptive proof of either guilt or innocence. And that conduct is an attempt to avoid suspicion by concealing evidence of his guilt - by fabricating false and contradictory statements - by the destruction and removal of proofs tending to show who was the offender. These are such artifices as are commonly according to experience and the maxims of the law, resorted to by the guilty. We shall show you not only that the prisoner has attempted to conceal the evidences of his guilt - not only has he fabricated false and contradictory statements, but that he repeatedly attempted to suborn witnesses to testify for him.

When before the inquest, the day after the murder, he denied that he had attempted to negotiate money with any one, when he had in fact been in negotiations with Gilman & Gray. He denied that he had an arrangement with the deceased for money. We shall show that he had. He denied that he wanted an interview with the deceased on Wednesday. We shall show you that he sought an interview, - visited him in the street, and had such interview with him that night in his back office. We shall show you that when he knew that John Mathews had said he wanted money of deceased for speculative purposes with J. Potter, he went to George Gilman, of whom he had attempted to negotiate money, professedly for the same purpose, and by offers of large sums of money and other inducements, endeavored to persuade him to go before the inquest and state that he had not wanted money of him. That he attempted to induce Gray to do the same thing. That when before the inquest he stated that he let deceased have two $100 bills on the night of the murder, and not being able to show where he got but one, he went to Wm Hill and tried to induce him to go before the coroner's jury and swear that he let him have one of the bills. He denied that he had any agreement with the deceased for money, or wanted any of him, or that he had an appointment at his office with him on the evening of the murder, or that he had written him a letter. He carried on what he supposed to be a secret negotiation for money, and was to assign to him his books, which assignment deceased was known to make. He had in fact written a letter to deceased to meet him at his office that night.

When by the *post mortem* examination it was ascertained that poison was found in the stomach of the deceased, he caused the acid bottle to be destroyed, and the brandy bottle to be cleansed.

When Flint went into the back office and found the deceased lying upon the floor dead, he was told by prisoner that he had fallen in an epileptic fit, while drinking a glass of brandy - that he had beaten him on the head to carry the idea that he had fallen in the street, and that he must assist in getting him from the office, or they would be suspected of having murdered him - that after various proposals to carry the body to the river and the street, it was finally arranged to deposit it in the cellar where it was found. That the prisoner went below to clear the way, came up, and carried the body to the place where it was found - that he afterwards returned and removed all traces, as he supposed, of the murder, and remarked that all was right - that Flint then went to the tavern, and not long after prisoner followed. That on Friday afternoon, after the disclosure that deceased was to let him have money, he told Flint there was $100 under the carpet under the safe, and which he desired him to move. That after physicians had reported prussic acid in the stomach of the deceased, he told Flint the empty phial had better be broken, and requested him to replace the other on the shelf and fill it up with water, at the same time to throw the watch which had belonged to the deceased into the river. We shall show that at the *post mortem* examination prisoner took the direction, removed the stomach, examined the wounds on the head and pronounced them fatal - that he poured the contents of the stomach into a bowl, remarking that they scented of brandy and had better be thrown away.

Thus unconfounded by the deed, with impious and bloody hands, like the guilty and murderous Macbeth, he

"Bends up each corporeal instrument to the terrible feat,"

and with unshrinking fratricide baffles the searching suspicion of the lookers on, and aims to put beyond the reach of proof the agencies he had employed in the execution of his baneful project.

Evidence for the Prosecution

David Shorey, sworn. I keep a shop under the office formerly occupied by the prisoner, and did on September last; saw the body of the deceased on Friday morning, Oct 15th; saw a body lying on the wood with the feet out a little way of the door in the cellar; this was between 8 and 9 o'clock I should think a number of persons were present, among them Mr. Doolittle, now dead, and Mr. Ira Doolittle; my attention was called to the body by

48

some circumstance; the outside door of the cellar was pushed in, leaving a space about a foot and a half I should think; the body laid on its back a little inclined to the right side, the feet pointing outward from the opening, The doors were very heavy and made to swing inward; the door could go back no farther than it did, on account of wood piled behind it; it is a door made of two parts; I was not present when the body was taken out; it was removed while I had gone to my shop for a short time; I did not recognize the body, though I knew the deceased when alive; the hat was off the head, and lying near by; I think touching the leg; noticed that the deceased had on clean boots which appeared to have been newly blacked; they might have been slightly soiled, and I think looked as if a person might have walked in them a short distance; there was a black coat on the body the brace on the pants was unbuttoned, and the vest and coat had the appearance of being pulled up; when I arrived at the place where the body was, there were the Messrs Doolittle, Mr. Savage, Mr. Fairfield, and I think a number of other persons.

[Witness took a plan of the room and showed to the jury the stairway leading from Coolidge's office to his shop on the lower floor]

The door which leads to this stairway was fastened on my side with an iron bolt, on the doctor's I think with a bolt and lock; the doctor kept medicine and fuel in the cellar, and the door was left unfastened to accommodate him passing and repassing. The cutting board in my shop is now where it was on the night of the murder, as is also the stove; I don't know at what time my help left the shop on the night of the murder, but they came to my house a few moments after nine there were three men and five females who compose my help that came to my house at a few minutes after nine, together with two boys. The boy who opened my shop in the morning was at his work taking off the blinds when I arrived, but I do not know whether or not he had been in the shop; one of the boys is about 16, the other 19 years of age.

Cross examined. The partition between the two shops is framing set up, and lathed and plastered on both sides; a door leads into my press room, the control of which rests with one of my lads, and is fastened usually when the shop is closed; they usually stay in this back shop until 9 o'clock when it is closed; I left chairs in certain positions in my shop when I left at night, one of which touched a stove, as shown on the plan; I found the chairs in the morning as I had left them the night before; I had been cutting a coat, and left say at about 7 o'clock; I left the coat partly cut; found it in the morning precisely as I left it; the door which leads from my shop downward is fastened with a small iron bolt, a removal of which leaves a free passage downward. The several inner doors are of the ordinary thickness; the wood which is in the cellar allowed one of the doors to swing back, further than the other; the wood was thrown loosely into the cellar from the outside of the doors; a man would have to stoop considerably to get into the cellar over the wood pile; I found the door of my back shop unhooked in the morning, as had frequently been the case for some time; this cellar door is a basement door, but there are no steps from the door downward; there is access to the cellar by passing through Mr. Williams's yard, adjoining. I have one room in the second, one in the third story; one flight of stairs to the third story, for all the occupants of all the rooms in third story occupied at that time by tenants.

Day Two: Wednesday, March 15, 1848
Evidence for the Prosecution, Continued

Before giving the account of the proceedings in this trial on the 2d day, it may be remarked that the prisoner through the whole of yesterday, manifested the most perfect cool self-possession. This was particularly shown during the selection of the jury. He had a list of the jurors drawn before him, with a pen in hand to mark as each one was sworn, challenged or set aside for cause. As each juror was called he passed along close by the prisoner and stood near by him during his examination. And when the clerk said "Juror look upon the prisoner - prisoner look upon the juror," almost every juror seemed to drop his eye, or turn his head aside under the fixed and steady gaze of the prisoner; but he never quaked. And during any discussion between Counsel and the Court, he would quietly place his pen on his ear resting his cheek slightly on one hand with his elbow on the side of the box, and watch the progress of the discussion.

Once when the Reporters sitting near him had been unable to catch the name of the Juror called, he discovered it and very politely furnished the name from his list. Most of the jurors who were peremptorily challenged, were challenged very promptly. One, however, came forward, and it was evident from his answers and whole appearance, and the long consultation of prisoner's Counsel, that they were in great doubt, and were very uncertain, whether certain principles, which one accustomed to criminal proceedings could not fail to observe had governed them in their selection, would exclude or admit this juror. Mr. Noyes passed from his seat to the prisoner, and consulted with him. During this consultation he turned his eyes upon the juror who was within reach, with such a fixed, intense, scrutinizing gaze as was noticed by all the spectators. One plain, farmer-looking man not far from a Reporter's seat was heard to whisper, "See how he eyes him!" The juror was challenged.

This complete control of mind over his outward appearance is the more wonderful from the fact, that his whole appearance indicates him to be physically and naturally of a nervous temperament. In connection with this way he stated a fact that Mr. Morrell yesterday said would be proved, that at the Coroner's inquest Coolidge conducted the examination; he himself removed the stomach remarking as he emptied out the contents that "it had the smell of brandy," and this was after suspicion had been directed towards him. During the recital of the terrible detail of facts and circumstances against him, the prisoner retained the same calmness of expression without any perceptible change except that a hectic flush might have been observed spread over a portion of his countenance.

Joseph Hasty, sworn. I saw the body of deceased on the morning after in the wood cellar; that body was in a sitting position on the wood, facing the door; his right boot, I think was behind the open door, and his left extended out a little at the opening; a man in the street might have seen the body in the position it lay; his vest and pantaloons, as well as coat, were pulled up towards his head; I think his coat tail laid back on the wood, but was not under him or over his shoulder. I noticed that his boots were clean I think also that his pantaloons were drawn up so as to expose the boot legs; I took the body out of the cellar alone; I could not at first get the body out, but some one went around into Mr. Shorey's shop and removed the wood, when I succeeded. The wood was so firm behind the door as to prevent its going back further; I think the wood was piled up about four feet from the top of the door; the coat I think was unbuttoned; first discovered that the dead body was that of Mathews after I had taken it out of the cellar; as I was carrying it along some one said "it is nobody else than Ed Mathews;" I then looked, wiped the froth from his nose and mouth, and saw it was Mathews; I saw him the day before at the Parker House, and on the same evening of the same day in front of the Parker House, in a wagon. I noticed that he had his gold watch chain on at the time; I don't know where the body was carried from where I found it, but I afterwards saw it in the hall in Williams's tavern; I was at Williams's tavern Thursday night; I don't remember that I saw the deceased's hat at any time; the clothes on the deceased were not muddy when I saw them; they were the same he usually wore; I had been riding that day, and remember that it was somewhat muddy; think the night was rather a light one.

Cross examined. Mr. Tutts, Mr. Simpson, and about thirty others were at the cellar at the time I arrived there; did not measure the distance the door was open, nor do I know whether David Shorey had been there when I arrived; the wood in the cellar was not packed in, but thrown in loosely; the arms of the body were extended when I saw it; I saw no boxes, or lumber about the door; it was an old plank on which we laid the body; I then left the body with other persons and returned about an hour afterwards; there were one or two pairs of steps from Shorey's back shop to the cellar; Philip's store is a half store; very narrow; the wood did not rise from the body towards the stairs, but I think the body was about on the top of the pile, in a sitting position a little inclined backward · the rigid character of the limbs did not allow the body being taken out at the door, until some of the wood was removed; had it been in a flaccid state, I think it might have been removed without disturbing the wood; it was the evening before that I saw him in his wagon at Williams's tavern; there was no light in the tavern except in the bar-room; the stage leaves at about 4 o'clock in the evening; I saw no members of Mr. Williams's family in the tavern, but I saw Dr. Chase, another gentleman and the driver; I think the froth on the mouth of the deceased was of a yellowish color, the streets were muddy on Thursday evening there is a crossing at Williams's, but it is usually below the surface of the earth in muddy weather.

[Witness pointed out on a plan of the town of Waterville, the position of the prisoner's office in relation to the Parker House, &c, showing also an open space in the rear of the block of buildings in which the office is situated.]

David Bronson, sworn. I saw the body of the deceased on my return from the Supreme Court. I think it was in a building in the rear of Williams's tavern at which I breakfasted; I did not know the body at the time; there were present about half a dozen individuals, one of them I think Joseph Hasty; the body at the time was lying upon the wood, so near the door that the head was resting upon the edge of the door; the door is composed of two half doors; the body was lying upon the wood, the head turned down, the tarpaulin hat partly on the head so as to partly cover the eyes; from the right nostril a membrane projected about half an inch, which was filled with air; the coat was raised up close under the arms, as if some one had been lifting it; I can't say where one of the legs was out at the door or not. Some one, I think Hasty, asked me if the body could be removed before a coroner's inquest was held, and I replied there was no objection, but that all the circumstances ought to be carefully remembered; I discovered no soil upon the boots, or any indications of the body having been dragged there.[1] Mr. Flint came along directly; I shortly afterwards ordered my horse and went away; I did not know the body except from hearsay; did not discover that the surface of the hat was broken, did not notice the position of the wood inside the cellar between the outside door and the stairs. The body might have been seen at some distance by approaching it from one direction, but not readily from any other. The part of the door towards Williams's was closed.

Cross examined. There had been no attempt to remove the body before my arrival, it having been supposed improper by the persons present to disturb it. The wood in the cellar rose above the head of the body I should say, I am not quite certain with regard to the position of the body.

Cyrus Williams, sworn. I saw the body of Edward Mathews on Friday morning, in the doorway of the cellar, at say between 7 and 8. My attention was drawn to it by Mr. Lothrop; some half dozen persons were present when I arrived. It lay in a partly doubled up position, with one arm over his head; the dress was drawn up considerably; the clothes were clean. The body could not be ready seen in passing by it; I was not present when the body was taken out, neither did I enter the cellar; I should say the door was open three or four feet; saw the body a second time before it was removed, and afterwards lying on an old plank on a pile of stones near the door; I examined the wounds on the head; saw no watch on the body at the time, but do not know that the jackets were examined; I first recognized the body as it lay on the pile of stones; afterwards went with the body as it was taken into my hall; was present at the coroner's inquest, and saw the stomach removed by Dr Coolidge, put into a task basin, and handed to Dr Thayer; Dr Thayer took the basin, smelt of it and said it had a strong smell of brandy; the bowl was afterwards set down on the board that the body laid on; after a few minutes, Dr Coolidge remarked that I had better take it out, it might scent the room; I took the contents, carried them down the back stairs and hid them behind an old hogshead. They remained there sometime and then were put into the ice house, and kept there until called for by Prof Loomis, at perhaps 9 or 10 o'clock, A.M.

---

[1] The Maine Farmer account here inserts "Mr. Evans – Mr. Bronson. We do not wish you to argue."

Dr. Plaisted was present when I delivered the contents of the stomach to Prof Loomis; the contents were under lock and key in the ice house, and I had the key in my pocket.

Cross examined. I delivered the contents to Prof Loomis at the head of the dining hall on the second story; I had permission of Dr. Thayer and the coroner to take the contents of the bowl away; there were present the coroner's jury, the council, and physicians; I saw the contents taken from the stomach; left them out of doors and did not seem them again until they were out in the ice house; Mr. Soule came in the evening, asked me if the contents were thrown away; told him they were not; he then asked me to put them in the ice house; I told no person where I had put the contents of the stomach until they were locked up in the ice house; there was nothing in the ice-house but sawdust; I delivered the contents in the bowl to Prof Loomis; my hostler had lost the key of the stable which fitted the lock of the ice-house and could not find it; I therefore could not open the ice house when I took the bowl from the room where the coroner's inquest was held; when I saw the body in the cellar, the feet were extended outwards I cannot tell how long the body was laid in the open shed before removed to my house; I do not know who called the physicians that held the post mortem examination, think it was Simeon Kelley; I accompanied the body when it was taken into my hall; the hogshead I speak of was an empty one lying on its side; the basin was not covered in any way when I left it behind the hogshead; it was a common earthen wash basin; I do not recollect whether I took it from one of the sleeping rooms or from the hall; think I took it from the hall; Dr. Coolidge had boarded with me about four years and left horses at my stable; he had an extensive practice to which he attended carefully; his general standing was good so far as I know; he has been my family physician since he boarded with me; it was known when I took the contents of the stomach out of the house, but I heard no one speak of it; the place where I deposited the contents was not observable by passers by, yet it was approachable; the wash-bowl was a glazed white one which had been used a year or two.

Prof Loomis, sworn - I executed this and the accompanying plans. [They are the same as those forwarded you with the difference that mine are in more detail. The object of this portion of the examination was to show the position of the shop, office, &c as shown in the drawings and marked] I received from Mr.

Williams a bowl, on Saturday noon, Oct 2d, at about 9 o'clock, a white wash-bowl, containing a liquid; several persons were present at the time; I think Dr. Plaisted and Mr. Shaw; I took it from Mr. Williams at the head of the stairs and was proceeding to my laboratory, when Dr. Plaisted suggested that it be put in a bottle; I and Dr. Plaisted proceeded to his shop, put the contents into a bottle, and then proceeded to my laboratory; I went from thence to Dr. Boutelle's, taking the bottle with me; I kept my eye on the bottle all the time, and allowed it out of my hands but in one or two instances; I was directed to analyze the contents of the bottle, and applied chemical tests to it first for the purpose of ascertaining if there was a presence of prussic acid, that being the most volatile of all poisons; the matter was strained through a linen cloth and half an ounce or more was placed in a retort and subjected to heat; a portion of the contents had been subjected before to a test and found to exhibit indications of prussic acid; the test was common copperas; I took the distilled portion from the retort and divided it into three parts, and placed each into separate test glasses; to one portion I added sulphate of iron, potassium and muriatic acid; when the potassium was put in there was a tincture of blue, when the muriatic or sulphuric acid was added there was a deep blue, which indicated distinctly the presence of prussic acid; a second portion was tested in a different manner and gave the same result, a presence of prussic acid; I made another test with the third portion, commencing with nitrate of silver (lemon caustic) which gave a curded precipitate; that indicated prussic acid and several other substances though the curded appearance is produced only by prussic acid, brought into contact with nitrate of silver; this precipitate was dried and placed in a swell retort and subjected to the heat of a lamp; had there have been prussic acid enough present to have filled the retort it would have produced a flame, which did not appear; I afterwards distilled over another portion of the same fluid from the retort, and also washed the solid portion which was left in the cloth through which the substance was strained; this working was added to the substance in the retort, and again a distillation made; I added to the whole of this nitrate of silver, and curded precipitate was produced as before but not so dense; this I put into a very small retort, after having been dried; this retort was placed in the flame of a spirit lamp, and another lamp was so placed that it would ignite any inflammable gas which might escape; an ignition of a flame was produced which is produced out of the gas which forms the basis of prussic acid; I did not get the flame in a third experiment, but on repeating it on Monday more carefully, it was produced on the same portion of the fluid.

I was present on Sunday at the post mortem examination, and saw present Dr. Thayer, Dr. Noyes, Dr. Plaisted and Dr. Boutelle; the head was forced open, and on exposing the brain, there appeared something which I supposed to be unnatural. The brain was then taken out, and I smelt of it, but am not confident that I detected anything like a peculiar odor; the brain was then taken and put in a vessel for further examination. The abdomen was then examined. The mucous coat of the stomach was found to be very much softened, and other portions very brown. The interior surface of the abdomen was very much corrugated. The darkest spot on the stomach was confined to a space of about two inches. The spleen was very much enlarged, but was not examined at the time minutely; one of the kidneys was removed for further examination. The liver was blood, from the position in which I stood; the blood that I saw was all virous. The lung were of a very dark blue color, with the exception of a small portion at the lower point; the anterior surface was more uniformly blue than the posterior surface; this discoloration of the lungs extended through the whole mass.

On Monday there was an examination of the brain, a part of the liver, the lungs, a kidney and the spleen; the substances then examined had the same appearance as the portions of the body examined on Sunday; the spleen was very much softened. No further examination of the lungs or liver was made, but the kidney exhibited no unusual appearance. The brain was found to be very much softened; a knife was passed through it several times, and the interior found to be white. When the thorax was opened, I detected a peculiar odor, which I have no doubt was prussic acid. I have frequently witnessed the effects of this acid on animals since this examination, having made experiments in order to test the truth of the experiments made on the body of the deceased, and have found that the effects of prussic acid, when thrown into the stomach in considerable quantities, will produce death in from three seconds to fifteen minutes. An acid which I made, of half the strength of the pure acid, put in the eye of a cat, produced death in ten seconds; the quantity was less than a drop. I am not able, from experiment, to say how soon death could be produced in a man. In one instance a dog ran, after taking the acid, about 19 feet and fell dead; a shrill might be produced from the effects of the acid, but when injected into the stomach, it would be the death shriek. The acid always produces on the stomach dark spots, and generally a discoloration of the liver and lungs; I have never seen an instance where the lungs were not somewhat discolored; the blood in the veins is always rendered fluid; I have not always discovered odor from bodies so poisoned, but have observed it about sixty hours after death so produced, when ejected into the stomach with brandy; I have applied the chemical tests I have described, to the animals I have experimented upon, and the results have been in every case the discovery of the acids by the iron test and the copper test, and in one instance by the silver test.

Cross ex. - Have had considerable experience in morbid anatomy; I have never been a medical student, but have frequently seen dissections performed at the medical college in Philadelphia. Morbid anatomy is not a part of my profession, but anatomy and physiology are sciences I teach; I have attended post mortem examinations, but am not aware of an instance where death was caused by poison or apoplexy; the bottle in which the substance was subjected to chemical tests were placed, I did not examine but supposed it contained nothing; prussic acid is a compound substance, which will rust, nor will its parts so combine as to produce the results mentioned in my chemical experiments; I speak of this as you do of any other well known chemical fact; none of the substances alone which compose prussic acid, will alone produce odor except syanagin, which is a gas - the odor from this is slight; syanagin alone will produce a [?] slow flame, such as was produced by my experiments; I know of no instance, and know of no authors, who say that prussic acid may be produced in the stomach by heat, but I think I have seen somewhere that it is said such a result may or has been produced by heat in the stomach; I have found no accredited author who makes such a statement, but know there is such a supposition; almost all substances contain the elements of prussic acid, but it is not common to find the odors of that acid in the human system so far as my own experience goes, or from what I have seen in books; I knew very little about prussic acid until called upon to make the experiments I have described; in none of the substances which I analyzed from the stomach of the deceased did I discover brandy; I think the oil of vitrol could not be mistaken for hydrocyanic acid.

Adjourned to 1 o'clock P. M.

Cross ex of Prof Loomis resumed. - Hydrocyanic acid may be produced from various substances there is a difference of strength to the different sorts of this acid usually sold by the apothecaries; that made by a certain chemist will be of uniform strength, that is to say, different chemists produce it by different modes, and usually attach their names to the bottles containing it; the flame arising from Prussic acid is always the same color; do not know whether Guild says the same is a purple one with a blue or [?] not; Christison may call it a rose red flame, I am not able to say with certainty; the experiment was made at about 3 o'clock in the day, but I cannot tell whether it was a clear one or otherwise; the room where the experiments were made is ordinarily lighted; I know the natural history of the substances I was experimenting upon well enough; Christison says the acid may be found in organic matter in various places where it is not supposed to exist; Guy says that hydrocyanic acid may be found in the stomach; do not recollect whether Guy says the brain has an odor which commonly resembles this gas; this was the first time I ever experimented on a human subject with a view of ascertaining whether death was produced by poison; I have heard it said that a dose of brandy will kill a cat, but am not aware that it was ever a notorious fact; I passed a tube into the stomach of the animals I experimented upon, then ejected the poison through the tube and I feel certain none of it could have got to the lungs; the first test that I applied was for prussic acid, though the preliminary tests, which I did not consider solid, were one for morphia, the other for prussic acid; had there been morphia, an orange red color would have been produced, - failing to produce it, however, I applied tests for prussic acid, finding indications of that poison; there appeared to be about a pint of the contents of the stomach which I experiment upon, a portion of it vegetable and a portion animal.

[Witness here described plans of the rooms of Dr Coolidge and Mr. Hovey.)

The distance from the cutting table is three feet four inches to the wall - the passage way is three feet, or about the same distance; there were several shelves in Coolidge's office, but I did not see the wood box as marked in the plan; Fairfield's house is situated about 8 rods in the rear of these buildings; the plans are not all made from actual measurement; I went into the cellar several times - its height is between five and six feet; the windows in the rear of the building are something more than the ordinary width.

Dr. Plaisted sworn - Saw the body of Edward Mathews on Friday at about 9 o'clock, in Williams's yard, and observed two cuts on the head; I was in the presence of several gentlemen at the time; next saw it in the hall of Mr. Williams's house, and at this time observed another cut, also a fracture of the skull. Dr. Thayer, Dr. Coolidge and Mr. Flint was present at this time. The scalp was not removed. The cut on the top of the head was perhaps half an inch long, and as deep as it could be before hitting the bone; the flesh was not swollen. I think Dr Coolidge removed the stomach; it was filled with food partly decomposed. The wounds on the head were the result of three distinct blows; I examined the body again on Sunday in the presence of Prof Loomis, Dr. Thayer, Dr. Boutelle, and Dr. Noyes. We examined the body again and removed the scalp when we found the brain very much congested, of a bluish color, and emitting a prussic acid smell; there was less blood on the brain under the fracture, than is usually found when living persons have received equally severe blows; the liver, the lungs and the spleen were more congested, and exhibited a more bluish tinge than I ever before saw at a post mortem examination - the blood was bluish in the veins and flowed freely when the vessels were cut; I saw Mr. Williams give the bowl containing the contents of the stomach into Mr. Loomis' hands; Prof L. took it and went with me to my office, where we put it in a clean bottle and he proceeded with it to the College; I did not see it after; I observed two or three small cuts on the thigh of the body inside the leg.

Cross examined. Dr. Coolidge and Mr. Flint made the incisions on the body, as is common in such cases, they being jury men; they offered it to us first; I observed a smell of brandy emitted from the stomach, but no other smell that I noticed; have frequently seen the coatings of stomachs where persons have been addicted to drinking brandy, but this one exhibited quite a different appearance; I thought from the quantity of brandy found in the stomach at the time, that it was sufficient to produce intoxication; Mr. Williams carried off the contents of the stomach; he asked what he should do with it, and Dr. Thayer or Dr. Coolidge said throw it out, or else assented to its being thrown out; next examined the body in the presence of the mother of deceased; you could see where wounds had been inflicted by discoloration of blood; whole brain showed more of prussian blue than I have ever seen upon a similar examination; internal appearance of lungs much the same as upon the exterior; one of the cavities of the heart contained blood; in my opinion the color from the brain was that of prussic acid; for any thing I may know, the brain may afford in its natural state this odor; did not notice anything particular about the eyes; thought I recognized the smell upon taking out the brain; not a familiar smell to me at the time; thought wounds upon the head might have been inflicted with a billet of wood; that upon the leg with a sharp weapon; such a blow as the one farthest back might have produced death; did not wash the bottle into which the contents were put, not apply any test to see what was in it; don't know from where I had it or how long I had had it; don't use prussic acid, only once had it in my office; one of my students had it; saw upon the throat of the deceased an appearance, might have been made by lying upon the wood or by hand; also a mark upon his back which I thought might have been produced by lying upon some hard substance; no one objected to the examination of the stomach; Dr. Coolidge's instruments were used at the first examination; upon the second mine; I never bought, never sold, nor had any prussic acid except what my student left about four years ago.

Dr. Noyes, sworn[2]. I saw the dead body of Edward Mathews on Sunday morning, the 3d day of October last; Dr. Thayer, Dr. Boutelle, Dr. Plaisted and Prof. Loomis were present.

On opening the body the lungs had not collapsed; the right cavity of the heart was found empty; the blood flowed freely from the arteries that were opened, and I observed it was of a dark color; an odor the same as that proceeding from Prussic acid was distinctly noticed to be exhaled from the brain and stomach; I noticed that the spleen was highly gorged with blood; the tongue at the first examination was protruded from between the teeth, and the eyes were considerably dilated; I noticed the marks of finger mails upon the left side of the throat, but am not able to say as to both sides; the wounds on the thigh might have discharged blood or might not, they were of very slight depth.

---

[2] Dr. J. F. Noyes had been a medical student of Dr. Potter in Waterville. He was the brother of Edwin Noyes, one of the counsels for Dr. Coolidge.

Cross examined. Only one wound upon the head where the skull was fractured; wound in the groin might have been deep enough to discharge blood; no particular examination of it; no examination of the passage of the mouth to the windpipe; both the cavities of the heart were found empty; have never attended a post mortem examination of one who died by poison; have attended post mortem examinations where death was by apoplexy, and it resembled this case in come particulars, more especially as regards the fluids; am not acquainted with morbid appearances where persons have died of intemperate habits, from observation it is stated in the authorities that the brain sometimes or always exhales an odor as of prussic acid; works of authority are Christison's, Guy's Forensic medicine.; physicians sometimes keep prussic acids, druggist generally; it is an article of medicine and of different degrees of strength; in the case of apoplexy which I mentioned there was not a large amount of blood on the brain, but do not recollect distinctly how it was in the veins.

Dr. John Hubbard sworn. The three principal tests of prussic acid are, prussiate of iron, cyanite of copper, and cyanite of silver. In a case of poison, the odor and other sensible properties will throw light on the agent producing the death. To those familiar with the odor, it is as reliable as chemical tests. No three witnesses testifying to the same point, would be more reliable than the chemical tests. Witness would expect if an animal or person died from prussic acid instantaneously, the odor would be discovered in any of the cavities of the body on opening it. Witness refers to a case where poison enough is administered to produce instant death. One grain of concentrated acid would produce death in one or two minutes; this would be equal to fifty grains of the medicinal acid. Would not expect to find the odor in the brain so readily as in other parts, because less vascular. The general morbid appearance would not be very dissimilar to those in some other cases of sudden death; if there is any difference, it is in the peculiar bluish hue given by prussic acid to the parts. Witness has seen experiments with prussic acid on animals – producing instant death. The odor may be discovered at least 64 hours after death, according to witnesses' observation. Six or seven days after death, it has been discovered, according to the authorities. Witness has used prussic acid in his practice, but has not kept it as a medicine a fifteenth part of the time of his medical life. Thinks medical men generally do not keep or use it at all. Has had occasion to administer it to only two or three patients; not used more than one ounce in his practice. The strength of medicinal acid is only 2 per cent; knows of but one degree of strength kept by apothecaries; the standard of the U. S. Pharmacopoeia. Should he wish it stronger, he should probably apply to a chemist. Supposes wholesale druggists in large cities may keep it stronger. Acids are used in different strengths by physicians, and diluted when necessary. Have heard the descriptions of the wounds on the head; should judge from the descriptions they were inflicted after death. Witness judges principally from the absence of all appearances of inflammation. Had they been inflicted but a short time before death, they would have produced inflammation.

Cross examined. Has never been present at a post mortem examination of a person who died from prussic acid. Cannot say what modification the fluids of the system would exercise; but if he discovered the odor, he should believe it; should rely with perfect confidence on either the odor or the chemical tests. There may be cases where the odor would not be perceptible, but chemical tests would discover it; this would depend on the suddenness of the death and attending circumstances. It is said that the odor may be discovered in cases where no prussic acid exists in the system, and that the acid may be generated by the decomposition of bodies; these statements are made by authors vaguely and without personal knowledge, and are not entitled to confidence. Witness has attended the examination of many dead bodies, but never discovered anything of the kind. Has examined standard works on the subject. – Cannot say whether acid taken in brandy would be retained in the system more certainly. Prussic acid was used some thirty years ago with great confidence for consumption; thinks if it had any efficacy it was in a disordered state of the stomach. Has seen an experiment where brandy and acid were administered, and after 14 hours and again after 40 hours, the acid odor was perceptible, but the odor of brandy was not. Has known chemical tests applied with success in cases where the acid was administered with brandy. Witness knows that Dr. Coolidge kept on hand all kinds of medicines; supposed he had a greater variety and kept a large stock on hand than almost any physician of his acquaintance. Cannot say whether physicians who have students purchase articles for them to experiment upon. Thinks brandy would have no material influence to prevent the effect of prussic acid; has seen an animal destroyed in one minute by a mixture of the two. Has examined several persons who died from habitual drinking and found nothing peculiar in the stomach; the liver was always strongly marked; thinks congestion of the brain would be likely to occur in those cases. Has known Dr. Coolidge four or five years, and as frequently met him and been called to his patients. He had an extensive practice. Never heard aught against his character as a citizen; thought him humane in his practice.

The examination of this witness here closed, and the Court adjourned to half past 8 in the morning.

Day Three: Thursday, March 16, 1848
Evidence for the Prosecution, Continued

The prisoner still continues solemn and collected in his demeanor, exhibiting very little anxiety or emotion. Heard it said last night by an officer who frequently sees him alone, however, that he gives way to emotions of the most poignant character as soon as he leaves the court room. Should he be proved guilty, the circumstances connected with the post mortem examinations of the body of Mr. Mathews, &c, show a degree of cool-blooded depravity on the part of the accused, which we can hardly conceive of. Think of a man concerting a plan to murder his nearest friend, and that for scarcely any reason, who, after having committed the deed, goes and deliberately examines the body of the victim, look his murdered companion in the face with all the professional coolness of a surgeon, and actually conducts post mortem examinations on the body and you have an idea of the position of the accused in this case. I do not believe that in the whole annals of crime, any thing like a parallel to this can be produced.

As the trial progresses, the excitement increases, and the indignation against the accused occasionally breaks forth with marked violence – I believe that should he be convicted, the populace will demand his immediate execution, so incensed are they at the enormity of the offense charged.[1]

The Court met pursuant to adjournment. The crowd of ladies and gentlemen in attendance as spectators continues as great as at first – in fact, it seems to increase from day to day.[2]

Dr. Noyes re-called. Saw Prof. Loomis's bottle containing the contents of Mathews's stomach, in Dr. N. R. Boutelle's office. The bottle was on the table when witness entered, with a stopple in it – Witness removed the stopple, smelled of the contents of the bottle, and detected an odor of prussic acid – Presumes Dr. B. is in Philadelphia – he left Waterville the last of October, and has

---

[1] Boston Daily Times.

[2] Northern Tribune.

65

not returned since. Dr. B. likewise smelled of the contents of the bottle.

Cross examined. Witness was a student in Dr. Coolidge's office a part of 1845 and 1846. Dr. C. kept prussic acid amongst his ordinary medicines – kept a larger assortment of medicines than physicians usually keep. Does not know that his students used the acid for experiments. Dr. C. has been in the habit of keeping students. Dr. Boutelle was a student there – afterwards Mr. Flint. Does not know that Dr. Thomas was a student there – he was with Dr. Potter. Has been acquainted with Dr. C. ever since he came to Waterville – knows nothing against his good reputation as a citizen, or as a humane physician.

Question by Mr. Morrill. Have you not heard things against the character of Dr. Coolidge at any time, aside from this transaction? This question was objected to by Mr. Evans. The Court said the inquiry must be confined to general reputation. Mr. Morrill then asked if the witness had heard reports prejudicial to the character of Dr. Coolidge. He answered that he had since this tragedy, but did not remember having any unconnected with this affair. Has been in practice in Waterville recently, and has been amongst the people in that vicinity.[3]

Question by the Attorney General. Have you heard any other charge against Dr. Coolidge, than that of murder? Objected to, and not allowed by the court.

Dr. H. H. Hill sworn. Not much acquainted with the case of prussic acid from practice – has never used it but one or twice in about 11 years practice – It is not much kept by physicians, nor used. The actual strength usually kept by apothecaries. Has never used more than half a drachm, and prescribed it only one or twice. Has seen it administered with brandy and water to a dog; it was of 16 per cent strength Animal life was gone in half a minute; organic life in a minute more. In this case the left cavity of the breast was emptied, and the blood forced into the veins. The lungs were gorged with blood and congested. This is not always but usually the case. The eye glistened and staring for some time after death. No other reliable indications peculiar to poison. Frothing at the mouth is said to be common in such cases; should suppose it would be so in case the poison produced

---

[3] This brief cross-examination provides a good example of the differences that occur in different versions of the testimony. See appendix.

convulsions. The reliable tests of prussic acid are copperas, blue vitirol, and lunar caustic or nitrate of silver, and the odor. Heard part of Prof. Loomis' testimony, He stated the same tests. – Witness has seen them used; considered the tests very positive. Should expect to detect prussic acid by applying his nose to the part nearest accessible. If it was in the cavities of the body, he should expect to find it there, if not too long afterward. In a dog, he has found it 62 hours after death in the cavities of the stomach; could not say it was so distinct in the brain. After it had been exposed to the air over 4 hours, the acid was detected by all the tests; the animal had been dead 14 hours before the dissection. Brandy in this case was given with the acid, but could not detect its color. Witness heard the description of Drs. Plaisted and Noyes of the wounds on the head; judging from the description of appearances, witness thinks the wounds were inflicted after death.

Cross examined. The animal he referred to was killed last Saturday night. Dr. Hubbard and Prof. Loomis attended during the experiment. This was the only case he had been present at. The same tests were applied as he had spoken of here. In this case the acid administered was 16 per cent. Never was present at a post mortem examination of a human subject killed by poison. Has been present at such an examination of a person dying of disease of the heart. The liver usually exhibits the effects of ardent spirits most certainly. Never attended an examination of a person who died in a rum fit; in such a case should expect to find the lungs somewhat gorged. Has seen statements in books that it is not improbable that prussic acid may be generated by decomposition of animal substances; but witness thinks it quite improbable. Has examined authorities; never saw it stated that this is "very apt" to be the case. The volatile oil of bitter aloes is spoken of as having an odor similar to prussic acid, and the only thing that can be mistaken for it. Would expect to find the odor more strong immediately on opening the body than after exposure.

Direct resumed. In the case of the animal, the odor was strong when the body was opened, and again in 80 hours afterwards; but the body had been closed up. Observed in the body of the dog a peculiar blue tinge; more strongly marked in the lungs than elsewhere. The liver had something of it, but not so marked. Never met with such appearances before. The liquid prussic acid is colorless when pure. Should think hydrocyanic acid is never generated in the stomach, or if it is it would be dangerous to have a stomach. Has no knowledge of its ever being generated there before or after death.

Cross examination resumed. Has witnessed the dissecting or dissection of many animals of different kinds, and never saw anything like the blue appearance mentioned.

William Tobey sworn – Prisoner was in debt to witness on the 30th of September last, for borrowed money, for about $115. One note was given in 1846 for $50. The other in March, 1847, for $40. Prisoner has attempted to borrow money of witness at various times. In March last was the last time; he wanted at first from $400 to $500 at ten per cent, and would keep it five years if witness desired. Let him have only what has been stated. He applied for $400 or $800 in Vassalboro', in October, 1846; witness partly promised it to him. In Nov. 1846, he again called in Waterville for the money; witness told him he must have good security; prisoner asked if his security was not good. Witness replied that it might or might not be. When witness lived in Fairfield, in March, 1847, he received two letters from Dr. Coolidge, on the same subject; afterwards saw him in Fairfield; then in Waterville, at Dr. C.'s office, and let him have $40. Dr. C. wanted more money, and told witness to charge the $40, and he would give him his note for the full amount when witness let him have more. Told him explicitly that it was the last he would let him have; did not apply to him for money afterwards. Told witness from the first to let no one know it. Saw the prisoner in his office on Saturday after the murder; called on him for the amount of the notes. In the forenoon, went into the office, and had some conversation with him; Flint only was present; said nothing then about the money. Called again after dinner; went into the back office with Dr. C.; left Flint in the front office, Asked Dr. C. for the money; he said it was impossible for him to pay it then; was in trouble; wished witness to wait till his trouble was over; asked him to secure witness by a note or notes to the amount; he said he could not, for *he had agreed to make them over to Mathews, and was liable to be called upon at any moment.* Saw him again in his back office, an hour or an hour and a half afterwards; thinks Daniel Moor was in the front office then. Witness said to him he could not see why he could not secure him with note or notes; Dr. C. gave the same reasons. Witness told him if he was called upon for the notes, he should have them. Dr. C. said some witness might not be there, and it would be some trouble to send to him. Prior to talking about the notes, had been talking with Dr. C. about the death of Edward Mathews. Called several times in the afternoon and found the door locked. Cannot say whether Coolidge was there.

Cross examined – Dr. Coolidge did not say what Mathews was to have the notes. In 1847, and usually when Dr. C. asked for money, it was under injunctions of secrecy. When witness called for the money, there was a suspicion against Coolidge, and he was excited; appeared to feel bad. Coolidge's first application for money was in September, 1846; had had business dealings with him before, and had an account. Lived in Waterville three years, and returned to Fairfield in Sept., 1846. Had been very familiar with the prisoner; prior to this accusation, know no harm of him. He had practiced in witnesses' family and neighborhood.

Direct resumed – The first time he saw Dr. Coolidge, Saturday, the Dr. mentioned the murder himself. Thinks the third time he went into Dr. C.'s office, E. A. J. Baker was there, Thinks the door from the front to the back office was not locked. Witness went to the door; Coolidge wished witness to retire a few moments, did so, and staid away half an hour, or an hour, and returned and found Coolidge in the front office; did not see Baker. These notes are paid; witness sued the notes that day, attached and got the money, Cannot say that Coolidge came to Vassalboro' on purpose for the money. Thinks the prisoner had practice in Vassalboro'; saw him there once before; he had an extensive practice,

David Smilie sworn – Prisoner owes him about $200, by note, for borrowed money; borrowed in June last; note is dated June 21, 1847; payable on demand; $5.08 cents indorsed on the back, Jan. 21, 1848; this was an account Dr. C. had for services. Witness lives in Winslow. No agreement as to interest; nothing said about it. Nothing said about keeping it secret.

Cross examined. Does not lend money frequently. Never pressed Coolidge for payment. He asked for $200 or $250. Has known Coolidge since he lived in Waterville; practiced in witnesses' neighborhood; his character was good prior to this affair.

Isaac Britton sworn - The prisoner is indebted to me by note for borrowed money, something like $200; I live in Winslow; five years interest and a small endorsement is paid on the note; I once met the prisoner and asked him if he knew the note would be due shortly; he said he did, and asked me if I wanted it; I told him when the interest was promptly paid I sometimes let notes lay over. He paid me the interest on the day the note was due, and I never have spoken to him since about it.

Cross examined. He has practiced in my family and his general character was good so far as I am aware. Witness lived in Winslow, about three miles from Waterville.

Daniel Moor sworn – Prisoner owes him two notes, one he thinks was given 3 years ago next May, for $25, borrowed money – payable upon demand, not a cent paid on it. Has turned the notes into Mr. Noyes with others to get a dividend. The next note was for $100, given in October, 1845, payable on demand – prisoner said he should have it in 24 hours if he wished; not a cent paid. Prisoner said he did not want it known he was hiring money. Never mentioned it till after this affair happened. Not a cent of interest paid. The interest on the $100 note was put in 12 per cent.

Warren K. Doe sworn. The prisoner is indebted to me by note $100; the note is dated Sep 25th, 1847, and is "on demand". Since his affair happened, $8 has been endorsed on the note; the indebtedness is for borrowed money which was loaned him at Waterville; nothing was said about the note or interest; live in Sebasticook.

Cross examined. The prisoner practiced in my family and neighborhood; his character is good.

John R Philbrick sworn. Prisoner owes him $150 borrowed money – note dated April, 1845, payable in one year. Nothing paid but interest up to October 1846. – Prisoner had promised him 'good interest.'

Cross examined – Lives in Waterville. Has known the prisoner – character good.

Jones A. Goodwin, sworn. Prisoner owed him Sept 30, 1847, something less than $10. Had not a note against him at that time – had one in May last for $180. Sold it to Lorenzo Crowell. Don't recollect the date – think it was given the winter before, payable on demand. Had an account for Clothing, for which the note was given, none of it borrowed money. Kept a Clothing shop and furnished prisoner in the way of business,

Job Richards, sworn. The prisoner owes me between $400 and $500, by notes, dated Feb. 10th, 1847, payable on demand, and one dated Aug 1847, payable in eight days; nothing has been paid on these notes, with the exception of $100, which was paid by letting me have a horse. There was no agreement as to interest on the first $300, on the last $50 he was to give me $5 for the use of it eight days; There was no injunctions of secrecy concerning the loan or loans.

Cross examined. I did expect the $5 when he asked me for $50 eight days; I have known accused ever since he came to Waterville, know nothing against his character; he has had an extensive practice in my neighborhood.

Robert Drummond, sworn. The prisoner owes me $100 for which I have his note, given June last; it was for borrowed money and made payable on demand.

Cross examined. I live in Sidney, about five miles from Waterville; the prisoner practiced in our family, and I never heard anything against his character.

Augustine Perkins, sworn. I am cashier of the Ticonic Bank at Waterville; I believe on the 30th of Sept. the prisoner had two notes, one for $100 and one for $150 in the bank, which had been over due six or eight months; they have been taken up since by the prisoner's sureties. On the 30th of Sept. Edward Mathews had a note discounted at the bank for $1500. (Note was produced and read.) The blank on which the note is written was procured on Thursday at about 10 o'clock, A.M., and in the afternoon I paid the money to Edward Mathews, the surety on the note is Charles P. Mathews; Edward Mathews had a note in the bank at the time, and took up on I think of $1000 on the Monday previous; the money on the note I hold was made Thursday, but is dated the Monday previous according to the rules of the bank; on 27th Dec '47, John Mathews paid $750 on the principal and half of the interest on the note as endorsed; there is also another endorsement on the note, dated March, 1848.

Cross examined. Prisoner paid up the interest on his notes when called upon, and said he would take up the notes they held very soon.

Charles R. Phillips, sworn · The prisoner owes me about $83, I think, $64 of which is by note, given in March, 1847, and running "on demand." I keep a furnishing store at Waterville; the prisoner applied to me for $500 in July or August last, for six months, but as he wished me to keep it a secret, I concluded not to let him have it. He offered me 10 per cent of rate use of it at one time. He had hired considerable money of me two or three years ago, in sums from $1 to $100; the last I loaned him was $100, in June, which has been paid since. Nothing was said about interest, but when he settled he throwed down a small amount, which might have been the legal amount or not.

James F Gray, sworn. The prisoner is not now indebted to me. In September of 1846 he borrowed about $200 of me, payable on demand, and it was paid in January last by process of a suit which I commenced. He was to give me 12 per cent for the use of the money: he applied to me in August or September last, for enough to make out $1000 with what he owed me then, at the same time saying he wanted about $300 in all, to send to Dr Potter, as he was going into a land speculation with him; he offered me $500 for the use of $1000 six months, and told me he would secure me with his books, by assignment or some other lien; he asked me to say nothing about the desired loan, as I think he said he did not want people to know he was engaged in speculations. He told me also, that a week or two before, he had received a letter from Dr Potter. I think this conversation was between two and three weeks before the death of Mathews, at the door of the prisoner's office. I did not tell him at the time whether I would or would not let him have the money, but agreed to see him again; subsequently I met him again, when he asked me about the loan, and I told him I was not sufficiently acquainted with business matters to do it. He said he would convey his books in such a manner as to make it satisfactory, but did not wish the conversation known; he asked me again about the loan on the day the body of the deceased was found. At the time I met him as he was coming from the coroner's inquest, went with him to his back office; he closed the door and locked it, and we were left alone. He put his hand on my shoulder, and as we walked to the window he started back and asked me if I thought those two men were watching us, pointing to two persons who were sitting on a log back of the office. I replied that

I guessed not; he then asked me if I had been at the coroner's inquest; I told him I had not; he said he had and feared he would be suspected; I had lost the notes for the money he owed me, and asked him to renew them, having had his promise the day before that he would do it; he replied that he was excited and could not do it that day, but would the next, and asked me to say nothing about his application for money to send Dr. Potter; I was about the leave the office when he desired me to stay, and asked me that if I should go before the jury what I should say I had been in the office for; I told him I didn't know; he desired me, in case I should go before the jury to say I was there for the purpose of having my lungs examined, but I replied that I was pretty healthy and people would not believe it; he then mixed a bottle of medicine and gave it to me; I put it in my pocket and went out; I gave the bottle to Mr. Shaw the coroner.

Cross examined. I am a boatman, sometimes hired and sometimes on my own hook; I am not in the habit of having large sums of money, but I think I could have raised a thousand or so; I had the conversation with the prisoner about the money in the latter part of August, I think; I was a witness at the coroner's jury and there stated the same facts I have stated here; I have never said I should not have made any disclosures against Coolidge had I not been suspected not so intimated to anyone, think, indeed I am quite positive I was in the village of Waterville on the night of the murder; left Mr. Sprague's, went to the store house down by the landing at about 1 o'clock; I then went to Williams's and from there to my boarding house, and went to bed at about two o'clock; I don't know as I am obliged to tell why I went to the store house in the night; it was known and spoken of in Waterville, on the day I went to the office with Dr. Coolidge, that I had been out the night before; I was asked by the coroner, when before the jury, where I was on the night of the murder; I was in the back office with Dr. Coolidge half an hour or more; while there, I think Coolidge told me he was suspected of the murder, said something about finding brandy in his stomach; I did not any time ask Coolidge what I should say before the jury, nor did I, in the course of the conversation tell him that I was also suspected or any thing of the sort; the warehouse I went to is about 20 rods from Williams's tavern; I rode down in a wagon; while at the warehouse I got brandy and drank it. To a previous question whether he had drank anything that night while rambling about, he answered "no," but explained by saying that about that time he had done rambling. I had the key of the warehouse, and the brandy drank was from my bottle which I kept there;

Direct resumed. Went to Getchell's party about 7 o'clock. Witness's brother and two sisters were there, and some others, Left Getchell's at 10 or 11, and went to Craig's with two Misses Craig, and staid till one o'clock. Has married one of the young ladies since. Returning he met Joseph Hasty with a wagon – got in with him – rode down Main street to the storehouse, drank some brandy, then put up the horse, stopped at Williams's, and then went home. Saw James Hill coming off the Ticonic bridge about 20 or 30 minutes past 1. Passed him and saw no more of him. When in the office with Coolidge, witness did not know that he (witness) was suspected; had no conversation with Coolidge as to suspicion of witness. Does not mean to say what distinct amount Coolidge wanted to raise. Thinks it was $3000 or $4000; cannot say with certainty,

Charles Gilman, sworn. About the 1st of June 1847, lent prisoner $100, payable on demand – he wanted it as long as he could have it – when I wanted it I was to have it – he wanted it to buy a horse – paid it about the last of July. In August 1846, lent him $60, on demand – paid it about the middle of September 1846. Has applied for money at other times – at various times for small sums, or not very large – from $10 to $100. Since the last loan witness has not seen him. Prisoner did not owe witness at the time of the murder.

Eben Shaw, sworn. Was called as coroner to summon a jury on the body of Mathews; during the examination noticed a discoloration on the throat of the deceased, more visible on one side than the other; there was a cut across the thigh of the pantaloons below the pocket, which appeared to have been made with a knife; I also noticed that the pocket had been fastened up with a breast pin, and afterwards forced open, as was shown by the pin still remaining. Witness was shown a bottle which was brought before the coroner's jury, as he said, by Mr. Gray. A man call his name Howe came into the hall and informed me privately that he had discovered some money in a wood pile, and I with a number of the jury went to the spot, and the money was taken out in our presence: the amount of money found was $150; a watch was exhibited to me, but I do not recollect by whom, but my impression is Mr. Allen brought it in; a boy named Butterfield came in and testified that he found it; there was an appearance of blood upon the back of the watch and on the key when I first saw it; the crystal was also shattered; I observed the boots of the deceased, and noticed that they were clean, giving indications of having been newly blacked; a hat was brought in, which they said was found on the head of deceased, that had blood inside of it, but I observed no traces of violence on the hat; the clothes were pulled up, the coat buttoned, and I think the lining torn out; I arrived at Waterville at 10, and got a jury in about an hour; Dr. Plaisted, Dr. Thayer, Dr. Coolidge and Mr. Flint were the first persons summoned; I cannot say at what time they commenced their examinations.

Cross examined. I arrived at about 10 o'clock, and the examination commenced about an hour afterwards; it was by my order that physicians were called, but I did not select who should be called; don't recollect who directed the taking out the stomach; neither do I recollect who suggested the examination of the stomach; Mr. Boutelle and Mr. Smith remained after the *post mortem* examination had closed; the body remained in the hall, after the first examination some time before taken charge of by the coroner's jury; I stood very near the head of the body while the prisoner was making examinations on the head, and heard him say that he discovered a fracture on one part of the head which in his opinion was sufficient to produce death; think there were three wounds on the head altogether; did not remain by the body all the time it was in the hall, but the constable had general charge of it.

Joseph Hasty, recalled. A watch was shown the witness which he did not recognize, but had seen Edward Mathews wear a chain like the one attached to the watch. There was a peculiarity about the chain which he had noticed also about the chain deceased wore.

Cross examined. Could not swear that was the chain Mathews wore the day before his death; but he wore *a* gold chain that day; I heard a conversation in Chandler's office at one time in which James F. Gray took part, but don't know that I can say distinctly what he said; think he said, however, that he should not have said anything about Coolidge had he not been suspected himself; this I think was in reference to his testimony before the coroner's inquest; Mr. Chandler requested me a month or more ago, to charge my memory with this remark of Gray.

Joseph Nudd, sworn. There are certain phials in my possession which were found in Coolidge's office in Waterville, (witness here exhibited two small glass bottles,) - they were found in a small closet between the shelves, where were usually kept his most costly medicines; Mr. Flint and the Attorney were present when the bottles were found; the was on Sunday; the bottles have been in my custody ever since; (three letters were shown which witness said were in the hand-writing of the prisoner, he should judge) - I noticed marks upon the throat of the deceased, which were black and blue, - there were two upon one side and one upon the other of the throat; I saw the body in the cellar where it was discovered, not far from 8 o'clock, on the morning of the murder; there were from three to five persons present - Ira Gould, David Leighton, and I don't remember the others; I saw the body removed, and at the time noticed a frothy substance which seemed to come from the nostrils and side of his mouth; I noticed the marks on the neck after that body had been taken out and laid on a plank; the prisoner had left some bills with me to collect sometime before this, from June to August, or about that time; I assisted in taking an inventory of the prisoner's property not far from a fortnight after the murder, the nominal amount of which, in personal property, was not far from $1600; this included medicines, &c, but not his books; I paid a note which prisoner owed to Lorenzo Crowell, to Mr. Smith, which was in amount something over $200; I paid this about the last of January, I think; (an account book was shown which witness said was prisoner's) - there is a charge here which I know, reading thus: "Edward Mathews cash lent, $200" under the date September 30, 1847; I was requested by the coroner to go to the office and get this book; I went there, told Coolidge my errand, and he opened the books and showed it to me; he asked what they said about the his book, and what he ought to say; I replied that if it were my case I should state the truth; when I went for the book he was standing near it, and this charge was there the last one on it; I was in the jury room when he was requested to go and get his book, and as soon as he left I was requested to go after him - he left the chair in which he had been testifying, when he went to the office; during that testimony he stated that he had loaned Edward Mathews $200, which were charged on this books, but that he took no note.

Cross examined. I went to Coolidge's office at the request of the Attorney general, with him; he (the Att. Gen.) was there nearly all day looking over papers, &c. I had taken charge of the office the day before, having had precepts so to do, being a deputy sheriff. I filled a cask with bottles which were there, and also observed a hatchet and some pieces of a broken jug. (Witness described the position of the body when found in the cellar as previous witnesses have done.)

During the week while I had custody of the office several persons visited it, the town committee among others. The inventory I have referred to included the medicines in the office and the library of books; I should think the space between the top of the wood on which the body was found, and the floor about was something over four feet.

Miller M Paine, sworn. Witness recognized the chain on a watch shown him to be the one worn by Edw'd Mathews, but could not recognize the watch. About the 15th of August Mathews swapped another chain for this one; the watch which Mathews wore would compare with this on every well; have seen this chain a number of times.

Cross examined. There is a peculiarity about the key, also the slide, by which I am able to distinguish it; it is of a peculiar construction.

George Gilman sworn - The prisoner applied to me for a loan of money while I was standing in the street, one day he accosted me with "How are you, George? How are you off for money?" I told him I was poor; he said he wanted to make a raise of $2000, as he was going into a speculation with Dr. Potter - that he had been in one speculation by which he had made 3000 or $4000, and was going into another; he said he would give me $500 for the use of $2000 3 or 4 months; I then left him, and presently while passing his office he called me, and said I had better try and raise that for him, that it would be good chance for me; Mr. Wheeler and Mr. Southard coming up, we entered into other conversation; Coolidge then went towards Williams's tavern, and I coming up shortly after, as he was getting into his carriage, he called me and said he would want the money in the course of a month; that was all the conversation I had with him at the time; he has asked before to loan him small amounts of money; before leaving him, when in the street, told him I would think of it; drank some cider bitters at one time in the Doctor's office, which his boy got for me, but never any liquors; talked with prisoner on Saturday morning following the death of Mr. Mathews behind the entry stairs at Williams's; had said that when he was before the coroner's jury they questioned him concerning his application to me for money; I told him that when I heard that he had applied to Edward Mathews for money, I told that he had applied to me; he said that he did not request money of me, but that he told me there might be money made at the West or South, and asked me if I couldn't fix it somehow so; I told him that I should state it as it was; He then exclaimed, "My God, I am a ruined man; George, if I can only get rid of your evidence I'm clear - I can prove Edward Mathews a liar, by my uncle in Hallowell; that I was going into no speculation with Dr Potter, and I never wanted money of Mathews. I am doing $20 worth a business a day, and have no use for money; my reputation will clear me." He said he must get rid of Potter, and also said "My God it is too bad for an innocent man", that he must get rid of my evidence if he could; that he would give anything to do it, and spoke of making me a present of fifty dollars. He wanted me to state before the inquest that the conversation he had with me was, that we might make good speculations West or South.

Cross examined. I lived in Waterville at the time, and was 21 years of age in May last; I had dealt in horses some, say to the amount of $2000 or $3000 a year; I had a capital of $500, perhaps $700, most of which was borrowed at 7 or 8 per cent interest I don't know where I could have raised $2000 at the time Dr. Coolidge applied to me for money, but I think he desired such a loan, and hoped to get it of me; I was very intimate with Dr. Coolidge; the doctor did not seem to be very much alarmed at the time I saw him behind the stairs, at first, but was very anxious I should go before the coroner's jury and testify as he desired; the conversation behind the stairs was from fifteen minutes to half an hour, during which time some one passed; at this time there was a good deal of excitement in the neighborhood, and Dr. Coolidge's name frequently mentioned in connection with the affair; I did not know at that time that Dr. Coolidge was watched in all his motions; I am now in the hide and leather business in New York, in company with Mr. Miles; I put in $5000 capital;

the business of the firm commenced about a fortnight ago; when in Waterville I collected rents for my father who owns real estate there; when before the coroner's jury I did not state the conversation behind the stairs, as I did not feel like it; my father let me have the $5000 which I put into the firm where I now am.

David Leighton, sworn. I had a conversation with the prisoner on the Saturday after the murder in the entry way of the office; I went into the office previous to this, where was also Mr. Richards; he said to the doctor, "what an awful thing this murder is." The doctor said "yes, I have lost mother, brothers and sisters, but never had anything to effect me like this;" I asked the doctor when if he had heard anything new on the subject, and he said he had not; he then touched me on the shoulder and I went into the entry with him, when he said, "I suppose I have got to prove where I got a $100 bill I let Edward Mathews have, and have forgotten, will you allow me to say I got it of you, and not deny it?" He seemed agitated, and was walking the floor with his arms folded; I went into the Dr.'s office in the first place to see how he appeared.

Wm W Goodwin, sworn. (A letter was shown witness, which he said he had seen before.) First saw that order in September last, two or three days before the 21st. It was presented to Mr. Burnett; I am an apothecary; do business for Mr. Burnett at Boston. The order was executed by me in part, and afterwards found among the old papers and rubbish in the cellar.

It was read by Mr. Morrill, and runs as follows.

Waterville, September 17, 1847
Dear Sir · Shall I have the pleasure of making you acquainted with Mr. Phillips, a gentleman from this village.
You will give him an abdominal supporter measuring 27 inches above the hip bones. Give him the kind that you think will be best. The patient suffers much from a bearing down, and charge the same to me.
Also wish you to send by express the rest of those tubes.
1 oz of Hydrocyanic acid as strong as it can be.
1 bottle of Cologne, opt.
1 lb Zinc Muriate Iron
Also any new preparation that will be worthy of trial.
Yours, respectfully,

V. P. Coolidge
      Joseph Burnett, Esq.
   * Sulphate Quinine 2 ox.
   * Measure around the hips 25 inches - around the small of the
back 25 inches.
   Perhaps all *this* measurement will not be needed.
 The letter is superscribed
   Joseph Burnett,
   No 33 Tremont Row,
   Boston

Mr. Burnett put up the shoulder braces, the hydrocyanic acid
I put up myself. (Witness recognized the bottle which was a dark
colored one) The liquid is colorless, but was put in this bottle to
protect it from the light, which injures it. It is of the strongest
kind; we imported 4 ounces of it; this is one ounce; this kind of
acid is never sold for medicine, the ordinary medicinal acid is
much weaker. The demand for this kind of acid is very small; we
imported it for the Eye and Ear Infirmary, where I suppose the
vapor of it is used, but I do not know in what manner. The bottle
is about two thirds full, nearly or quite the quantity we sent. The
handwriting on the bottle is my own, and was put there after the
liquid was put it; don't remember ever selling this sort of acid
before except in one instance, that was to a physician who wished
to experiment on animals. We have only the manufacturers
mark to indicate that it is the strongest kind of acid. When I
poured the acid from the large bottle into this one, the vapor was
very perceptible, and produced giddiness.

Cross examined. I have frequently handled this kind of acid,
in its medical form - we put it up as often as once a week; it is
used by the best physicians in Boston and elsewhere. All the
medicinal acid is put up in ounce bottles and labeled, 'minimum
dose, one drop[4]," that is the strength we always expect to find it.
I don't know that we have ever sent any of the acid to the Eye
and Ear Infirmary. *Fort.* On the bottle means *fortissimus*, which
is *strong*; it generally means, as applied to our business, 'the
strongest,' or 'as strong as can be.'

---

[4] The Boston Daily Times gives "ounce" instead of "drop".

Benjamin Wales, sworn - (A paper was shown the witness which he did he received on the 18th of Sept last) It was received by Mr. Morrell, and is as follows.

Waterville, Sept 19th, 1847
Dear Sir: Will you send me one ounce of the strong Hydrocyanic acid as strong as it is made.
If you have not the strongest, send as strong as you have.
Yours &c,
V. P. Coolidge
[Mr. Wales is a man doing business in Hallowell - Rep.]
I gave a bottle of acid to the same man who gave me the order - bottles were shown witness which he thought were not like the bottle he put the acid in; the degree of strength was not put upon the label, consequently I suppose it was the medicinal acid, which is two per cent strength; had it have been otherwise, I would expect to see it marked on the label.

Cross examined. I knew Dr. Coolidge, but had never before executed an order for him.

Mr. Goodwin recalled - Have frequently answered orders for Dr Coolidge but never before sent him any Prussic acid.

Wm N Phillips, sworn. - I was at the prisoner's office on Sunday, the 13th of Sept; I went to his office to carry a measurement of my wife's person, to have him send to Boston for a supporter; he was writing when I went in; I went with him to the back office and took up a bottle which he said was a very powerful poison, Prussic acid; he said if he hold put one drop of it on my tongue I should fall dead as quick as if struck by lightning. He said he had tried it on a cat; after finishing his letter, he read to me that portion referring to my own business, (Witness was shown a letter which he thought was the one he carried to Boston and delivered to Mr. Burnet.) I received the supporter, and ordered the other things to be sent by express. After my return, he was one day standing at my desk writing a direction for some cough medicine, and asked me how the supporter suited I told him very well; I then asked him if he had go his things, and se said "Yes, all right." This was on the 29th.

Cross examined. When in his office did not notice the medicines but took the first bottle I put my hand on; have known him ever since he came to Waterville, and know that he has an extensive practice; his education was as good as that of young men generally,

Direct resumed. Has heard hints thrown out against Dr. C.'s character; cannot say where,

Dr Jonathan A Smith, sworn. Had a small quantity of hydrocyanic acid of poison about the middle of last August – near commencement day at Waterville. It was about two drachms, but was not weighed. It was for a patient of witness', who had been visited by Dr. C., and who had recommended its use. Cannot say how large a bottle Dr. C.'s acid was in; thinks from 2 to 6 ounces. The bottle was in an envelope, to protect it from light. Saw the bottle and it appeared about half full. Had seen the acid some eighteen years before, in the lecture room at Brunswick. Supposed this to be of medicinal strength; he was to put 15 drops in a 4 ounce cough mixture.

Augustine Perkins, recalled · A quantity of bills were shown witness which he said were the same denomination, and the same bank as some he had let Edward Mathews have. They are on a Providence Bank and are not generally circulated here; there are six ones, two twos, and three threes of Exchange Bank, Providence; of the money I let him have there were $300 on banks out of the State, and $1000 on bills on banks in the State.

Cross Examined. Don't know how much money I paid out that day; am certain bills I let Mr. Mathews have were of the Exchange Bank, Providence.

Day Four: Friday, March 17, 1848

Evidence for the Prosecution, Continued

Daniel Moor, Jr, sworn. Prisoner was indebted to witness in September last, in one note of $125, dated Oct., 1845, payable in four months; another for $100, dated Dec., 1845, on interest, no time mentioned; both for money lent. Interest paid to Feb. 1847. Settled an account with prisoner at that time, and he allowed 12 per cent for the money; said it was cheap enough – as cheap as he got it elsewhere. 12 per cent was agreed upon when the money was borrowed. The notes were secured by notes turned out by Coolidge to a lawyer who had had my notes for collection. Witness received about $220 from the notes turned out. Witness was on the inquest.

Cross Examined. Frequently lets money at that rate when he has it. Attended the post mortem examination. The physicians were standing near the body; Dr. Coolidge remarked, that it was impossible to tell whether the wound was sufficient to produce death, unless the scalp was opened and turned over. After a few moments, Coolidge said, if we are going to do anything, let us do it. They determined to do it, and Coolidge took a knife and opened it. Does not recollect who directed the stomach to be opened. The physicians concluded that the fracture of the skull was sufficient to produce death – Drs. Thayer, Plaisted and Coolidge. Some one proposed further examination; cannot say it was Coolidge. Cannot say how long the contents of the stomach remained in the room after taken out. After examination, the body was removed from the room. Cannot say it was removed into the entry. The cut was directly across the deep wound on the head, and the scalp was turned up to see the effect of the wound. Thinks Dr. Thayer was the first to announce to the jury that the wound would cause death.

Question by Mr. Morrill. What was the credit for pecuniary ability of George Gilman in September last? Objected to by Mr. Evans, and not allowed by the Court.

Franklin Dunbar, sworn - I live in Windsor; the prisoner is indebted to me in the sum of $100 - on 30th of Sept last he owed me $500, $100 of which was borrowed in January 1846, and a note given, on which nothing has been paid; he borrowed in the June following $400, and surety given; John Kendall, who was surety on the note, has since paid it; after the note was given at the time the money was borrowed, Coolidge remarked that he would give me 10 per cent interest; the money was paid into the hands of Coolidge, though Kendall asked me for it, saying it was for a particular friend.

Cross examined. Kendall made the application for the money; I live about two miles from Waterville, and have known Coolidge a long time, his character is good, so far as I know, and his practice in my neighborhood very extensive.

J. A. Goodwin, recalled - Prisoner called on me in April last for $400, and said he was willing to pay 10 per cent; I have loaned him small sums at several different times; when he applied to me I told him he could get the money very easily of Mr. Daniel Moor, he said he would rather get it of me, as he did not want people to know he hired money.

Emulous Butterfield (a boy about 13) sworn, - I found a watch, I believe on Monday, about four days after Mr. Mathews death, in Dr. Coolidge's sleigh top; Tilton, Sloper boy, and several others were present at the time; the sleigh was right over a little office in Williams's shed; I climbed up over the carriages and got into the sleigh, when I found the watch right between the swell and the seat; I was looking in a stove pipe, and a boy saw a piece of white paper sticking out; hostler told me to pull it out; it was thin white paper; Mr. Tilton picked it up and said it was a gold watch; he carried it with the paper up into Williams's hall.

Cross examined. I then lived at Orea Doolittle's; other boys and men searching there; three or four had gone up there before me; don't know what they did; first time that I had been searching for anything; good many there in the yard generally; Sloper boy, smaller boy than I, first found paper; no cushions in the sleigh; I was looking for nothing in particular, but was with some other boys looking around - beside the sleigh there was old stove pipes, and one thing and another in the shed; know it was Dr. Coolidge's sleigh because I have seen him ride in it; have seen him ride in other sleighs, Mr. Freeman's; did not unwrap the paper before it was thrown down.

Examination resumed. Don't remember who it was went up before Sloper boy and myself; that person went up and came down before I went up; he did not stay up long; 2 or 3 went up before see, the same way; don't remember who they were; was hunting, because I did not know but what I might find something, watch or money; some money had been found before that time.

Eben Shaw recalled · Witness produced a third paper in which he said the watch was brought into the hall by a man whose name he thought was Allen; don't remember his Christian name; don't remember his person; the paper has been in my possession ever since I first saw it, with the exception of a little time while it was in the Grand Jury room.

Cross examined. Was left in the possession of the grand jury; I left it there; that did not occur to me; left it with the grand jury one day and took it the next; found it next day in grand jury room locked up in a desk; some one gave me the key; various parcels of paper, of same quality and size were brought into the jury room; some members of the committee produced paper of the same kind; was an attempt made to see how general the use of such paper.

Oliver Paine, sworn. Identifies the paper in which the watch was wrapped. Saw it in Williams's hall with the watch in it. Identifies the watch. Rev. Mr. Tilton brought the watch in; compared this paper in the hall with some taken from Coolidge's office by witness, Monday forenoon after the murder, The watch was brought in Monday; witness got the paper from the office afterwards. The paper compared very nearly or exactly – could see no difference; witness was on the inquest. First saw the body in the cellar between 7 and 8 o'clock. But few persons were there then – Joseph Hasty, Mr. Flint and others. Saw it on the plank, in the shed, and afterwards in the hall. The handkerchief was pulled up a little – not much out of form. Saw the cut on the pantaloons, near the left groin, below the pocket. Searched the pockets; found a small memorandum book, a buck-horn handled pocket knife, and an article of perfumery, called cachou. Thinks the article is called cachous aromatic. Did not find the same thing on the floor of prisoner's office; was not in there the next morning. – There was no box in the pocket; the cachous were loose. Saw no pocket book, wallet, purse or money. Cannot say if there was a handkerchief. Saw nothing unusual about the collar. On one side of the neck were three rakes, like the marks of three finger nails – about a third of an inch wide, and an inch or an inch and a quarter long; some on the other side, They looked reddish – did not bleed. Thought the skin broken or scratched off. Remained in the hall during the inquest; the body was taken from the hall to the room adjoining, to be laid out. All the examinations were before this removal. They were made in the presence of the whole inquest. Noticed a pin in the side of the pocket – it hung in the side – it was somewhat uncommon – supposed the pocket had been pinned up. Thinks the pin was not crooked; cannot swear positively as to that. The boots were not much soiled.

Cross examined. Besides the paper brought from Dr. C's office other sheets of paper were brought in by other persons, before the inquest. The paper was similar; one sheet was of the same texture, but larger. Got nearly a quire from Dr. C's office. Thinks it was given to the coroner. Believes this to be the same paper the watch was in, but does not swear positively. Found the same kind of paper at Mr. Crooker's, bookseller, jeweller; also some at a shoe store. Cannot say how many of the aromatic pills were in Mathews's pocket, quite a number. Said to be used to give the breath a flavor or smell. Did not taste them. Does not know who suggested the removal of the stomach. The inquest was examining witnesses whilst the physicians opened the body. It is said the aromatic pills are used after smoking to purify the breath; the manufactures so states; does not say anything about drinking. Does not know whether Mathews was in the habit of drinking or smoking,

Emulous Butterfield, recalled. The Sleigh body was here exhibited, witness pointed out where he found the watch. There was no runners. It stood on some boards, the front part towards Williams's house. Witness stood a little one side of the dash board, and saw the paper in the opposite corner. Has no doubt this is the same sleigh.

Cross-examined. Does not remember that Coolidge's sleigh was highly gilded. It was a single sleigh for one person. Is certain that Coolidge's sleigh was not a gilded one.

Harrison Smith, sworn. Testified to prisoner's signature on several papers shown him; they are statements which were made before the coroner's jury by Dr. Coolidge.

The paper was read by witness and is in substance as follows:

Day Four: Friday, March 17, 1848

Statement of Coolidge, Saturday, 1ˢᵗ of October

I saw Edward Mathews yesterday afternoon, about 2 o'clock, near Charles Mathews's store; he asked me if I was going into my office; I told him I was; soon after he came into my office; he wanted to hire some money of me; two hundred dollars; said he was going to let two gentlemen have it who were speculating in lands at the West; he did not name the gentlemen, nor where they were from; I said to him, I have not the money to spare I had rather you would get it somewhere else; but I said if you cannot, I will let you have it; did not let him have it at that time; he said if he could not get it anywhere else he would call again at 8 o'clock, and wished me to be at the office; he took a glass of brandy which set in a row with other medicines and went out; this was about 3 o'clock in the afternoon; he was in my office from five to ten minutes; I do not know which way he went from my office; I next saw him a few moments after eight o'clock in the evening; I did not see him between the times above mentioned; when I saw him in the evening, it was at my office; he then came in and said - "Doctor, I must have that money, and I will pay you in the morning; I let him have a one hundred dollar bill that I had of W. R. Doe, of Sebasticook; I do not recollect on what bank the bill was - and one hundred dollars in other bills, making two hundred; he then took his money out of his pocket, and counted it; he had two thousand dollars, including the two hundred he had of me; he then put the money into his pantaloons pocket wrapped up in a paper; Mathews said I have now got the complement for them and am ready, and immediately stepped out of the office; I soon followed him, and when I passed out of the office I saw Mathews in company with two gentlemen with cloaks on, before David Shorey's shop door; as soon as they saw or heard me, they moved off down street, towards Stevens' store. I saw two men that I supposed to be the same above named, near Goodwin's store the same evening before I saw them in company with Mathews; they were strangers to me; I had never seen them before; I was not so near as to distinguish their faces or describe them; I was in Dow's Tavern in the evening about 7 o'clock. I stepped in to see the Register; I saw Charles Mathews in the door; I think I did not have any conversation with him at that time; I might have said 'good evening;' the day before, that is the day before yesterday in the afternoon, I had a conversation with Edward Mathews about signing a note at the bank with him; it was at my office; he came in and said, I have got some money to raise - and said, will you sign a note with John Mathews for $1500 to the bank; I said, No, at once; it was four or five o'clock in the afternoon; no one was present; deceased wished to keep the business a profound secret; wished me to tell no one for my life - meaning, both the purpose he wished the money for, and the fact that he had applied to me to sign the note; I never received any letter from Dr Potter informing me that I could make a great speculation, and never communicated any such fact to the deceased; I think I received one letter from Dr Potter within two months; not quite two, certainly not more than one; have not within one week past received any letter from a person in Cincinnati; in the letter I had from Dr Potter he spoke of speculation - and said if he had $5000 he could make $4000 in six years; I once swapped notes with the deceased; he had my note for a safe I bought from him, and I gave him a note against Hodgdon; in a few minutes after I left the office as I have before said I returned to it once afterwards, in the course of the evening, say at about nine or half past nine, I again left the office and went into Williams's hotel to call Mr. Flint; I wanted him to look up some cases in the books; he returned to the office with me; Mr. Flint stayed there about one hour, and went away about ten or eleven; I soon after left the office and went to bed at Williams's; this morning at four o'clock I went to Mr. Bassett's in Winslow; I returned, and at six o'clock I started to Skowhegan; I had no call last evening to visit my patients abroad; I did not write any note to the deceased last evening or at any time deceased did not solicit me to become interested with him in any speculation; when deceased was in my office Wednesday afternoon; he appeared to have drank too much; I did not notice he was under the influence of liquor - at any time yesterday; I received a letter day before yesterday from my brother in Greenwood, Mississippi; I have had a consultation with George Gilman about a speculation, but did not solicit him to join me in it. It was in relation to land west and south; I did not recollect that I asked him to lend me money; I have looked for letters from Dr Potter since I testified as above in relation to letters from him, and find none later than April; I have received letters from him since that time, but cannot find them, nor can I tell how recently I have received them, I have my day book which I now exhibit; I made the charge of two hundred dollars to deceased this morning after I returned from Skowhegan.

V. P. Coolidge

There is also a certificate with the names of V. P. Coolidge and Stephen Thayer attached, signifying concurrence in the opinion of Dr Plaisted relating to his testimony before the coroner's jury concerning the post mortem examination of the body of deceased.

Second statement of Doctor Coolidge, before the Coroner's Inquest, Oct 2, 1847.

I did not have a medical consultation at Skowhegan on Thursday, not any time this week. I have never told any person that I had. I was at Skowhegan on Thursday last. I visited the family of Joseph W. Porter. I have an uncle in Hallowell of the name of Coolidge. I have not visited him nor had any consultation with him, except that I called on him on my return this summer from Boothbay. I have made no application to him for money. I did not take a letter from the Post Office Wednesday from any person in New York or Ohio. I did not see Edward Mathews last Saturday that I recollect after his return from Brighton – he was not at my office last Saturday evening. I have not within ten days past written a letter or note to Edward Mathews. I did not see a book of forms shown me by Edward Mathews. I did not tell Edward Mathews that I had received a letter from Dr. Potter stating that a time when he could make a profitable purchase would expire. I have not delivered my books of accounts to Mr. Nudd for collection. I have drawn off some bills for him to collect. I cannot say whether I had a conversation or not with George Gilman in relation to any subject. I might have said something to him near the north end of Williams's platform, but I do not recollect whether I have or not had any conversation with said Gilman at any other place. I do not recollect that I even asked him how he was on it for money. Sometime with ten days I said something to him about speculating, that if a man had money he might make something of it, and might then have asked him how he was on it for money. I did not tell him I had made two or three thousand dollars out of one speculation. I recollect of saying that a man might make two or three thousand dollars by speculation if he had the money, or something like that – but I do not exactly recollect – I did not say to George Gilman that if I had $2000 to make up $15,000, I could make a grand speculation, nor anything to that effect. I have stated all that I have ever said to him on that subject. I have heard the testimony I gave yesterday read over, and find it correct, and do not wish to make any alteration in it. I was at Skowhegan at Joseph W. Porter's on Friday morning.

When I started from Williams's hotel on Friday morning at 6 o'clock, I went first to the house of Johnson Williams 2d, to visit a patient; from there went to John Beals'; and from there out to Poole's, in Skowhegan, crossing Pishon's Ferry. I did not call Edward Mathews into my office on Wednesday last. I went by him on Wednesday, near Mr. Percival's store; Mathews said, I will see you directly; I said "well," and passed along. A few minutes after, he came into the office. I have not written any letter to Dr Potter within two months past; I have not written any letter to him since yesterday morning, nor has any person in my behalf. When Mathews talked with me about the speculation he was about to engage in, he did not say particularly who it was with, or who was concerned with him. I supposed it had all come up since he returned from Brighton. I have had a conversation with David Leighton today, I asked him if he would allow me to say that I had a $100 bill of him; he said he had had no money lately. I thought that as I had stated that I let Edward Mathews have a $100 bill which I had of Doe, and as I had also let Charles Griffin have a $100 bill, I might be called on to account where I got the other; and therefore I asked Leighton to allow me to say that I got it from him. I now think I had the other $100 bill of Reuel Howard. I sold horse to Howard for $130; he paid me $100 down; it was at that time I took the bill of Howard; I had made an appointment to meet Dr Johnson, of Canaan, in consultation at Mr. Poole's in Skowhegan. I think it was this week, but am not sure. I did not communicate this to Mathews, or to any other person that I recollect. Mathews did not spend any time in my office Saturday, nor Sunday, nor any other evening until Thursday evening. Wednesday afternoon was the first time he was in my office this week. I have not played cards or any other game with Edward Mathews since he returned from Brighton. I did not mean to say that I made an appointment with Dr. Johnson to meet him in consultation at Porter's; but that I was called there to visit a patient, and expected to meet Dr. Johnson there. Mr. Leighton is accustomed to go into my office considerably.

V. P. Coolidge

Cross examined. This narrative was made from the answers to interrogatories put principally by Mr. Boutelle, and I believe is just the language he made use of, he sometimes adopting the language of the question, sometimes making use of language of his own; all his testimony was taken down, for the reason that at that time he was suspected of the murder, or supposed to have more knowledge of the affair than some others; he knew that he was suspected and told that he could have many witnesses called to testify where he was on *that* night.; a Mr. Robinson was called at his suggestion; I do not know that persons were appointed to watch Dr. Coolidge but such was the report; the course of the examination was such as must have caused Dr. Coolidge to suppose he was suspected; I knew that committees were appointed to search the town, and that the town was divided into districts, in one of which was situated Dr. Coolidge's office; these committees were appointed on Friday, the first day of October, and requested to proceed immediately with the search; the doctor did ask particularly that Mr. Robinson should be examined and testify where he was on Thursday evening, but he did not desire that Mr. Flint should be called; he left at a certain point of his examination, and went to his office for some letters - on his return he brought his day book and exhibited it, saying, I think, that he made the charge of $200 against Mathews since he went out, but of this I will not be positive; the doctor's testimony was read to him by me, after he had related it, and he pronounced it correct with one exception, in which case I have made a correction.

Elbridge L. Getchell sworn. I saw the prisoner and Edward Mathews on Wednesday afternoon, Sept 29th opposite the store of Mr. Phillips; I wanted to see Mr. Mathews and therefore hailed him; he came across, and while I was in conversation with him, Dr Coolidge came up and told him he wished to speak to him; he left me and went in the direction of Dr Coolidge's office, in which direction also the doctor had gone a few moments before.

Benjamin Ayer sworn. Was at prisoner's office on Wednesday afternoon before the murder about half past 3 o'clock. As witness entered the office, Mr. Dingley and Mr. Flint were there – thinks Edward Getchell the office boy was there. Asked where the Dr. was. In a short time Geo. Robinson came up the stairs, opened the office door, and made a remark. Saw Coolidge come from the back office with Edward Mathews in a short time, about ten minutes after witness went in. Mathews came along and entered into conversation with witness and Dingley. The Dr. inquired about his horse. Some one said his horse and carriage were at the door. He took his medicine, and went down the stairs towards the street – the Dr. returned and called E. Mathews into the stairway – they remained there but a short time – not over a minute – as Mathews opened the door to return into the office, heard Dr. Coolidge say something like this: "Keep dark" – this was the amount.

Cross examined. Witness will not say but the Dr. said – "all right" – thinks Coolidge said, "Keep dark." Remained in the office but a short time – thinks he left Mathews there when he went out. Mathews was not in witness's store Wednesday, but was there Thursday afternoon, at two different times – was there nearly an hour. Cannot say whether Mathews had been drinking then – he was lively and sociable – cannot say if he was more so than usual – not enough acquainted with him. Saw Mathews again Thursday night just before dark, opposite witness's store, going towards Charles Mathews. Never knew Edward Mathews to be in witness's store before.

Direct resumed. Does not recollect any one coming out of Dr. C.'s back office with him and Mathews – thinks they were alone. The door was shut whilst they were in there. – When Mathews was in witness's store Thursday afternoon, he had a gold chain and watch – took his watch out there – cannot swear that this was the same watch or chain. As near as witness can recollect, the words used by Coolidge in the stairway were – "Keep dark."

Julius A Bartlett, sworn – Saw Edward Mathews on Thursday evening about half past 6 o'clock, near Chick's store, on the side-walk, opposite Williams's tavern – met him there. Had not seen him for three or four weeks, · Had some conversation, and then walked leisurely along towards Dorr's tavern or the Parker House. Returned up street, and then walked down Main street to Mr. Smith's store, next building to Ticonic Bank. Stopped there a few moments and then returned the same street, and went down again towards the Dorr House, opposite side from the one we walked the first time. Went down opposite the Dorr or Parker House. Mathews crossed the street to speak to some one. Does not know whom. Had seen the prisoner – thinks it was not he. When Mathews returned, went with him up to Chick's store ·witness went in there, and

Mathews went into the barber's. Mr. Carter was with the witness and Mathews in walking up and down the street. Witness and Carter had on cloaks. Carter is in College at Waterville. Did not see the prisoner that evening. Knew him, but was not intimate with him. Carter had been there but a few weeks – prisoner, probably, had not seen Carter. It was about 7 o'clock when they got through their walk.

Cross examined. – Witness's only acquaintance with prisoner was only has he had met him at parties. Cannot say if it was dark earlier that evening than usual. Thinks the stores were lighted up. Did not enter Smith's store, or the Parker House. Went to the College after leaving Chick's but not immediately. Cannot say how long ago he first met prisoner.

Eliphalet P. Simpson[1], sworn. Saw Edward Mathews at the Parker House on Thursday evening. There was a party of young company there. Saw him several times in the course of the evening – the last time was about a quarter before nine. Cannot say whether Mathews may not have gone out in the course of the evening. Noticed that Mathews had his boots blacked at the Parker House that evening. When Mathews left there he went up Silver street towards Main street – towards Goodwin's tailor shop. If witness had started from the Parker House to go to Dr. Coolidge's office, he should have gone in the same direction that Mathews did. Witness came out of the Parker House and talked a moment with Mathews on the steps. Went to the stable for a small cord for the young folks, returned to the house and handed the cord to John Paine in the entry, and witness then went directly home – about 50 rods. The 9 o'clock bell rang while he was on the steps of his house.

Cross examined. Cannot say the exact distance from the Parker House to witness's house. Was requested to get the cord. Saw Mathews go up Silver street towards Goodwin's shop. Should go that way if going to Boutelle's office or the Colleges. Did not pay particular attention to Mathews after he left. Cannot say whether the shops were open at that time. Witness went up Silver street to go home; cannot say which side of the street he went. No sidewalk on that street. It had been raining that day, and the streets were some muddy – it was rather a dark, foggy night, No crossing below Williams's. Thinks Mathews went up

---

[1] Some sources give name as Eliphalet E. Simpson.

north side of Silver street until you get to Main street. There is a private avenue leading from Silver street.

A F Tilton sworn. Identifies the watch and paper enveloping it. On the first day of October, he was standing in William's back yard; something was thrown down from a loft above the shed which connects the house and stable occupied for carriages. Witness took it up, opened the paper and found it was watch. The watch was entirely enveloped in the paper when he took it up. Witness carried it into the hall occupied by the jury of inquest. On recollection, it was not the first day of October – it was Tuesday. Cannot say whether he delivered the watch to any one, or laid it on the table in the hall – thinks Mr. Shaw, the coroner, took it.

Cross examined. Witness had been in the back yard perhaps half an hour. Thinks it was about 11 o'clock. He was there on account of the excitement arising from the murder, and the search that was being made for the watch and other articles. Was standing in the stable east of the shed when the watch was thrown down. Thinks the watch fell on the floor of the shed – was thrown from a height of ten or twelve feet. Took it up himself, and carried it to the hall. Cannot swear positively to the paper – thinks it the same. Recognizes the watch by the blood on the case – there is not so much of the stain now as then, nor is it so deep. Witness lives in Waterville. Many persons were about when the watch was found. Witness was acquainted with Dr. Coolidge in Waterville – he has practiced in the witness's family – knows nothing but his character was good.

George Lincoln sworn. Lives in Waterville. Was in Shorey's employ last September. Was in the shop at work on the night of September 30th. In the second story. The room is on the same floor with the prisoner's office. Left the shop immediately after the 9 o'clock bell rang[2] – in five or ten minutes. There were in the shop Gilman Fellows, Herrick Barton, and William Lincoln, witness's brother. Witness was there all the evening. The others came in about eight o'clock. All went out together, left the building immediately, and all went directly home. There were others of Mr. Shorey's hands in the room overhead, (third story). There were five girls there. The entry leading to the room above

---

[2] The Boston Daily Times gives 8 o'clock, but the Northern Tribute, the Maine Farmer and the Portland Advertiser all agree on 9 o'clock.

is connected with the front entry. The girls in the room above left just before witness did. The door was locked by H. Barton when the witness went out. Those with witness were talking and laughing while there. Heard persons between 8 and 9 o'clock, going up and down stairs – thinks they must have gone into Dr. C.'s office, because he cannot tell where else they could go. Cannot say whether ordinary noises in the doctor's office could be heard in witness's room. There is the width of the stairs between. Shorey keeps goods in the lower shop. Barton was employed most of the time above. Came up that evening about 8 o'clock. He was in the lower shop until that time. The cutting room is in the room below.

Cross examined. Does not know whether the door at the head of the stairs was open or closed. Carter has an office in the third story – the persons who came up the stairs may have gone into Carter's office. Has a distinct recollection of hearing some person going up the stairs once, if not more. The fact was spoken of, because two of the boys were playing checkers, and they threw the board under the table when they heard someone coming. The persons playing were Joseph Fellows and a Davis boy – they came in the early part of the evening – they went out soon after. Thinks there was no playing after Barton came up. Thinks it was about the time that he came up that the steps were on the stairs. Some work was done in the shop that evening, but not much. Coal was burned in the room where witness was. The wood for the room above was kept in the cellar. Thinks there was no fire above that evening. Fire was kept in witness room to keep the irons hot – witness thinks he did some pressing, Shorey's wood was in the south side of the cellar – Philips' on the right side. Witness went down stairs when the body was found, but did not notice the wood. Could hear persons speak in witness's room from below – frequently called by Shorey – sometimes he came up – only one partition. Witness is 18 years old.

Direct resumed. Carter's room is over prisoner's – had the impression no persons where in there that night – heard none up there, or ascending the stairs leading to Carter's. Thinks the steps coming up did not go up Carter's stairs. Cannot say if there was any light in Carter's that evening.

AFTERNOON

Herrick Barton sworn. On the night of Sept. 30, witness was about Shorey's shop from 6 to 9 o'clock. Was in front shop till nearly 8 – went there about 6 that evening. Closed the shop before leaving it. Points out shop on the plan. At 8, went up stairs into the press room. Three or four boys there – George Lincoln, William Lincoln, Gilman Fellows, Joseph Fellows, and Amasa Davis. Closed the blinds of the shop before he went up stairs, and locked the door. Shorey was in about 7 o'clock – went out and did not return. Went up stairs on the inside – did not go down again that night. Went from the room above soon after 9 – the boys went out, and witness locked the door, The girls overhead had previously done. Witness opened the shop next morning, and found everything as he left it.

Cross examined. Found nothing disturbed when he came back in the morning, Is usually employed in the sewing room. Was reading in the lower shop after Shorey left. Jesse Mathews was in that evening – left just before I went up. Did not go into the third story. About an hour after I went up, the girls left. The door was open between the press room and the entry leading down the back stairs. The door into the front entry was not open. Two boys played checkers a few minutes after witness went up. Has been with Shorey a little more than a year; is 15 years old. Saw the girls when they came down – they did not come into the press room. Went down stairs after wood the next morning; wood was on the south side. The wood on the north side sloped off towards the stair and the cellar door. Cannot say if he would have to bend much to get over the top of the wood. Thinks the wood did not rise abruptly from the stairs. The highest point of the wood was between the stairs and door. Saw the body before it was removed. It was towards the door – could see it from the stairs.

Direct resumed. Was sweeping out the rooms above when Shorey arrived at the shop in the morning. Made fires above and below. Went down cellar for the wood – did not then see the body.

James Hill, sworn. On the night of the death of Edward Mathews, saw the prisoner on Water street, back of Williams's tavern. Water street runs parallel with Main street. Where he saw the prisoner is not more than 10 rods from the river. Water street is back of the block occupied by Dr. C. Dr. C. was alone, going north. Witness was going south – passed prisoner within a few feet; witness looked round after prisoner passed, and noticed him when about a rod distant. This was just before ten o'clock. Witness went down and crossed the bridge to Winslow; saw no more of prisoner. Returned about 1 o'clock – met two persons in a wagon near the bridge on the Waterville side. Recognized Joseph Hasty – not the other. Went up Main street – had a dog with him – the dog near the bank all at once jumped and howled, and ran across the street. This is but one building from prisoner's block. The dog disappeared behind the buildings. Witness walked a little faster at first; the dog came to him near West's shop, some 40 or 50 rods from where he left him. Saw no other persons that night in the street.

Cross examined. Has not the dog with him; dog about two years old; howls when he has occasion. The last he saw of the dog was nearly opposite the Bank. When he started from home the night was rather dark; when he returned, the moon shone, but was foggy. Heard the town clock strike two, after he got over into Winslow; it wanted 20 minutes to 10 when he started from home. There was a young lady with witness; walked rather slow. No moon when he started; thinks it was starlight. Dr. Coolidge had on a white hat; could not tell the color of his coat; recognized him by his countenance. Saw his face distinctly enough to know him. Did not speak to nor salute him. Dr. C. was walking slow. Did not see anything on his arm or in his hand. Did not mention his meeting the doctor there for three or four weeks after the murder. Never went down that street on any other evening. The next day's occurrence remined him of the fact of meeting Dr. C. Was led to mention it by the young lady's speaking of it. Was at the Division of the Sons of Temperance Wednesday night. The doctor passed witness on the right; when witness looked back, the doctor was looking towards him. Did not pass any signs of recognition, One of those in the wagon spoke to witness when they met, but he did not answer. Saw the doctor but a short distance ahead, before they met. Met the doctor two rods north of the south end of Water street, between Gen'l Fairfield's house and Williams's stable. The cross street into Water street is above Williams's stable; there is a passage way below through Fairfield's yard. Several houses are on Water street; does not know who live there. Thinks there are not fences all the way on Water street. Is certain that he met Coolidge and Hasty the same night.

Joseph W Freeman sworn. I saw Dr Coolidge on Thursday night at about half past 8, or 9 o'clock, on the platform of Williams's hotel; he came there looked through the sitting room window, passed off the platform and went away; Mr. Flint and Emily Williams were sitting in the room at the time, as I know from having passed through the room fifteen or twenty minutes before.

Cross examined. I left the sitting room, went into the bar room, and from there to the door, where I stood talking with the hostler; I think the sitting room window was curtained but do not know; I did not notice his dress at the time, or whether he had on an outside coat; I did not notice where he went when he left the platform; I did not testify before the coroner's or the grand jury, but first spoke of it accidentally to Mr. Moor the late Attorney General.

John Bowles, sworn. I saw Dr. Coolidge on the evening of Thursday, under Mr.Williams's hall; I was greasing the axletrees of a coach as he came up and passed me on the left, and went towards the door which leads to the bar room; as he passed I said "Hullo, doctor," he relied "Hullo," and passed on; this was about a quarter past 9 o'clock.

Cross examined. It was not uncommon for the prisoner to be passing about the house, as he boarded there; any person coming from Main street would go through the same door he went through; he did not appear agitated at the time; I harnessed the doctor's horse for him the next morning at about 4 o'clock as he ordered, he saying he was going to Winslow to see Mr. Barrett; a messenger who had called him was just going away as the doctor called me.

Nelson Adams sworn. I saw Dr. Coolidge on Friday morning after the death of Mr. Mathews, at Williams's bar-room a few minutes when he came in from out of doors; a man soon came in and inquired for Dr. Coolidge, and I told him he had just passed out; when I saw him he was coming from the direction of the stable, and from the shed where the watch was found; he called John Bowles and said he wanted his horse; no other persons were present.

Cross examined. The Huntress stage had just left when Dr. Coolidge came in.

Day Four: Friday, March 17, 1848

George L. Robinson, sworn. I saw the prisoner at about 11 o'clock in the evening; he came into the bar room and asked me to call him at 6 o'clock the next morning. I next saw him at about half past 4 o'clock the next morning, as he came into the barroom and desired me to order a breakfast for him. I had not called him; he soon called up the hostler and went away. The week before the death of Mr. Mathews, the Doctor asked me if I knew when Mr. Mathews would be home from Brighton; he also again asked me, and at the same time inquired if I knew how much money he took to buy cattle with; I told him I understood he took $2000[3] from the bank; he told me that when Mathews came home he wished me to let him know, as he wanted to see him on his return; on the Wednesday before his death I saw Mathews in the street and went to the office to tell the doctor; at one time he said he had lent Mathews some money that he did not take a due bill for and felt uneasy about it, this was, he said, the reason that he wished to see him; when I went to the office I saw Mr. Flint, Mr. Dingley and young Getchell.

Cross examined. No person slept with Dr Coolidge; know nothing of an exchange of notes between Mathews and the Doctor, or between the Doctor and Hodgdon.

Asa Fernald sworn. I was in Dr Coolidge's office on Thursday forenoon, and saw Mr. Flint, Mr. Dingley and Getchell the office boy; while I was there, Mr. Mathews came in and remained a short time; I saw Mathews take nothing from the safe, or any other place in the office.

Edward S. Getchell, 13 or 14 years of age, sworn. I saw Edward Mathews in Dr. Coolidge's office on Thursday, but do not know what he came there for; I once saw a letter in the office for a Mathews, but do not know whether it was Edward Mathews, and do not know when it was taken away. When I came to the office the next morning at about eight o'clock, I did not build a fire, but noticed there was a fire in the stove about 9 o'clock; I first saw Dr. Coolidge that morning drive up to Williams's and get out of his carriage; saw a spot on the carpet near the door which opens into the back office, and called the attention of Mr. Flint and of Mr. Dingley to it; Mr. Flint stooped down and scratched it with his finger nails; I should say the spot was as

---

[3] The Boston Daily Transcript says $200 for cotton, The Portland Advertiser and Northern Tribune both agree on $2000 for cattle.

large as my two hands; saw a hatchet there, the one I was in the habit of using to split up my wood with.

Cross examined. The piece of carpet on which the spot was, was a separate piece one width, and stretched across the floor of the office; the spot I speak of was not immediately in front of the door, but close to the book case, within a foot of it; don't know the color of the spot, neither do I know it was not there the day before; this was, however, the first time I discovered it. I did not see Mr. Baker in the office that morning. Mr. Flint, Mr. Dingley, the Doctor and myself, each had a key to the front office.

Amasa J Dingley sworn. On Wednesday prior to the murder, saw Edward Mathews in Dr. C.'s office in the afternoon. He came in with Dr. C. They went into the back office, remained there a few minutes, then they came out, Mathews went out alone and went down stairs. Saw a letter in the office that week directed to Ede Mathews, abbreviated for Edward· it was the first of the week. Did not know the hand-writing; it had been there almost two weeks. Does not know what became of the letter; cannot say when he last saw it, nor whether he saw it after Thursday. Was not in the office Thursday evening – left about quarter before six, by the town time. Had had some conversation with the Dr. about getting a subject. Dr. C. said there was a man in Clinton having fits. He did not think he would live; if he died he would make a good subject. Cannot say if the Dr. attended him. On Thursday afternoon Dr. C. said the man in Clinton had died, and would make a good subject, Witness said it was so far off, it would be difficult to get him. The Dr. said he did not want any help when he went after a subject; said he was hell on a subject when he got started.[4] Witness went home soon after. Returned to the office about nine o'clock the next morning. The body of Mathews had been discovered. Witness observed a spot on the carpet near the door leading into the back office. Identifying the carpet – says the spot is not there, but has been rubbed off. Did not examine the carpet closely; cannot sat on what colors the spot was. The spot was not very distinct where witness stood – he looked over Flint's shoulder. Had seen a cask in the closet prior to the death of Mathews; does not know how it came there,

---

[4] All four main transcription sources report this precise phrase; the Northern Tribune italicized it, the Portland Advertiser put it in quotes. So it was considered very striking. It seems likely the cask in the closet was intended to hold a "subject", but there can hardly have been a plan to place Mathews's body in the cask.

Cross examined. Did not examine the spot again. Saw the Dr. extract teeth; did not see him perform other operations in the office. – Had been in the office about three weeks. – Had been in the office Tuesday evenings, but other evenings returned home across the river about six o'clock. Cannot say if Getchell was in when he went in. Thinks the Dr. and Mathews were in the back office on Wednesday about fifteen minutes. Does not know what they did, nor whether any brandy was drank there; had never seen Mathews in the office before. Don't know whether the closet was finished, nor whether it was kept locked. Had several conversations with Dr. C. about a subject. Witness was studying medicine; had attended two post mortem examinations before this time; had studied at home from May till he entered the office. Had books of Dr. C. Had not attended any surgical operations, nor made any chemical experiments; did not know of any being made in the office. The Dr. was out of the office most of the time – suppose he was on his business; had frequent calls at the office; saw nothing out of order in the office when he went in Friday morning except the spot; cannot say that he expressed a wish to have a subject; does not recollect – is not certain who commenced the conversation. Witness was desirous of experimenting on a subject; does not recollect that Flint talked about a subject at all, either when the Dr. was present or absent. The second conversation, the witness said, Doctor, you must keep your eye out for a subject. He replied, that person in Clinton is dead, &c. Nothing was said about the mode of obtaining a subject; did not propose to help; did not ask the Dr. if he wanted help; did not ask him who it was; does not know how extensive his practice was on that side of the river; he often said he was going that way; had a conversation with Dr. C. in the spring about a subject; Dr. C. introduced the matter; was in the office Saturday after the murder; does not recollect seeing John Richards there; a number of men there, in and out; does not recollect whether the Dr. was much in the office; numbers were in and out Friday and Saturday; they began to come in soon after witness got there Friday; Samuel Doolittle was in, and examined very closely; looked in the wood box; witness was there till Doolittle went out; cannot say how long it was; did not see Doolittle look at the spot; does not know where the hatchet was discovered.

Direct resumed. Does not know who built the fire in the office, if there was one. Doolittle was in between nine and ten,

Edward S. Getchell, recalled. The hatchet now shown to him is not the hatchet, he thinks. Thinks the office hatchet was about as dull, and about the same size; there was a hatchet there; saw it there after the murder; it was there the last he saw of it; thinks this is not the same.

William Howe, sworn - I saw Mr. Flint on the evening of the 30th of Sept. last in the sitting room of the hotel, at about half past nine o'clock, and was in his company twenty or thirty minutes when he left and went into the front entry which leads towards the bar room; he had a lamp in his hand when he left the room; I found on the 4th Oct last in the wood-shed a quantity of money, tucked down by the side of a passage to the privy the amount was $155, it was in a position where it might have been seen without removing anything by any person looking that way; I had however been seeking in that vicinity previously in company with the coroner.

Cross examined. Flint and Emily Williams were playing back gammon in the sitting room when I went into it; Flint went out first, and in about five minutes Miss Emily followed. My curiosity was started by seeing the plaster started; got up and did not see any thing; afterwards took another position and saw it readily; Coroner was there, and search continued after I found the money; remained in the room 10 or 15 minutes after Flint went out; I retired that night at a quarter past 10.

Day Five: Saturday, March 18, 1848
Evidence for the Prosecution, Continued

Charles K Mathews, sworn. Last saw Edward Mathews at the Parker House, a little past 8 o'clock in the evening of Sept. 30th. Witness went with him to the Parker House, went into the room where there was a small party; Edward called witness to his side. His next act was to leave the room.

Question by Mr. Morrill. Where did Edward Mathews say he was going? Objected to by Mr. Evans, but the Court admitted the question, as part of the *res gesta.*

Does not know as he said where he was going in so many words. After what witness said to him, Edward said he supposed it was time for him to be going, as witness understood it, to Dr. Coolidge's office. He then went. He had left the Parker House that evening or one prior to that; went towards Dr. Coolidge's office; witness understood him to say then, that he was going to see if he could see anything of the Dr.; understood him that he was going to see Dr. Coolidge. From the time he first went to see Dr. Coolidge, till he went last, may have been 15 or 20 minutes. He was absent from the Parker House perhaps a minute the first time; a very short time; long enough to go 10 or 15 rods, if he had gone quick. The last time before witness saw Edward Mathews at the Parker House, he saw him about 6 o'clock at the barber's shop; don't know what his business was there. Witness saw him at his store between 4 and 5 o'clock; no one else present. Saw him in the forenoon at his store about 10 o'clock; Edward then had a letter from Dr. Coolidge; Dr. Coolidge's name was signed to it; supposed the letter and signature to be in Dr. C.'s handwriting at the time. The last witness saw of this letter, deceased put it about his person somewhere; cannot say what pocket; did not see it afterwards. The letter was in Dr. Coolidge's handwriting; has seen Dr. Coolidge's writing in prescriptions and directions for taking medicine for witness and for the family where witness boarded. Thinks he has seen the Dr. write. Has not seen Dr. C's handwriting frequently, independent of prescriptions. The letter was read in witness's hearing by Edward Mathews.

Question by Mr. Morrill. Whose letter did Mathews say this was, and where did he get it? Not allowed by the Court.

Mr. Morrill then proposed to ask what were the contents of the letter. The court said it must first be proved that the letter was lost. Mr. Morrill said it was proved to be on the deceased's person on Thursday, and that no such letter was found about deceased after his death. The Court said it must be shown that search had been made in deceased's papers. Mr. Morrill said he could show this by the administrator. Examination on this point was suspended here.

Witness identifies the note to Ticonic Bank; witness's name is on it; Edward Mathews and witness's father were present when he signed it. Edward disposed of the note about his person and left the store. Does not know as he said where he was going; went towards the Bank; saw him again in one or two hours; In the afternoon Edward came in and exhibited a pile of bank bills; witness did not examine the money; witness saw it; it appeared like quite a large amount; Edward was in the store but a short time. An hour or two before he came in with the money, Edward was in witness's store took a blank instrument for a mortgage of personal property; witness read it; witness keeps a bookstore; deceased took the blank mortgage from witness's store; deceased took a book of forms and filled the blank mortgage from that book, as he would any instrument for conveying personal property. After writing a few lines, deceased stopped – laid it aside – took another similar instrument and filled it out in full. Witness looked over deceased's shoulder while deceased read it to him. Deceased put the instrument about his person; this was the last witness saw of it; witness identifies a paper which he saw in his store the same afternoon the mortgage was written. It was written before the mortgage. (This paper was exhibited to the Court, and decided to be inadmissible.) Edward was in witness's store an hour or an hour and a half at the time of the writing of the instrument. When Edward left the Parker House, his dress was clean as usual; did not observe his boots. Thinks deceased put the money in his pantaloons pocket; does not know exactly. Edward Mathews put the form book in one of his pockets; cannot say which; witness saw deceased pin up one of his pockets.

Cross *examined.* Never saw Dr. Coolidge write but a few times. Does not recollect distinctly seeing him write but once; he wrote a prescription of medicine at witness's boarding house. Don't know who took the prescription; witness read the prescription before it was sent; it was sent to the Dr.'s office to be filled. Has seen other writings of Dr. Coolidge – said to be so by other persons. Saw some letters Dr. Boutelle said were written by Dr. Coolidge – witness read them – there were two. Cannot say to which of three persons the letters were addressed. Knew the Dr.'s writing by his peculiar style – means the peculiar form of the letters. Has seen some of Dr. C.'s writing since that instrument was written; witness's store is near the center of the village. Saw one of the letters referred to at Gardiner; they were letters thrown in at a fair – they were not signed. Did not see them in Dr. Boutelle's possession. Witness repeated some of the contents of the letters, and Dr. Boutelle said he saw Dr. C. write them and address them to the persons they were directed to. Did not say that when Edward left the store with the note, he was going to the Bank – went that way. Don't know that there were students in the store at the time. Saw Edward turn to the right down Main street. Is certain Edward pinned one of his pantaloons pockets – cannot say if the money was in that pocket – thinks he pinned the left pocket. Thinks he so stated before the inquest. Was but a short time in the barber's shop; parted with him after that – cannot say if it was dark, or whether the shop was lighted. Thinks it was a pleasant, starlight evening – rather wet under foot; was standing in the front door of the Parker House when Edward left the first time – was in the entry till he returned. The last time Edward went out, witness did not go to the door; witness left the Parker House about 11 – thinks it was a pleasant and starlight evening then. Cannot say if it was foggy any part of the evening. The prescription witness saw written was for himself – was sick – the Dr. said he was sick – was sick about a week; perhaps longer than he needed to be; thinks it was the cholera morbus; was sick once before with the measles – once with the cholera morbus – cannot say at which sickness the prescription was written – both were last summer; witness's eyes were not sore when he had the measles. The prescription was written in the room – thinks he saw the Dr. writing it. Was confined to his bed a day or two. The blank used by Edward Mathews was a printed form. At one sickness, witness was confined to one room – at the other, in another room – cannot tell what room the prescription was written in, nor what part of the room. Will not say certain that he saw the Dr. write; it was written in witness's presence; thinks he saw the Dr. write it. Has seen other directions for medicine – did not see the Dr. write them. The money Edward had looked like a large number of bills – does not know the denomination of any of the bills. Edward wrapped up the money in a piece of paper in the witness's presence. Took it from about his person; cannot say if it was wrapped up in anything there. Is cousin to the deceased.

Williams Mathews, sworn. [Mr. Mathews is Editor of the *Yankee Blade*, Boston] Is administrator on the estate of Edward Mathews. Is brother to the deceased. Has custody of deceased's papers. Has not found amongst deceased's papers any paper such as described by last witness. Has found a mortgage of personal property – a mortgage of an interest in the Yankee Blade newspaper establishment by Mr. Norris, one of the partners, to Edward Mathews – no other mortgage. Has examined the papers and letters of the deceased – found no letter of Dr. Coolidge. The mortgage found was dated last May. Deceased kept his papers in his travelling trunk and writing desk. Deceased lived at Clinton – was in partnership with Philander Soule – business just commenced at his death. Before that resided with his mother at Waterville; has looked in drawers there and his late father's trunk for papers of Edward Mathews; found the Yankee Blade mortgage there. First saw the body Sunday after his death – it was in the coffin.

Cross examined. Received his writing desk and some account books the last of October or first of November. Received the other papers whilst witness was sick; was sick from Oct. 6th till February. The keys were handed to witness by his mother or sister. Thinks the writing desk was kept locked. Examined the desk and his father's trunk in December. Edward and the witness had access to the trunk; since his death only his mother had access. The trunk of Edward was not locked. Most of his letters were there – mostly filed. The papers were in the top of the trunk. Looked over the papers and burned the useless ones. Was in Boston when Edward died.

Chas K. Mathews recalled – Mr. Morrill asked him what were the contents of Dr. Coolidge's letter, which witness saw in the hands of the deceased. Objected to by Mr. Evans, but after consultations allowed by the Court.

Witness read the letter over the deceased shoulder. Read two times himself. The letter requested the deceased to come to the office that evening, and reveal it not for your life – those last words were underscored with a very heavy dash – reveal it not for your life. This is the part of the letter distinctly recollected by witness. The first part of the letter did not make impression enough on witness's mind to cause him to recollect whether he has looked over that part as to see whether deceased read it right. (This part of the letter was not allowed to be stated.)

Mr. Morrill offered to prove the contents of the mortgage. The Chief Justice decided that this could amount only to the declarations of the deceased; it is not proved that the prisoner had any knowledge of the paper; the evidence was held to be inadmissible. – The Attorney General cited a case from Pickering – the Court said it was not a similar case.

John Mathews sworn. Mr. Evans inquired if witness had not been in attendance, contrary to the order of the Court. He said he had, the last two days. – Mr. Evans moved that he be excluded. He said this was sufficient cause. Mr. Morrill said he did not know the witness was attending here – it was his personal act – the government was not responsible for it, and should not lose the benefit of his testimony on that account. The point was reserved for consultation, and the decision of the Court suspended.

Philander Soule sworn. Resides in Clinton. Last season was in partnership with Edward Mathews in purchasing a drove of stock – does not know exactly what it cost or sold for. Can tell very nearly the amount of money laid out for stock – it was nearly $1800; not all of the stock purchased was driven to Brighton – some of it was sold about town. Thinks he and Mathews started with the drove the 6th of September – returned on Sunday about the last of the month, near the 28th[1]; not certain as to the day. Saw the deceased on Thursday; he staid at witness's house Wednesday night – left witness's store about 8 o'clock. Previously to that, witness was at his stable – Mathews came out, and after some conversation, they went in, and took some books of forms – witness took Curtis' Conveyance – deceased took the Business Man's Assistant, a small pamphlet, and turned to a form and passed it to witness; the form was an assignment, and also then the form of a mortgage, or else the mortgage first. Thinks Mathews took the Business Man's Assistant with him. Next saw Mathews in Williams's hall on a board. Discovered a cut on his left thigh; after the body was placed in the entry, Dr. Wright and others were looking at his

---

[1] The last Sunday of September in 1847 was the 26th.

throat. Witness saw three marks, resembling the scratching of finger nails, in a line on one side of his throat – one on the other side. Put his thumb on the mark to see how it agrees with the mark. When in the hall, he noticed a reddish appearance round the neck, as through the handkerchief had been pulled up. When Mathews found the forms, he made some remarks. (Not permitted to say what were the remarks.)

Cross examined. Don't know who or what Dr. Wright is – knows him by sight. Jos. Marston, one of the jury was there. Don't know who, if any one, had charge of the body, nor how long it was in the entry. The cattle were bought by witness, deceased, and S. B. Stinchfield – only knows the amount by the records they kept. Don't know when deceased came to witness's house Wednesday night – did not see him till Thursday morning. Was usually at witness's house nights, when at home, after July came in.

Direct resumed. Witness has (and exhibited in Court) the boots, hat and clothes of deceased. Points out the cut on the pantaloons, also marks of blood inside the hat. Received these clothes from Edward Mathews's mother the next Sabbath after the murder. The pantaloons are now when witness first saw them, in reference to the cut.

The court, after consultation, decided not to exclude John Mathews from examination on account of his disobeying the order of the court. The court decided that the English rule rejecting a witness who remained in the court contrary to their order, had not been adopted in this country, and permitted the witness to speak.

John Mathews. I saw Edward Mathews on the afternoon before his death in Charles Mathews's bookstore, also the same day in the forenoon at the same place. (A paper was shown witness). This is a note on which my name appears as principal with Edward Mathews. I came into the store at about 4 P M and saw Edward Mathews writing at a desk, he left that desk and came into the front part of the store where was another writing desk and showed the writing to me; it was of the tenor of a mortgage deed; I signed this note in the presence of my son, at his bookstore. I once held a note against the prisoner for $100, for money borrowed on which he agreed to give me 12 per cent interest, and so wrote the note, but I objected to that and the interest was stricken out; I saw the prisoner on the day after the death of Edward, in the street and walked with him to Williams's hall, when I asked him if Edward Mathews was in his office the night before he said "yes, he was in my office twice." I asked him if he came here to loan him (the Dr.) money. He said "No; he came to borrow money, and I loaned him $200 which I did not take a due bill for, but charged on my books, as he said he should pay it the next morning. It was then objected that I should put more questions to him.

Cross examined. When I came into the hall with the Doctor, a number of persons were present, you (Mr. Noyes) were there yourself and are the person who objected to my questioning Dr. Coolidge; two or three questions were put to Dr. Coolidge before I questioned him, but by whom I don't recollect; I do not know that there was an organized meeting in the hall, and do not recollect that I was requested to leave it; I do not recollect that you (Noyes) told me all persons except the committee of search must leave the hall, but do recollect that Mr. Boutelle told me it would be proper for me to remain.

Thomas Flint's Testimony

On Thursday evening, Sept. 30th, not far from 7 o'clock, returned from a visit to Clinton, took tea and went to the office. After sitting there a short time, Dr. Coolidge came in. We conversed on various topics. After talking about the patients we had visited, we commenced speaking of getting a subject, a matter we had previously spoken of. – Dr. C. introduced that subject. He said he had made arrangements to meet Charles Stackpole that evening about 8 o'clock; if he came in, wished me to leave the room. About 8 o'clock, some one came to the door, the door was fastened, the blinds closed. – Witness waited to see if the Dr. would tell him to open the door. The person went quickly down stairs. The Dr. asked witness if he thought it was Charles. Witness soon after left the office, it was perhaps a quarter past 8. Went to Williams's tavern; found there a child with an enlarged head; talked with the parents, measured the head, and went to Percival's store and measured the string with which he measured the head. After talking further with the parents, played a few games of back gammon with Emily Williams, and then talked awhile with those who were in. It was about half past 9 – took a light to go to bed. As witness opened the door, met Dr. Coolidge; he took the lamp from witness's hand, blew it out, and set it on the stand where the hats are placed; saying at the time he wished me to go to the office. We went to the office; as we passed in, the Dr. made me pass in by him, witness stood by the side of the table at the right hand of the door; there was a dim lamp burning fluid on the table. After locking the door, Dr. C. came up before witness, and said, I am going to reveal to you a secret which involves my life. Said he, that cursed little Ed. Mathews came in here, drank some brandy and fell down dead; he now lies in the other room; I have thumped him on the head to make folks think he was murdered. I then set down in the chair which stood behind me; a rocking chair. He then asked what he should do with him; I replied, I did not know. We sat a few minutes without anything being said. He then said, I must get him out of the office; did not say at that time any place to carry him; said he wished he was in the river. Witness told him he did not think he could get him there; it was very light. The front street was spoken of; and the place back of the buildings. Finally I told him we could not safely carry him further than the cellar, it was as far as I could go with him. He objected to placing the body in the cellar, said it would be found there. – Witness told him probably it would be found before 9 o'clock the next day; it could not be concealed. After hesitating a short time, Dr. C. took the hand lamp, the only one there, and walked towards the door between the front office and the back office. I did not follow him. He turned around and requested me to follow him. – I did. – On going in there, I saw a pair of drawers lying there folded. On those drawers was the impression as if made by a person's head; did not see anything on the drawers. Near where they lay, was a spot looking as if blood had been wiped up. We passed on to the back window, the lower sash of which was then raised to its utmost height. There was in front of the window a temporary counter; beyond that and the window, the body lay. Did not see the whole of the body. Dr. C. set down the lamp and went down into Shorey's Shop to open the door. He returned, and asked me if it was not best to put something round the head, as it was bloody. Witness said he did not know but it was. He went behind the counter, and placed something around. He then dragged the body from behind the counter, to near the door which goes down into Shorey's shop. I saw, after he dragged him there, a hat drawn down over the face, tight on the head. He then said, it was best to take off our boots, avoid making a noise.

We removed out boots. I went into the front room, to take off my coat. He spoke to me; told me to be quick and come back. After putting on an old coat that I had there, I returned to where we had put the body. I went to take him by the feet. Dr. C. told me I had better take hold of the shoulders; I could carry him better then he could. I took hold of the shoulders; he the feet. I raised up the arms; found they were then rigid. We started to go down stairs, Dr. C. forward, carrying the feet. After we had got partly down stairs, the body slipped forward; the coat was drawn up partly over the breast the arms were drawn up level with the body. We continued down stairs, through Shorey's shop; down the cellar stairs; on the wood, and left the body at the outside door, which was partly open. The Dr. then removed what he had tied round the head; had some difficulty in getting it off. The hat was left off the head. We then returned to the office. Dr. C. took the lamp and went down stairs to close the door and place everything as he found it. He then removed a spot or two from behind the counter – on the floor between the counter and the window – he came round, and threw what he removed from the head – and towel which we used in wiping ourselves, and the drawers, into the stove in the front office.

He then asked what it was best for him to do. I told him it was best to keep on about his business, and let the matter come out as it would. He said, people cannot suspect me; my popularity will shield me. He then said he was going away early in the morning to Skowhegan, and I must come in before breakfast, and see how things looked there. He told me that there was a cask in the closet, which should be headed up. I then left, asking him to go into the house with me. He said it was not best for both to go in together. I left him there, to go into Williams's hotel. As I stepped in, I saw Geo. Robinson coming out of the sitting room with a lamp. I took the lamp which Dr. C. had set down, and lighted it by the one Robinson carried. He asked me where the Dr. was; I told him he would be in soon; would be in at half past 10 o'clock. He looked round and said it was nearly that time now. I asked him what he wanted of the Dr. He said a Mr. Morse wanted him to go down on to the plains. I went up stairs, and had partly undressed, when Mr. Baker, my room mate, came in. I went to bed; got up in the morning when the first bell rung in the tavern; this was a bell rung for the boarders to get up. I dressed myself and went down to the office. I found a note from the doctor lying on the floor, directing me to sweep both carpets, saying that he found a shirt button there. I destroyed the note. I swept the carpet in the front room, and also the oil cloth carpet in the back room. I saw in the back room the same spot I saw the night before, near the old book case. I also found another spot of blood on the mop board under the window. I found one on the floor, some aromatics; a little thing they have to scent the breath with – *cachow aromatics*, I think they are called. I then went to head up the cask; found the head out; got the head partly replaced and discovered some blood on the head; rubbed that off, and replaced the head, and drove the hoops. Before getting this done, some one came into Shorey's shop – cannot say whether above or below – heard the door open. Discovered that one hoop had been left off – that I threw in the stove. Found a fire already there. I then went to my room to prepare for breakfast. After breakfast, went to the office again; found Edwin Getchell there, the office boy. He was sweeping the carpet. He noticed a spot in the back room, on the oil cloth carpet; he did not know how to account for it. He was sprinkling the floor – I told him he might sprinkle it, and sweep it up. In a short time, I went out of the office and left him there sweeping. About that time the body was found. I was in part of the time, and out a part of the time. I was called up to Mr. Boutelle's office. After returning, Edward called my attention to a spot upon the carpet in the front office between the door and book case. I examined the spot and found it was blood – thick clotted blood – with a few hairs. Went down Shorey's stairs and saw the body. Between 11 and 12, I saw Dr. Coolidge in his carriage near Dr. Thayer's house. Dr. Thayer was then talking with him. Witness went up to them; told Dr. C. the circumstance of my being called into Mr. Boutelle's office; does not know whether Dr. Thayer heard or not. Dr. C. having driven away, witness turned and went back into the office. As witness went into the office, saw Dr. C. charging Edward Mathews $200. He then took the account book and went out; said he was going into Williams's hall. Witness remained round there a short time, and was summoned by the coroner's jury. Dr. C. came in before witness left the office. He handed me some money that was in his pocket book; said they might ask for his pocket book, and he did not know but there was too much money in it; told me to take care of what he handed me. A short time afterwards went into Williams's hall. Preparations were there being made for the post mortem examination. Dr. C. sent me for instruments. I went to the office and took the instruments to the hall. They were used in the examination. The physicians were sworn about that time by the inquest – Drs. Coolidge, Plaisted, Thayer, myself and other. Dr. Coolidge did the cutting; I assisted when he required it. After we had finished, I sewed up the cuts we had made. After the post mortem examination, witnesses were examined by the inquest, and I was sent out of the hall. Sometime between Dr. C.'s return from Skowhegan and night, Dr. C. gave me a letter to destroy, I tore it up in the street as I was walking along. After the post mortem examination, I placed the money which Dr. C. gave me in the wood pile where it was found, in Mr. Williams's woodshed. After we had been released from the coroner's jury, I went into the office. Dr. C. came in; he said there was $1000 under the iron safe under the carpet; he wished I would take care of it. I told him I did not know what to do with it; he thought it would be safe in my trunk. I did not remove it at that time. I was round in various places a while. After supper, I went in, took a part of the money and put it in my pocket. There was a small quantity of money which he gave me in the afternoon, which I placed in a crevice inside of the door which goes up into Mr. Carter's printing office. I saw Dr. Coolidge that evening afterwards; he told me he wanted a part of that money. After dark, after tea, Mr. Baker and Dr. Coolidge went down to the office. I remained out. Went up the street a little way; as I returned to Williams's, he told me I must go down to Dr. C.'s office; Dr. C. was there taking on, and I must go down and quiet him. I went down to the office; found Dr. C. much agitated; expressed a desire to see Dr. Thayer. I went to Dr. T.'s and found him near a store on the side walk. Dr. Thayer went down, and after talking with Dr. C. a while, he became more quiet. Dr. Thayer went home, accompanied by Mr. Baker. Dr. C. and myself returned to Williams's hotel. Dr. C. went to his room; wished me to go in and sleep with him. I hesitated somewhat, he urged it and I went in. After we went in, Dr. C. took some of the money I had in my pocket, selected out some of the bills, and put them in his pocket book. The money he returned to me I put in my pocket. We then went to bed; had some conversation about taking care of the money. I wanted he should take it. He thought I could take care of it better. We finally concluded it would be safe to put it in a jug and let it set in the office. Did not sleep much that night either of us. I was awake most of the time, and the Dr. was. In the morning, I left the Dr. in his room, and went down to the office; placed all the money I then had into a jug.

The jug was set away in one of the small closets under the medicine shelves.

AFTERNOON

Thomas Flint. On Saturday forenoon, Dr. Coolidge was requested to go to Clinton to visit Philip Emerson – it was through me – I was out there Thursday. Dr. C. did not wish to go – told me to go and I went; do not know at what time I returned. In the afternoon Dr. C. transferred his property to me – the business was done by Mr. Baker and lawyer Chandler. We were together much in the afternoon – talked more about the property than anything else. That evening speaking of the money, I tried to get him to take care of it. He did not seem inclined to. About 7 o'clock I went into the office, broke the jug, and threw the money into the stove. That is the last I had to do with money. On Friday morning, the day the body was discovered, Edward Getchell and I examined the hatchet to see if there were any marks on it – could not find any decided marks. That forenoon, I brushed some froth from the side of the old book case. That forenoon, an examination was made of the office by the Selectmen I think – I recollect Joshua Williams. Mr. W. was in there in the forenoon, and examined, previous to the discovery of the spot of blood which was found near the new book case before witness saw it. On Friday night after we went to bed, Dr. C. spoke of the witnesses he had heard of before the inquest, and there importuned me very strongly never to reveal what I had discovered. Do not recollect anything more particular as to the conversation that evening. There are many things that took place then, that witness cannot fix the time of – Saturday night the chief conversation was about a letter which purported to be written to Edward Mathews. He had heard there was testimony before the inquest about a letter from Coolidge to Mathews. I asked him of that letter was not in existence. He said it was not – on Friday morning, he went down and took it from the body and destroyed it, so that it could not be produced as evidence against him. On Saturday, Mr. Noyes was called in as his advisor. On Monday morning, the Dr. told witness there was a bottle that had contained prussic acid standing amongst the medicine vials in a glass case which should be destroyed, and inquired what bottle it was. He said one I had never seen – it had no label on. It came from Hallowell. I asked why he wanted it destroyed if no one had seen it. He said William Phillips had seen it. He also said Esq. Noyes thought it best that the vials on the shelf should be replaced – Dr. C. said the bottle which he obtained of Burnett should be filled two thirds full, as there was some gone out of it. I filled the Burnett bottle, as I guessed, two thirds full, and replaced the vials. The empty bottle I broke, and put the stopple in the drawer where he kept stopples. I removed the old bottle containing prussic acid, and the Burnett bottle, first to the old book case, and then to witness's trunk. Witness did this because Wm. Phillips had suggested that the Dr. in his rage might destroy himself – witness himself had like apprehensions. Dr. C. also told witness to rinse out the brandy bottle, and throw out the water in the sink; witness took the brandy bottle, but did not rinse it. Told Mr. Baker to empty out the water in the sink – afterwards found he had only changed the water from the basin to the pail in the sink. Witness threw the water out. Sunday night, Dr. C. told witness where the watch was – wished witness to get it from the sleigh and throw it in the river. Dr. C. told witness the watch was in his sleigh stowed away in the loft – witness told him he could not attempt to remove it then and he had followed as far as he could go – he must let things remain as they were. Recollects nothing further about the watch, or connected with the affair. Dr. C.'s books were finally transferred to Esq. Noyes for the benefit of the creditors, as witness understood it. The papers transferring the property to witness were destroyed Wednesday or Thursday. Does not recollect the particular time when the books were transferred to Noyes – Mr. Baker had the management of it – it was Wednesday or Thursday. Slept with the prisoner Friday and Saturday, and perhaps Sunday night. Had not slept with him before. Dr. C. urged it then. Thinks Mr. Baker slept with him Sunday night. A great deal of the time when witness was with the prisoner, Dr. C. directed his conversation to witness, urging witness not to divulge what he knew to the public – once he expressed fears that witness would do it.

Cross examined. Is in his 24th year. Lived at Augusta the first year and a half of the last five years, at home and at school; was at school in North Yarmouth. Since that has been at Waterville two years last October; went there to study medicine with Dr. C. – Was at Philadelphia five months, a year ago last winter, attending medical lectures; returned about the middle of March. The next season he spent mostly in Waterville; left Waterville at the time of the murder – came down here; stayed here from

Friday till Sunday morning; went back to Anson; about the 1st November went to Philadelphia again; left Philadelphia 8th January for the trial – went to Anson after the postponement, and again went to Philadelphia the last day of January. Returned to this place a week ago today. The first person he mentioned these facts to, was partially to his father, on Thursday night, a week after the murder, in witness's room at Williams's hotel. Witness partially stated them to Mr. Baker on Friday morning coming down here. Talked with persons in the street about the death of Mathews previously – does not recollect whom; was called to Mr. Boutelle's office, and questioned if he knew of any business between Dr. C. and Edward Mathews, - said no, - was asked about a letter from Dr. C. to Mathews and said he saw one on the table the day before – witness first accounted for himself to the inquest – told them he was in the office – told them it was to examine books as to a case Dr. C. had at Skowhegan. Don't recollect what else he told them, if anything. Thinks he was not questioned at considerable length. Told them he was called into the office by Dr. C. to examine authors; was there on oath. Did not state to them any circumstances as to what took place in the office, which he has testified to today. Does not recollect what he did testify to; was before the inquest more than once; cannot say what day he was before the inquest the second day. Does not recollect being examined the second time; does not know that he ever signed his testimony but once. Did not state to the jury at either of those times anything about the money, the watch, the bottles of acid or his sweeping the floor. The usual oath was administered; presumes it was to tell the whole truth. Cannot say that he had talked with any person about where he was Thursday evening before communicating it to his father. Recollects being with Mr. Evans and Mr. Noyes, on Sunday or Monday evening – cannot say which. Does not know that he pointed out the table at which he sat or the books he read, Thursday evening. Cannot tell what answers he made when questioned – was questioned. Does not recollect saying that the body of Mathews was not there when witness came in and witness never saw it there. Thinks he went through the cellar on that occasion – will not say which way. Does not recollect speaking of the impossibility of taking the body down those stairs without disturbing the chairs or the cloth. Will not say whether it was so or not. Has not any promise from the government that he will not be prosecuted if he testifies.

116

Hs heard from Gen. Simonds and witness's father, that if he will testify he should have all the favor shown him which the case demands. Witness communicated enough to his father to let him know the position in which he was placed. Never told his father the residue of the facts entirely. Communicated to Baker when coming down to go before the grand jury – the last part of the jury – had talked of the matter before with Baker somewhat. Thinks he had previously told Baker the same as he had told the inquest as to his conduct Thursday evening. Does not know how Dr. Coolidge came to send for the acid to Boston – knew nothing of it. First saw the bottle when it arrived by express from Boston – opened the bottle to examine it – did not use any of it. Smelled of it – knew the odor of the acid. The odor is all alike. Smelled of it to satisfy his curiosity. Could not say it was prussic acid till he smelt of it. Did not use any of it. Baker asked witness if there was not something that ought to be done there in the office – told him he might empty out the water in the wash-basin. Gave him no reason. Did not tell him he had been trying experiments with prussic acid. Never tried any – never were any tried in the office in witness's presence. Had become acquainted with the odor in Dr. Coolidge's office. Saw it there, and examined it to know how it did smell, and how it looked. The bottle from Boston was put in a place where we keep all small vials, behind a glass door. Thinks Dr. C. was not in the office when it arrived. Does not know where it was put, or even saw it. Does not recollect showing the bottles to the counsel of Coolidge, and telling them they stood there precisely as they were, and just as full as they were, for some time. Will say that he did not. Does not recollect telling them there was no fire made in the stove Thursday evening, and had been none that night. Does not recollect saying the shutters were not closed or the curtain not drawn that evening. When Dr. C. called witness in after 9 o'clock, there was a hand lamp – no other lamp was lighted. That did not give much light, it was partly turned down; went down stairs in the dark; Dr. Coolidge was ahead; they turned the body at the foot of the stairs; when we started, we talked forward. Does not know that they touched anything on the way, except a stair, going down the first stairs. It was dark in the cellar. The body was not entirely laid down at any time – witness did not let go of the body at any time. Could not see it after got into the cellar. Found no difficulty getting over the wood, except in stooping, – Cannot say if they had their hats on; struck his head against the floor, when he straightened up, before they laid the body down. It was about an hour witness was absent from house.

Deceased was carried with his hat on. Felt the hat laying by the side of deceased when they left him. Witness did not take it off. Dr. C. must have done it. Saw no person on Main Street; heard some one go into Gen. Fairfield's just before they left the back office; head the door open and shut. The window was open. Don't know how much money he took from under the carpet; put it in his pocket; kept it till morning; put it in the jug – put all he had in the jug at the same time. Hid part of it in the woodpile to get rid of it; this was before he knew of any other. The money in the jug witness put in the stove Saturday night soon after tea; there was a fire in the stove, put the money in the fire so that it might be burned; supposed it was burned. Cannot say how long it was from the time he spoke to Dr. C. at Dr. Thayer's before he saw him making the charge; witness had time to walk to the office. The distance may be 30 rods; might walk it in 5 minutes; might be 10 or 15. Does not know that Dr. C. had been in the hall at that time. The post mortem examination had not taken place. – Does not know if the inquest jury had been formed. Witness had not then been examined. When the Dr. left, he took the book with him; and said he was going to the hall. Did not go with him. Does not recollect ever saying the body was put in a sack and carried down. Had had a conversation with Dr. C. about buying him out – witness expressed a wish to do it. Did not state to him his want of money as the reason why he could not do it. – Had not the means to do it. Did not say to him I could not get assistance from my father to do it. – Had had previous conversations with Dr. C. about obtaining subjects. Not very often – but when it happened to come up, witness had expressed a desire to obtain a subject. Had not read much on the effects of hydrocyanic acid. Had not read Christison. Don't know that he ever talked with Dr. C. about the effects. Never saw deceased drink brandy in the office. All witness knows of his drinking brandy there, was by the settling of the brandy in the bottle and what the boy told witness. About one third of the contents of the bottle were gone – the bottle would hold a quart. – Does not know how many times that day he had drank there or been in there. Cannot say how much the brandy had settled the day before. The bottle was empty Friday morning, witness thinks. Does not know that there was any brandy in it the evening the counsel were there. Does not recollect showing them the bottle, nor that anything was said about brandy. Does not recollect being asked why the brandy had not been analyzed, or if anybody had suggested it. Witness gave the bottle to Mr. Nudd, the officer, when on the way to Philadelphia. Understood the bottle was to be preserved when the other property was sold. Believes there was then nothing in it. The bottle was replenished from a jug which was kept in the office. Witness thinks he filled it Wednesday night or Thursday morning. Filled it so as to have it convenient for use. It was frequently used. On Thursday noon, one-third was gone – does not know of anyone using it. When the boy Getchell made a remark about it, witness made no remark – asked the boy about it – took his account of the matter. Was in the office Thursday forenoon most of the time. Saw no one drink brandy that forenoon – had as good an opportunity as the boy. The boy called witness's attention to the spot on the carpet in the front office. Witness stooped down and picked some hairs from the spot. Don't know how many hairs; the spot was dried blood about as big as the hand; did not examine the carpet below. Don't recollect making any remark; thinks Dingley was present; cannot say if they saw the hairs; Getchell was near; threw the hairs away; don't recollect where; cannot say if he threw it on the floor. Thinks that was all he did; cannot say whether he scratched it with his finger nail; took the hair up; there was no concealment about it; if the others were looking on, they saw it. Witness examined the spot more closely afterwards, and rubbed it a little. Took it in his hands. Did not obliterate it. Last saw it Sunday after he went from here – saw it there in the office – pointed it out to Mr. Nudd and Attorney General Moor. It was plain to be seen at that time; has not seen the carpet since. First communicated to the Attorney General his knowledge of these facts before the grand jury – recollects no conversation with him before. Was twice before the grand jury. – had no assurances from the Attorney General; spent a part of a day with him at Waterville. On Thursday night, Mr. Baker slept in the same bed with witness – witness rose first in the morning – cannot say if Baker was asleep or awake. Had some conversation with him that night before retiring – cannot say on what subject. Did not hear Dr. C. when he went to bed – could not unless he made considerable noise – did not sleep at all Thursday night. Did not hear Dr. C. when he got up. Heard a good deal of noise in the house; cannot say if any more than usual. Never laid awake before; suppose he heard the stages go out. – Witness went down

Shorey's stairs before breakfast part way; went down two or three steps, to see if anything was left. Was at the door of the office when Dr. C. gave him the letter he destroyed Friday; cannot say where the Dr. came from then. – There was a fire in the office – cannot say if there were fires at Williams's. Dr. C. took the letter from his pocket-book. Did not see the money in his pocket book then. Cannot say if any one was in the office – cannot say when he destroyed the letter, thinks it was within 5 hours. Kept the acid bottles in witness's trunk over one night – at that time it was not known to any body that witness took them away. Never made any experiments with acid, nor witnessed any.

Never saw any experiments with a cat or turtle; never witnessed any experiments with prussic acid elsewhere. Does not recollect being asked by Mr. Boutelle at his office whether he saw Mathews the night before, was there but a short time. Gave him no information about Edward Mathews. Mr. B. took him into another room, and asked him about the business and the letter, and witness replied. – Thinks he did not ask him if he knew where Mathews was the night before. Does not recollect when he carried the bottle to his room where his trunk was. It was the next day after the body was found. Placed the two bottles in the old book-case Friday evening – those were all the bottles witness then knew of. Mr. Baker was not in the room when witness went home Thursday night. Returned to the room Friday morning after going to the office. Slept with Dr. C. Saturday night. On Monday or Tuesday night, 4 slept in the same room; Dr. C., witness, Baker and Ayer. The curtains were down Thursday night before witness left the office at 3 o'clock, - Dr. C. put them down. The light was put in the front room before they took the body down. The money put in the crevice by witness; he afterwards put it in the jug. It was a small amount. – Had it of Coolidge Friday. Did not wrap it up – Never counted this money. Don't know how much was left under the carpet when he took the first out. Took out what was convenient to reach. On Saturday morning rolled the safe back and took the rest out. The object of exchanging the money with Dr. C. was that he might have only bills on the river banks, as less suspicious. The bills witness had, he rolled up, pinned with two pins, and put in his coat pocket. Made several attempts to remove the spot on the oil cloth carpet and mop-board, but did not succeed, and left them. The door down stairs was not open when witness went into the office – Dr. C. went down without the lamp the first time – took the lamp afterwards. Tied the lid on the acid bottle after opening it when it was first received. Cannot say it was with the same string. Cannot say if he tied it up again. Opened the bottle when Attorney Gen. Moor was there; don't know who tied it up. Opened it when witness filled it up – does not recollect if he tied it up. Does not know if it was tied up when Moor was there. Last saw the bottle in Nudd's hands – does not know it was tied, - does not know how much he put in the bottle – put in water. Does not know how many of those aromatics he found – threw them away – has seen such before – never saw Mathews have any. Never had any conversation with deceased about witness's desire to buy Coolidge out. Had not much acquaintance with Mathews. He was not frequently in the office through the summer. Witness was asked by many persons about the time what he knew; did not tell them; does not recollect what answers he gave. Thinks Coolidge expressed fears of witness's divulging on Wednesday. Had written to his father on Monday and on Wednesday – gave both the letter to Mr. Blunt, the driver – did not mail any letters. Witness's father came to Waterville on Thursday.

Mr. Morrill offered the letters Flint write to his father, but the Court ruled them out.

From the Republican Journal (Belfast, Me) March 31, 1848 – It was supposed, by some of the reporters, that Flint would break down under the searching cross examination which he would receive from George Evans, the senior counsel for the prisoner. The reporter for the Mail gives the following notice of Flint and his examination: --

"A brief description of young Flint, *the witness,* may not be unacceptable to your readers. He is about 24 years old, straight, genteel form, not so tall as Dr. Coolidge – very dark grey eyes, bright, sparkling, and somewhat prominent; complexion dark; no beard or whiskers; dark hair; well shaped head; temperament cool, and nerves not to be shaken with trifles. He could gaze into Evans's eyes as long as Evans could into his. Once during the examination there was apparently a trial of their skill in this regard, but the Hon. Senator yielded. I have never seen a witness upon the stand who was so little confused by a cross examination as Flint. He was immoveable – a statue, and withstood the "searching operation" with remarkable power. No ingenuity of counsel could ensnare him, and no power could make him quail. During the several hours of his examination he was Thomas Flint, and nobody else. He knew that he had prevaricated before the jury of inquest, and the object of the cross interrogatories was to show that he had perjured himself, but "*non mi recordo*" was his answer to many questions. Before the jury of inquest he was undoubtedly guilty of the *suppressio veri*, if not of the *expressio falsi*. His testimony is generally believed by the people here, but whether the jury will believe it, is quite another affair."

From the *Yankee Blade*, the publication edited by Edward Mathews's brother, as reprinted in the *Eastern Mail* April 13, 1848.

Thomas Flint. The following just and exculpatory remarks in relation to this young man, are from the pen of William Mathews, editor of the Yankee Blade, and brother of the deceased. In giving an account of the closing proceedings of the trial, the writer says:

"Of the various witnesses who took the stand during the trial, none acquitted themselves better, under the circumstances, than Flint. The circumstances under which he appeared were particularly trying, and it would have surprised no one, had he been greatly embarrassed and confused. He was, however, calm as a clock; told his story in the clearest and most succinct manner, without verbiage or contradiction; and finally stood the fire of a severe and scrutinizing cross-examination for nearly three hours, without flinching or embarrassment. Mr. Evans plied him closely with questions of every sort and shape; but it was evident, from the beginning, that the witness was more than a match for him, and, having the truth on his side, could not be involved in a contradiction."

Miss Emily Williams sworn. On Thursday evening, Sept. 30th, Thomas Flint came into the sitting room about 8 o'clock, at Williams's tavern. There was a gentleman and lady there with a child who had a very large head. Flint remained there an hour and a half – went out only a few minutes to measure a string which he put round the child's head. He next went out between a quarter and half past 9. – When he left, Mr. Williams, Howe and myself remained. When Flint opened the door, he met Dr. C. in the entry. He said to him, "look here, Tom." They both went out the front door.

Cross examined, Did not see Flint again that night, Saw the side of Dr. C.'s face, his arm and his hat, Heard Dr. C.'s voice distinctly. Was at the back side of the room. Remained but a few minutes after Flint went out. Flint had a light. – Saw the lamp afterwards on the stand in the front entry, Dr. C. spoke as if in a hurry when he addressed Flint. Thinks she then went into the dining room to see her mother. The curtains were down in the sitting room. Has conversed with Flint about this matter. Does

122

not remember his giving any account of himself after he went out.

Prof Champlin sworn. Was not in Waterville at the time of the murder. Commencement was on the 12th of August; on the 13th I called on Dr. Coolidge at breakfast time; found him at breakfast. Witness was obtaining subscriptions for the benefit of the College. Opened the subject to Dr. C. – he said he wished time to think of it. Saw him again a few days afterwards, in the back yard, and he said he had not made up his mind. Left town, and did not return before the 17th September. Called to see the doctor soon after; did not find him at first; found him there a few days afterwards. He was giving medicine to a person. After he got through, spoke to him about the subscription, Dr. C. said he had made up his mind he could not give – said he had made a large purchase with Dr. Potter. Thinks he mentioned the amount of $10,000, but will not be positive. He said he expected to make a large sum by the speculation, and if he did, he would at a future time make the College a handsome present. Witness soon after left, and went into Mr. Esty's store to make some purchases, The doctor followed him and requested him to say nothing about the subject of his speculation, At my first conversation with prisoner, he spoke of going abroad soon, as an excuse for not giving, but wished witness not to mention it.

Samuel Doolittle, sworn - I saw Dr. Coolidge on Friday following the death of Mr. Mathews, and asked him if the contents of the stomach had not better be examined; he asked me if they had been preserved, and I told him they had, he replied that they had lain so long nothing could be ascertained by them.

Cross examined. – Was in Coolidge's office Friday morning; searched round, but discovered nothing, He was in the hall when John Mathews came in; it was before the inquest had been organized, or the committees of search,

Mr. Morrill stated to the court that with the exception of one or two more witnesses the evidence for the government was all in, and it being near 6 o'clock, the Court adjourned to Monday morning at 9 o'clock.

Day 6: Monday, March 20, 1848
Evidence for the Prosecution, Continued

Joseph Freeman, recalled.   I saw Edward Mathews on Thursday evening at about 8 o'clock as I was going into the bar room of Williams's tavern; he was passing out of the bar-room under the hall, in the direction, of the Parker House.

Amasa J. Dingley, recalled. In the course of the conversation with prisoner with regard to a subject, Dr. C. came out of the back office, and said there would be a good place to dissect, and the subject could be kept in the cask or barrel in the closet. Witness asked if they could not dissect in the front office. He said they might if they used plenty of spirits. Cannot say at which conversation this was. Before the murder, saw a cask with iron hoops in the closet several times; it was a small cask. Does not recollect seeing it there afterwards. – Some time after the murder, saw a small cask with wooden hoops in the back office.

Cross examined. The cask was about the size of a half barrel. First thought of this circumstance since he testified before, Mr. Morrell remined him of it. Did not testify about the barrel or the subject before the inquest. Has conversed with Flint twice on the subject. Witness was charged by Attorney General not to say anything publicly about the barrel or subject. Flint was not present. Part of his testimony in writing was read to witness – thinks the whole was not. It was the same in part that Flint testified to here. Saw them turn over writing which was not read to witness. It was the 16th November when this was read to him. No other testimony was read to witness. Cannot say it was Flint's testimony before the Grand Jury. Attorney General Moor said it was Flint's testimony – did not say where it was taken.

Witness was in the office Friday evening – perhaps half an hour. Left the office about 8 o'clock, after dark. Mr. Baker was there, and no other besides Dr. Coolidge. Dr. Thayer was not in - don't know whether he was sent for. Coolidge was there when witness went in – it was about half past 7. Kept a memorandum of what he could think of – set down the date of the conversation with Attorney General – did not know but he should be called on.

Day Six: Monday, March 20, 1848

Mr. Morrill gave notice that the government would rest the case here.

Counsel for the Defense

Mr. Noyes then opened the case for the defense, substantially as follows: -

May it please your Honors, and Gentlemen of the Jury:

The government having concluded their testimony, it now becomes my duty to open the case for the defendant. The prisoner at the bar, gentlemen, stands charged with one of the most heinous offenses known to the laws, and you are set apart from your fellow men to adjudge impartially as to the guilt or the innocence of the accused. You are well aware, gentlemen, of the prejudices which have existed in this case, and you are here to adjudge of the accused by the evidence only, always according him innocent until proven guilty.

On the 30th of September it has been shown to you, that the deceased was about his business in the streets of Waterville; at 8 o'clock he was at a social party at the Parker House; he left there, and in the morning his body was found in the cellar under Mr. Phillips' store.

Let us look further into the matter. The prisoner was at his office in the evening of Thursday; he was seen to go to his boarding house, look into the window, and was afterwards seen in the public streets. Now, gentlemen, I propose to discuss this matter without taking into consideration the testimony of Thomas Flint, (I shall have something to say on this matter before I close,) but to review the testimony of credible witnesses, and such as the law declares to be such.

The prisoner at the bar, gentlemen, is a man of common sagacity. He is charged with the most heinous offense, and the act is alleged to have been committed in a building in a public street, at an hour when the rooms all around that in which the murder is alleged to have been committed, was full of persons, in the pursuit of various employments. Do you believe a man in the possession of his senses, could commit an act of this nature, when he was liable to interruption every moment; for it is proven that there were several keys to the office, and those keys in the possession of various persons. If indeed, you believe the death to have been produced by a secret and deadly poison, are you satisfied that it was not an accidental death and not a premeditated one. But let us review the evidence here.

Mr. Noyes then reviewed the tests which had been applied to what he said purported to be the contents of the stomach, and endeavored to show that they were not certain tests, placing considerable stress upon the testimony of Dr Hubbard, as well as that of Professor Loomis. He also referred to the uncertainty of the contents of the stomach not having been meddled with after taken from the hall and placed over night in the open air. Had not, inquired he, some chemical action taken place in the substance in the wash bowl, while standing there. He was certain changes had taken place, for when the matter was taken from the stomach, there was a presence of brandy enough as shown by the evidence, to produce intoxication, and when the same matter was placed in the hands of Professor Loomis, no brandy was found. Referred to the odor which proceeded from the brain and throat of the deceased, and stated that it was a certain fact that the extracted oil of bitter almonds has an odor precisely like that of Prussic acid. He also mentioned the fact that no odor was noticed when the body was opened in the morning, and declared that there was an inconsistency in supposing that had there been Prussic acid in the body at the time, an odor would to have been discovered by the learned physicians present. He would be willing to rest the case here, were it not that such a mass of circumstantial evidence of a vague character had been introduced, touching on so many various points that he felt bound to go over the whole ground, notwithstanding the government had entirely failed to connect a chain of circumstance which could bear upon the prisoner. In all considerations at present, however, he did not propose to touch upon the testimony of Thomas Flint.

It sometimes happens that innocent persons, when suspected of crimes, will take undue means to clear themselves from suspicion. - Gray, it has been shown, would not have testified against Coolidge, had he not been suspected himself, and it could not be supposed that when conversing with Gilman, he (Coolidge) under the excitement he was then laboring, could have been over particular in the language he made use of. It was a circumstance of little moment and ought not to be seriously considered. Read an extract from Lord Mansfield's speech in the Douglas case, where an innocent uncle had been convicted of murder of his niece, some person at the time having heard her, while he was correcting her for some offense, say "good uncle do not kill me." The girl disappeared, the uncle was tried for murder and executed, but some years after, she appeared again, and stated that she ran away and had been secreted since that time.[1]

The next thing that the government attempt to prove, is that the prisoner had the means. We grant it, but the means were such as every physician on the river ought to have in his possession. Ten drops of the medicinal acid would have produced death; then should the circumstance of having procured other acid be considered. He had poison enough always, and the fact of a physician, with a large practice, buying a bottle of hydrocyanic, it seems to me ought to go for nothing.

Referred to finding the deceased's watch in the prisoner's sleigh, and endeavored to show how easy it would be for any person to put it there, in order to throw suspicion on the prisoner. - In referring to the testimony of Flint, he said it was utterly impossible that the body of the deceased could have been taken down though Shorey's shop, more especially by the cutting board without disturbing the cloth lying on the board. We shall show you, gentlemen, that this witness Flint, with the oath of God upon him, has sworn on more than one occasion, that he knew nothing of this transaction, We shall show, too, gentlemen that he has given a different account of the transportation of the body to the cellar. He has lied before the grand jury, or he has lied here. If he had been convicted of perjury the law of the land would exclude him from the stand here. He has not been so convicted, and is therefore allowed to testify, but the fact that he has lied under oath, goes to so effect his credibility that you have no right to convict on such testimony. Cited authorities relative to the credibility of witnesses, &c.

---

[1] . This may be an error. Mansford gave a well-known speech in the Douglas Cause, a very notable case of inheritance; for an accessible account see *The Douglas Cause* edited by A. Francis Steuart (ed.), Glasgow: Hodge and Company, 1909. The "good uncle do not not kill me" was used in "Remarks upon Mr. Cornish's Trial, by Sir John Hawkes, Solicitor-General in the Reign of King William the Third". See *A Complete Collection of State Trials and Proceedings for High Treason and Other Crimes and Misdemeanors from the Earliest Period to the Year 1820.* Volume XI, London, 1816, Column 464. This is a famous and frequently cited reference used for defense in cases resting upon circumstantial evidence. The remarks are from ca. 1685.

We shall offer you evidence that the prisoner was not in want of money, when he is alleged to have committed this deed - that he had due him, at the time over $6000 - that he was in excellent credit not pressed by any body, and that his business, so far from being on the decline, was rapidly and permanently increasing. He referred to the prisoner's asking Gilman & Gray for money, men, who, he said, were not lenders of money, and if the prisoner ever asked them for such sums as they testified to, it was mere idle talk; there was nothing in these circumstances, which could convey the least suspicion of a motive for the commission of this grave offense.

He cited the law in relation to the force of evidence in regard to character before the offense charged, saying he should show that from youth up, the prisoner has maintained a most respectable standing in society, has been considered a humane, a moral and upright citizen - one on whom no suspicion of crime had ever before rested, and who could not be suspected in this case, but from a variety of unconnected circumstances, of little or no weight.

Evidence for the Defense

Mr. Noyes proposed to introduce the certificate of the physicians before the inquest to show cause of death. Counsel for government objected to its introduction. Court said it might be offered for the purpose of contradicting their statement there. Mr. Evans - we expect to show a variance in their testimony: that they stated before the inquest that the wounds might have caused death; that here they have said, that they did not.

The Chief Justice said, upon a comparison of the testimony of Plaisted before the inquest, with that here stated, that they did not perceive any variance.

Testimony waived by counsel for defendant.

Oliver Paine sworn. I was one of the coroner's jury on the body of Edward Mathews; the session commenced Friday afternoon, and Thomas Flint was called before the jury and examined on Friday, and also on another occasion; the first examination lasted about half an hour; he stated at this time that he had no knowledge of the murder of Edward Mathews, or any circumstance connected with it; he also said he saw nothing about the office to raise a suspicion that the murder was committed there; he said he saw Mathews in the street once after his return from Brighton, but that he did not see him on Thursday evening; he stated that he was in the office himself until 8 o'clock, and that he then went to Williams's tavern, played backgammon until half past 9; that he then took a light and was going to bed, when he met doctor Coolidge and went with him to the office, where he remained until about half past 10, looking up medical cases in the books in reference to a case the doctor had at Skowhegan, he stated that the doctor was sitting at a table with him; also that no one else was in the office; he did not state how long it was after his return to the town before the doctor came in; he was called again before the jury on Saturday, and interrogated with regard to what he saw about the office; with regard to a letter also; he at this time declared he had seen nothing to throw suspicion on the doctor and that he knew of no circumstance which would lead to the detection of the murderer; all of this testimony was not taken down on either occasion, as Mr. Smith stated it was strictly negative and not necessary to be recorded.

Cross examined. I think I have not stated all that he said; he answered several questions in the negative; he was not willing to go on and make a statement, but preferred that we should ask questions.

John Marston sworn - Was one of the coroner's jury and heard the examination of Thomas Flint: he was minutely examined as to his knowledge of the murder in any respect, and he replied that he knew nothing about it; one reply that he made was, that when he went to the office after having been called from Mr. Williams's, he found the office lighted as usual, and the door to the back office open; he also said he saw nothing unusual on the floor; said he could give no information of any character which would lead to the detection of the murderer; said he was employed that evening in hunting up cases in the books, and that the doctor was sitting with him at the table; am not certain whether he stated at what time the doctor returned to the tavern after he did, but think he mentioned about half an hour; he was examined at two separate times before the coroner's jury; have the impression that he said he saw deceased in the street on Thursday afternoon, but that he did not see him after that.

Cross examined. Do not undertake to give Flint's language exactly, but this is the substance; am not quite certain that he did not say that he saw deceased in the office, but think not; was present when John Mathews testified, but do not recollect what part, if any of his testimony, was taken down; he testified to one fact, I am certain, and that was with regard to his signing the note; don't recollect what he said about Dingley being in the office that day, but think he said Dingley was there; he said he left the office at 8, and returned after 9 sometime.

Benjamin Ayer sworn. I resided in Waterville at the time of the death of Mathews, and frequently heard Flint say that he know nothing about his death; these replies were frequently repeated, from Wednesday to the Thursday of the following week; he said he had no knowledge whatever of the affair, and could give no information with regard to it; I was frequently with him and the doctor at the hotel; I saw Flint on the morning of that the body was found, back of the building; some one suggested that the body might not be dead; Mr. Flint went to the deceased took hold of the hands, said they were cold, and that the person was dead; this was before the body was removed from off the wood; the space from the top of the wood to the floor, I should say was about 2 1/2 feet, it was not three feet; the woodpile sloped off towards the cellar stairs as well as towards the door; people frequently visited the doctor's office in the evening; I assisted in making a schedule of the doctor's effects, and recollect pretty nearly the amount; it was not far from - (Objected to and ruled out, the Court remarking that the schedule would be the proper evidence.)

Cross examined. I was not on the spot when the body was taken out of the cellar, and do not know whether the wood was thrown back or not, after the body was taken out; I frequently interrogated Mr. Flint as to his knowledge of the murder, because suspicions had rested on the doctor, and I told Flint that I wanted the facts to come out; was not boarding at the time at Williams's, but stopped there on Monday night, and on two or three night following; on a certain night Mr. Flint, Mr. Baker, myself, and Dr. Coolidge were in one room all night, making out a schedule of the doctor's effects; the prisoner talked of this affair at the time, and said he thought it rather a hard case that he should be accused of the murder; do not know at what time Flint's father came to Waterville, but know he was there on the Thursday night following the death of Mr. Mathews.

Direct examination resumed. I was on a watch raised to search the town, and was back of the building where Coolidge's office was, myself, one night; should think Coolidge was watched in his actions during this time pretty carefully.

Samuel Brown sworn. I reside in Buckfield; knew the prisoner in the fall of 1841, while he was a student at medicine with his uncle; he remained until he came to Waterville, with the exception of a time while he was attending medical lectures at Hanover; I knew him quite well while he was at Buckfield; his character was very good; he kept school once in our town.

Cross examined. I can't state at what time precisely he left Buckfield; never knew of his establishing himself in the practice of medicine elsewhere than in Waterville.

John Simmons sworn. I reside in Canton in this State; have known the father of the prisoner 25 years; prisoner was born in Canton, and I knew him from his birth till he left for Buckfield in 1841; he lived with his father most of the time until he was 20; he obtained his education at the town school, and of his uncle, who was a literary man; report said that he attended medical lectures at Hanover; in his early years he worked on his father's farm, and acquired and maintained, so far as my knowledge extended, an unblemished character.

Adjourned to 2 o'clock.

AFTERNOON SESSION

Isaac W Wheeler sworn. I was employed by Mr. Nudd to make out a schedule of Dr. Coolidge's property, soon after his arrest, and was assisted by Mr. Flint; I had heard that Flint had testified before the grand jury, but had not heard what he testified to; Flint told me at this time that they put a sack over the body before taking it down stairs; we were employed together two or three days, but before getting through he went away; when employed in this work, Flint filled up a pocket case he had with such medicines as he wanted; they were stated to be expensive medicines by the bills.

Cross examined. Flint filled up about a dozen phials; I remonstrated at the time, thinking the time occupied in filling up the medicines might be worth more than the medicines; he said he carried the body down in a sack. (Witness explained the apparent discrepancy in his testimony by saying Flint told him the body was put *in* a sack or a sack put *over* the body) I have spoken of this circumstance in the street, and to Mr. Noyes - perhaps to other persons.

Daniel Baker sworn. I reside at Waterville, and on the 20th of September last, was boarding at Williams's hotel; Mr. Flint and Dr. Coolidge boarded there also. While at the breakfast table I heard of the death of Edward Mathews, and with Mr. Kelly went to the place where the body was found; several persons were there, among them Dr. Hoyt; I had conversation with Mr. Flint at the time the coroner's jury was held frequently, and he invariably told me he had no suspicion as to the murder; I went to Dr. Coolidge's office in the early part of the day, and we went from there with Mr. Flint to the office of Mr. Boutelle, when he went into the back office and remained some ten minutes; I was in the office of Dr. Coolidge in the evening (Friday) and saw Mr. Dingley and Mr. Flint there; Dr. Thayer came in, by request, in the same evening; on Saturday, in the forenoon, I was in the office of Messrs Boutelle & Noyes, where I am studying; in the afternoon I was in Dr. Coolidge's office most of the time with Mr. Flint and Mr. Paul L Chandler; there was a good deal of excitement about and a good deal of suspicion; on some morning after Sunday, I called on Mr. Flint at Mr. Williams's, for the keys of Dr. Coolidge's office, he gave them to me, and at the same time asked me if I would pour out the contents of a pail which stood in the office; Flint remained at this room, No. 2, at Williams's; I went to the office with Mr. Chandler, unlocked the door, found the pail but did not pour out the contents; we went to Mr. Flint and asked him why he wished the contents thrown out, and he said because that a fortnight before he had experimented with Prussic acid, and some of the dregs might be in the pail; afterwards he told me he threw it out. Mr. Flint and I came from Waterville here together to go before the grand jury, when about four miles from this town, he said "I suppose I am a witness and have got to testify against Dr. Coolidge," but did not say what he should testify; up to that time there was nothing but common conversation; I asked him if he knew any thing personally of the crime alleged, and he said no; I stayed with him until towards night the next day, and went back with Mr. Howe; Flint remained, I have the impression.

Cross examined. I have the impression that was Monday evening that I and Chandler went to Dr. Coolidge's office - we went then to look round as we had frequently done, but I remember of no particular object we had in going there; we finally, after consultation, concluded we would not turn the water out, but let Flint turn out his own slops; the slops were somewhat dark colored; I enumerated to several persons the fact that Flint commented to me about the slops.

At the time Flint and I were riding together, he said he had got to testify against the doctor that the crime was enormous; the Doctor must be guilty; the time had come for him to testify; that there was no escape for the Doctor; he must be hung; but that he had no personal knowledge of the crime; did not say to him that his position was a dangerous one, and he ought to be careful in his statements; recollect telling him at one time that we were bound to state what we know - the reason why I did not go before the inquest and state about the slops, was that I did not know what the slops contained, and was not summoned before the jury of inquest; Flint's asking me to turn them out excited my suspicions, but not the appearance of the slops; the pail was nearly full, and looked like a slop pail where every thing was turned in; on Monday night I slept for the first time with Dr. Coolidge; on Tuesday night I slept with him; on Wednesday, Flint, defendant and myself were together, and from 8 o'clock Mr. Ayer was with us; on Thursday night I slept with Dr. Coolidge; none at all with defendant on Monday; very little on Tuesday; on Wednesday night we were together, until the Doctor retired and left us writing. I was anxious to keep those who came there on business that might harass the Dr. from seeing him; don't recollect telling Mrs. Williams that she must not permit people to talk to defendant about the murder, although I might; could not state how much of the time I spent in the defendant's office the Saturday after the death; might have been there from an hour to an hour and a half. I wrote a bill of sale from defendant to Flint, at Flint's request, of his horse and carriage; defendant signed the bill of sale; don't recollect seeing Paul Chandler within 24 hours; I witnessed the bill of sale; Mr. Chandler wrote other instruments; Mr. Chandler asked if it was a bona fide sale; it was answered that it was; afterwards the instrument was burned in No. 2; I consulted with Mr. Boutelle and he advised to have it burned, there having been another disposition of the property; did not see the consideration paid, or returned again;

Coolidge made the second assignment; knew nothing of the removal of the acid, by Flint; don't know any thing about the removal of the instruments; what they were taken for or why; had a conversation with the defendant about the stomach being analyzed on Sunday night; told him what had been found in it; never saw that acid bottle in No. 2.

Examination resumed. Was sent to Williams's by Mr. Noyes on Wednesday night, to make an assignment from defendant to Parker and Phillips; after examining the schedule they declined it. Mr. Noyes left home about that time; told me it must be made; it was finally made to Noyes. Have not been in the Court room during trial; have read the evidence thoroughly up to Friday; identified a book exhibited as the day book of the defendant; have heard Miss Williams's testimony read this forenoon.

Chas E Stewart sworn. I reside in Gardner, and saw the deceased at Gardiner on the morning prior to his death; also saw him the evening before in a room smoking and playing cards - gambling; he had a considerable sum of money which I saw him exhibit once during the evening; there were four persons in the room altogether at the time; we all came down stairs together, at 10 o'clock; one of the party, John Shackford, was a resident of Gardiner, had been there 3 months; stayed as he said at the Cobbossee House; he left next morning at about 9 o'clock, in a wagon alone; that was not the first time I had seen him playing. Counsel for government objected to testimony as irrelevant. (Court ruled the evidence to be inadmissible.)

Cross examined. The watch before exhibited in Court, was shown to the witness, and he testified, it was the same witness had sold to deceased in August; he had it that morning; when I last saw him he gave me $65 for it; gave me his note; it is not now paid; there is an endorsement on note of $20; I think upon the 7th of Sept; I had owned the watch one year; he had it 2 or 3 months before he bought it.

Henry Smith, sworn. Was acquainted with deceased; saw him some two or three hours on Friday evening previous to his death; at the Cobossee house[2]; as late as 1 or 2 o'clock; [The evidence was objected to. Court said it must be stated what was expected to be proved. Counsel said he expected to prove he was up late

---

[2] Cobbossee House, an inn established in 1827, and in business into the 1960's.

at night, drinking, and had those habits from which sudden death might be expected. Court said the question might be put.] Witness then stated, that he did not see him drink, but that he was then intoxicated; think I did not remain with him until 3 o'clock in the morning, although I might have so remained; think he was quite as much intoxicated as I ever saw him; he exhibited large sums of money to me when no one else was present; when I first saw him he was in front of the house; he invited me into the house; John Shackford and some others were present in the room with us; don't recollect that there was any thing to drink in the room; James M. McCurdy was in the room: he is my clerk.

Cross examined. Don't recollect the name of any other one; they were all acquaintances of mine who had formerly resided in Gardiner; some others and myself had been out serenading; did not see him when he went away the next morning; this was at the Cobbossee House; think I have seen the watch before. Witness was here asked if he had ever owned the watch. He declined answering the question, and appealed to the Court. He was directed to answer the question. Said he had never legally owned it; own it now; won it in a bet on Friday night previous to the death of Mathews. Counsel asked what the bet was about - [objected to - Court ruled it admissible] I won it of the deceased; bet against another watch, which I have here; I made but one bet.

Mr. Noyes, (attorney in the case,) sworn. Was present on Monday or Tuesday evening at the office of Dr. Coolidge in company with Mr. Flint, Chandler and yourself (Mr. Evans); Flint was asked if he was present in the office on the Thursday evening of the death, and he said he was, and pointed out the place where he sat, and where Dr Coolidge sat; he stated that on that evening the blinds and the curtains were open; we then went into the back office, and he pointed out where the acid bottles, as he said, sat on the morning after the death of the deceased. There was something in the brandy bottle which looked like brandy and which he said was brandy. He told us that the bottles were exactly as they had stood the day before. Said it had decreased for several days previous. Said nothing about having removed any bottles, and said, I think to one of us, that he found nothing extraordinary in the office in the morning after the death. I am assignee of the prisoner's effects for the benefit of such persons as became creditors to him within thirty days prior to the date of assignment. The assignment was made without my knowledge. Counsel was asked the amount of the assets [objected to. Mr. Wells asked the witness if the paper would not show the amount. Mr. Noyes stated that the assignment referred to two schedules, marked A and B. Mr. Evans stated that the books were unfortunately left at Waterville. The Court ruled that the documents would be the best evidence.] The witness stated that the Dr. had been engaged in an extensive practice, and from the individuals among whom he practiced should judge that it was a lucrative practice - was his collecting lawyer - most of the demands he left with me were litigated cases.

Cross examined. I have collected from his demand since the assignment some $1500 or $1600 from some of our most independent citizens; Mr. Evans and myself were engaged as Counsel for defendant at the time of conversation with Flint in the office of defendant, and we went there for the purpose of obtaining information; it was then expected that defendant would be arrested; I was myself absent from town at that time, except at night.

Counsel for defendant here stated, that they had a great many witnesses present to testify to the good character of defendant, but as they understood that the counsel for the government did not contest the point, they would not take up time by introducing witnesses.

Mr. Evans now desired to read from Guy & Chistisons, some passages in relation to the effects of chemical action on prussic acid, which would go to show that witnesses who had testified here, had not read all that was contained in those works relating to the matter. The Court decided that reading from books other than books of law was not admissible, on the ground that the authors of those works were not under oath when they were written. Mr. Evans said he would not undertake to say that the practice in the Courts of Massachusetts and New York was more correct than the practice here, but that in those Court such readings would be admitted.

Mr. Chief Justice Shepley[3], apparently somewhat affected, replied that he adhered to his decision, and intimated that Mr. Evans had made use of improper language; whereupon Mr.

---

[3] This is the Boston Daily Times reporter's error; Whitman was the Chief Justice.

Evans arose and feelingly disclaimed any intention of casting imputations on the Court, he had too much respect for the Court and for himself to do this. He thought he had been misapprehended by the Court; the witnesses had given their opinion as founded upon books; he proposed to show by the reading of those books, that they were mistaken. Justice Shepley remarked, I have only to say, sir, that all my remarks are correct. Chief Justice Whitman concurred with Judge Shepley, and gave a short opinion; it was also understood that Judge Wells concurred in opinion.

Mr. Noyes read to the jury Mr. Flint's statements, Oct 1st and 2d, before the inquest – also the statements of A. J. Dingley and George L. Robinson.

Statements of Thomas Flint before the Inquest 1st and 2d Oct

"Is acquainted with deceased. I saw him yesterday about ten o'clock in Dr. Coolidge's office. I am a student in Dr. C.'s office. He did not make known his business, not go into the back room. Coolidge was not present. I did not see him again after until his death. I am sure that deceased was not in the office again during the day when I was there, I was absent all the afternoon – Mr. Dingley was in the office yesterday. I left the office last evening about 8 o'clock. I left Coolidge in the office. I was absent about 1 hour or a little more. A little after 9 I stepped to the door, met Coolidge who requested me to go to the office and read books in relation to some case he had at Skowhegan. Some time after ten I left the office. Dr. Coolidge remained in the office – I returned to the house and went to bed.

THOMAS FLINT. Oct 1. "

Oct. 2d. – Last Tuesday or Wednesday I saw a letter on the table in the office directed to Edward Mathews, in Dr. Coolidge's hand writing, which Coolidge said might be given to Mr. Mathews if he called for it – I do not know that Mathews received the letter. I have not seen the letter in the office since Mathews was in on Tuesday or Wednesday. Coolidge was in the office in the evening of Thursday – I cannot say how long he was there. I saw him there before 8 o'clock. I left it about 8. Next saw him at Mr. Williams's door after 9 o'clock. He returned to the office with me, and stayed till after 10. I then left him in the office. I did not again see him during the night,

THOMAS FLINT.

The statements of Dingley & Robinson before the inquest do not vary materially from their testimony in this case, except in being less full.

Mr. Noyes wished to introduce the schedules of Dr. Coolidge's notes and accounts, but could not have them here till morning.

Mr. Morrill, for the government, wished to call a witness.

Additional Testimony for the Government

Philander Soule recalled. Has had a conversation with Daniel Baker, about the contents of the stomach, and he told him that Dr. C., when it was proposed to examine the contents of the stomach, said it was probably too late. Recollect who it was who made certain remarks to him. Thought it was Baker, and asked him about it last Thursday or Friday. He said he would tell me what he did say. – He said he had a talk with Dr. C. at his room, and said to Dr. C. he would bet $300 there was no prussic acid in the stomach, and would give $5 to have them sent to Brunswick and analyzed. Dr. C. remarked that if there was any prussic acid in the stomach, it would escape before it got to Brunswick. Baker also told witness he asked Flint if there was anything he could do at that office, and Flint told him to turn the water out, but he did not.

Cross examined. Is a relation to the deceased – he was a member of witness's family. – Asked Baker in order to draw him out. Did not write down his answers. Has conversed with Flint twice at the Mansion House in presence of Gilman and others.

Joseph Nudd, recalled. Counsel asked the witness to produce the brandy bottles. Objected to. Chief Justice said he did not wish for any brandy bottles. Mr. Evans replied that he did not if they had any acid in them. The evidence was objected to as new matter. Court said it could only be allowed if it was repellant in its character, and called upon the counsel to state for what purpose it was offered. The court permitted the witness to be examined. He stated that he took possession of the bottles on Monday morning; there were two brandy bottles; one empty; the other had a small quantity of water or something in it.

Cross examined. The bottles were placed on a shelf with several others; there were more than one shelf; there were several shelves of bottles. Have been the sleigh that defendant formerly used; it was gilded, with flowers upon it. The brandy bottles were exhibited in Court and identified by witness, two empty white bottles; the one that had something in it was emptied out by Mr. Moor; think it was never analyzed; the spoonful left was never analyzed, I think; a glass topper is tied to one of the bottles, I think by Flint, by direction of Mr. Moor.

Re-examined. The Dr.'s sleigh has been painted a darker color since; the one brought into Court the other day belonged to the defendant.

Dr Hubbard, recalled - The essential oil of bitter almond is said to be a deadly poison, and it has an odor like that of prussic acid; it is prussic acid in its native state, combined with vegetable matter.

The testimony on both sides being concluded, notice was given that Mr. Evans would commence his argument tomorrow morning, whereupon the court adjourned to that time.

Day Seven: Tuesday, March 21, 1848

George Evans, Coolidge's lead counsel, had just completed a term as a United States Senator. Henry Clay wrote "Mr. Evans knew more about the finances than any other public man in the United States." In an obituary notice of Evans, published in 1876, the writer noted "Mr. Evans masterly defense of Coolidge is still vividly remembered by all who heard it."

Day Seven: Tuesday, March 21, 1848

Mr. Evans' Argument[1]

I am now about to perform, feebly I am sensible, the duty which devolves upon me as counsel for the prisoner. I am about to address to you the last words which shall fall upon your ears before your decision settles the fate of the prisoner. Not in my hands, thank God, is the responsibility · it rests upon you, gentlemen of the jury. It is a fearful, terrible responsibility, for fallible men to pronounce the doom which sends to the unseen world, in the prime vigor of life, a fellow-being – even though deeply degraded – stained with many vices – one who has filled up the measure of his guilt. How still more responsible, to decide thus the fate of one whose life heretofore has been irreproachable, suspected of no vices, the center of a large circle – whose misfortunes have stricken many hearts? Mr. E. appealed to the jury to beware of any bias, until their verdict is agreed upon – until certainty fixes upon their minds, that the guilt of the prisoner is beyond a doubt. Bear in mind that the government must make the guilt of the prisoner manifest. There is in such cases to be no weighing of evidence no preponderance of proof. In capital trials, the proof is to be satisfactory and conclusive. This is the consolation of the jury – that they cannot be called upon to pronounce the prisoner's guilt, until every reasonable doubt is removed.

This case presents several strong and remarkable features.

That the deceased, Edward Mathews, came to his death on the night of the 30th September, cannot be doubted – and that after his death some person inflicted blows to convey the idea that he had been murdered. Who ever heard of such a case? Who ever heard of a case where after a murder, means were used to make that murder known? The effort is to conceal it as long as possible – to give the perpetrators time enough to escape, to enjoy the fruits of their crime. That here the intention seems to have been to secure immediate detection – to publish the fact immediately. – It would seem that these blows were inflicted, and this body left thus exposed, by some one who wished to turn suspicion upon one who was not guilty. Men to not desire to reveal their own guilt – to make known their own crimes.

---

[1] The Maine Farmer reports that Evan's argument lasted for seven and a half hours

Not less extraordinary is the accusation that the prisoner at the bar, enjoying great popularity, extensive business and ample means, and possessing an unspotted reputation, should for the paltry motive attributed to him, be guilty of the highest crime known to society. This is so wholly improbable as to call for the clearest and most convincing proof before it is believed. Who committed this crime, we cannot undertake to say – it is shrouded in mystery and darkness · and so will probably remain till that great day when all secrets shall be made known – when the earth as well as the sea shall give up all her dead – the light of the moon shall be as the light of the sun – the light of the sun shall be as of seven days – and until then it will be known only to Him to whom all hearts are open.

The government has taken up four days in examining some sixty witnesses – some upon the smallest and least important matters – the slightest circumstances have been pressed where they would throw the least light upon the crime. At last they bring in a witness who, if to be believed, they might have dispensed with most of their other evidence. This amounts to an acknowledgement that this witness is not to be relied upon.

Mark the difference in the mode of examination. In the other cases, the evidence was drawn out by a series of questions. But here the witness comes on the stand, and gives his testimony in the form of a narrative, without a question scarcely put to him. It would appear from this, that this testimony could only be presented in an imposing form in the way it was given. Mr. E. said he would consider the evidence first, independent of that of Flint. If Flint's were the only testimony, he believed that the jury would scarcely leave their seats – they would return a verdict without hesitation.

Mr. E. then asked, how stands the case as it was last Saturday morning. The death of Mathews none denied. He supposed that the idea was abandoned that the blows caused death. Although sufficient to cause it if inflicted in life, the evidences testify that the appearances indicate that they were inflicted after death. The evidence gives no light as to who inflicted the blows – if inflicted after death they have no bearing on the case – it is to be inquired, not only how they affected the deceased, but how they are connected with the prisoner.

Mr. E. then inquired if the death was caused by hydrocianic acid. He said it was extraordinary that of the skillful physicians, and the learned professor, called to testify in this case, not one of them professes to have known previously the effects of this acid on the human or animal system. Something was examined which is said to have been the contents of the deceased's stomach. But who says with confidence that this bowl or bottle contained the contents of that stomach. Here is a great chasm in the proof. These learned persons derive their knowledge from books, find a limited use of books. Physicians are not chemists, chemists are not physicians. What proof is there of the identity of substance examined? They were removed about 2 o'clock Friday afternoon, and placed in an exposed situation. The jury are not to judge if it is probable that the contents were not touched – it is enough that they may have been touched. Mr. Williams was directed by the physicians and the coroner that this substance was to be thrown away. The village was full of excitement. Who can say that Mr. W. was not seen in depositing it there? There it remained till morning, and then for the first time was put under lock and key. This is an acknowledgement that that was the only safe place. Now there are reasons to show that some change had taken place. Prussic acid was afterwards found in this substance. It is discovered by the odor and the tests. Where was this odor on Friday? All testify that they discovered nothing of it then – that when the stomach was opened, they found no such odor. Was there not something added? It may be argued that it was improbable -who had any motive for doing it? It might have been *done* – the acid bottles were absent from the office that evening.

Mr. E. said the counsel had stated there was blood on the hatchet. The hatchet is produced and there is blood, Mr. E. supposed, on it. Yet the boy says it was not the office hatchet, Flint says there was no blood on the office hatchet the next morning. Neither Flint, Dingley nor the officer says this is the office hatchet. Many persons went in and out of the office; they may have changed the hatchets. And if they changed the hatchets to lead suspicion in a particular direction, why may not the same persons have tampered with the contents of the stomach, and infused poison after death. When we find that the most sensible quality of this poison was not discovered when the stomach was opened, and when all admit that the odor should have been the strongest, and yet after the exposure of this substance, this poison, which would be constantly escaping, was found in it, does it not raise a presumption, a probability, that the poison had been added after death? It appears that some one had a desire to cause early discovery; and to remove all doubt of murder. Who can have had such a desire, but one who wished to turn suspicion in a particular direction?

Mr. E. contended that the tests of prussic acid in this body are wholly unsatisfactory. Those who made the experiments are inexperienced. They themselves confess that they were so. The gentleman who applied the tests admits he knew nothing about the matter before this occurrence. His knowledge is acquired since. He puts acid in the body of an animal – searches for it and finds it there. There is nothing remarkable about this. He has searched the books as far as his purpose required. A learned man says no man is fit to make experiments until he has made many. Do you know this acid is generated by the decay of the human body itself? That he does not know; it was not necessary to his purpose; he has seen or heard something of the kind. Prussic acid exists in many substances; it is a compound composed of various substances which exist in nature. Who can say what change takes place in the human system after death? The stomach in life is a great laboratory, in which chemical action is constantly going on. One learned gentleman, a skillful physician but not a chemist says that these tests are as conclusive as the testimony of three witnesses. How can he say that, when he admits he does not know but what changes may take place in the system which he knows not of? He knows what he has met with, not what others have met with. It is as conclusive as the evidence of three foreigners, whose language we do not understand – that is all we can safely say, There is then the uncertainty as to the identity of the contents of the stomach; the fact that it was exposed in an open place, and afterwards shut up in a close ice house, the ice out, and nothing there but foetid air, and decaying saw dust. Who can say what change this might produce?

Why was not the learned gentleman and distinguished chemist (Prof. Cleaveland[2]) called in this case, who could testify from what he know, and not from what he does not know?

The morbid appearances are relied on; the congested, gorged appearance of the viscera. But after spending a long time in describing these appearances, the physicians, Drs. Hubbard and Hill, say these appearances are not to be relied on. They cannot say what would be the appearances in the case of death from the

---

[2] Parker Cleaveland, professor at Bowdoin College from 1805 until his death in 1858. Best known for his contributions to the natural sciences, a fellow of the American Philosophical Society from 1818.

144

effect of ardent spirits, or other causes of sudden death. There is no proof here, no certainty; no one could say what appearances after death are peculiar to this species of poison. Nor is it pretended that the morbid appearances of animals are a safe guide in deciding upon the causes of the death of human beings. Mr. E. repeated that the chemical tests were applied by persons who had no experience. They rely upon them after experiments upon dogs and other animals. But no one says that the same appearances would be produced upon the stomachs of animals as upon those of human beings by the administration of the same medicine; on the contrary, they say this is unsettled. It is testified that the poison of certain substances will produce certain results. But will they say that nothing else will produce the same results? They talk as if they had arrived at the utmost height of human knowledge. It is true some sciences have reached their height. It is so of mathematics, of geometry. No one can ever make out that five times ten will make out more or less than fifty – or that the three angles of a triangle will square more or less than two right angles. But who shall say that other sciences have arrived at perfection. What was known of chemistry a few years since? What could these gentlemen have testified a half century ago on this very matter? And will they say there is nothing more to be known? How different from the great philosopher, who with true humility presented himself to be a child picking up pebbles on the shore of the great unexplored ocean of knowledge. Yet he had made greater discoveries than any man of his time – his true humility indicated true knowledge. Before the jury can decide that this substance cannot be generated in the decaying body, they should have the testimony of men of large experience that such is not the case. Is it improbable that the decay of matter should produce this substance? The constituent parts of prussic acid are the constituent parts of the very food we eat. Death produces a dissolution of the matter in the system – a liberation of the gases which in life are united with the solid parts and are not palpable. This is just in accordance with the experiments made. When the body is opened, no prussic acid is found. On Saturday there are indications, but there is no peach colored flame produced. On Monday after 48 hours longer decay of this matter, the flame is produced by a fresh distillation. Why is it, that this most volatile of all poison, which escapes on exposure, is found to grow stronger and stronger in this case, instead of weaker and weaker. It is not only so of the chemical tests, but of the odor. One gentleman finds it in the brain – another, in the thorax, and no where else. A very small quantity of the acid is found on Saturday, a very large quantity on Monday. Why is this, if this acid was introduced into the system before death, and not generated after death? But if satisfied that these tests are sufficient, then there is that great want of proof of the identity of the matter, If satisfied of that, then you must be satisfied that science has reached its limit, and that acid is not generated by decomposition after death.

The inquiry then arises, if this is all admitted; was the death caused by poison? There is no direct proof of this – no human eye saw it. It is said there was a train of preliminary investigation. He had been talking of a subject – as through he intended to get by this crime a subject well known to all his students. He is said to have procured acid – the strongest that could be had. All the physicians keep it – he had always kept it. In the very order which he sent to Boston for this acid, he sent to have any new medicines sent him which were worthy of a trial, showing that he kept up with the times – that he wished to try new medicines, This acid is volatile, easy to lose its strength – exposure to the light, or standing long, destroys its strength, What is there strange, then, in the fact that he wished to have an acid always to be relied on? He did not need the strongest to effect death – the weakest was sufficient for that. But he sent to Hallowell for some about the same time, a few days before. But who testifies that he received it? In the uncertainty which may have existed, as to receiving that from Hallowell, he took advantage of an opportunity to send to Boston, for this with other medicines. It is testified that the physicians about Boston constantly keep it – if physicians here do not, it only shows that they are a little behind the times. But Mr. Phillips testifies that he had a bottle there when he sent the order to Boston. That was doubtless the bottle he had long had, and was probably nearly exhausted, and therefore he sent for another. – But there were three bottles it is said. If there were, one was the old one – one received from Hallowell, and one from Boston. But if Dr. C. had had any intention to use the acid for any such purpose as murder, would he have told Mr. Phillips what it was? Would he have not told him it was cough drops, or that it was a vial of no consequence? But all was open – so was his sending for the acid to Boston and to Hallowell; thus multiplying the evidence against himself. Had he not acid enough in his office? Could he not have obtained it unknown to any one except some shop boy, instead of sending an order signed with his own name?

These mysterious conversations about a subject – his having these half barrels there – were all these things to prepare the minds of his students for his having the body there of a man well known to all his students? Mr. E. argued that this was incredible.

In the opening argument, we were told that it would be found that the prisoner was anxious to have the contents of the stomach thrown away, and the evidences of his guilt destroyed. But there is no such proof. The prisoner would not acquiesce in the opinion that the wounds on the head would produce death, until the scalp was removed. If he had administered this acid, would he not have been swift to concur in the opinion that these wounds were sufficient? Would he have proposed further examination? Who proposed to take out the stomach – no one is found to have proposed it – none of the physicians – not the coroner. It must have been the prisoner. The witnesses do not say it was not him. It is not shown that he directed then to be thrown away. He did suggest that they be removed; the smell was disagreeable to many there. The coroner and the other physicians concurred. They had done with them – they wished them removed. There is evidence that the next day when it was proposed to send the contents to Brunswick, the Dr. said it would be doubtful if any acid would remain by the time it reached there. The books say so; the physicians testify to the same thing. Is this evidence of guilt? How easy would it have been for Dr. C., if Flint is at all to be relied upon, to say to him to follow and see where the contents of that bowl were deposited, and see that they were destroyed. Or when Flint was about to sew up the body to say to him, put in some neutralizing substance, that there may be nothing hereafter found in the body to allow detection. Here was a ready instrument, who would have done his lightest bidding. At another time, when it was proposed to have the contents of the stomach analyzed, he inquired if they had been preserved, and suggested that no reliance could be placed on such an analysis from the lapse of time. Is not this a natural answer. Would not any medical man have said the same? It was not then too late to have the contents destroyed.

It is said the prisoner had a motive. He was in debt. He had borrowed money. He had enjoined secrecy. He did not wish his affairs known. Do not men generally wish to keep their affairs secret, especially borrowing money? Is it unusual? Are all such men ready to commit murder? Is this proof? Men generally run through the whole catalogue of crimes to get money, before they are hardened enough to commit murder. Because he borrowed money when he had no need of it, was proud, and wished to keep his affairs secret, is this evidence of his readiness to commit murder? He went to Waterville without means. He had his choice, to borrow money, or to drive up his customers sharply; he chose the former. He lived liberally; supplied himself with large quantities of medicine; had expensive horses. When he borrows money he must give a reason for it; he does not want to say that he chooses to indulge his debtors; he has to make some excuse; he says he was about entering into speculation; he has a correspondence with Dr. Potter. But who has pressed him; what has required this amount of money? What did he want of $1500? What prevented his getting it? Mr. Noyes has collected $1600 without difficulty since the murder. It was due from the wealthiest persons around Waterville. Could he not have obtained $1500 in 12 hours? Was there a necessity for resorting to murder to get it? It is said he had agreed with Mathews to lend him $1500. If so, the money was within his reach without the murder. It appears from his books that his practice the first year he was in Waterville amounted to $1000. It went on increasing, till the last six months he charged $2500. - $2500 is six months is a very respectable practice. Would a man so situated commit murder for the paltry sum of $1500? The human mind revolts against it. It requires the most positive proof to produce conviction of guilt in such a case.

Dr. C. gave as an excuse to Prof. Champlin, when urged to subscribe to the funds of the College, that he wanted his means for a speculation. Admit that this was a false excuse, is every man who gives such an excuse to be condemned as guilty of murder? If so, the Lord have mercy on the majority of mankind! It seems to have been the habit of the prisoner to keep his affairs secret.

It appears by some of the witnesses that after the murder, Dr. C., seeing what inferences might be drawn from those loose statements of his, wished to suppress the evidence of it. Is this unnatural? Gray and Gilman testify to something of this kind. They and all the other witnesses seem to commence with the preconceived opinion that the murder was already a settle fact, and their only business was to make it out. Some of them sought a conversation with him for that purpose. Gray says that the Dr. wished him to deny that he (the Dr.) had ever wished to borrow money of him. Gray was suspected himself – was out late that night, wandering about – very nearly contradicts himself in his own testimony about his drinking; not much reliance is to be placed on his testimony. Gilman says Dr. C. wished to borrow of him $3000 or $4000; the idea is absurd; he had no means. The Dr. had some conversation with him, for some purpose, but that he ever seriously through of borrowing money of him is not to be believed. When the Dr. was agitated and overwhelmed by suspicion, which he might have been if innocent, he applies to Gilman not to reveal his conversation with him. Much may be said on the other side of the boldness of innocence, but human history proves too frequently that the best and most pious men have denied the truth to save themselves from punishment. The boldest of the disciples of the Savior, though admonished before hand, denied his Master with cursing and swearing. The sons of Jacob, when the cup was found in Benjamin's sack, instead of asserting their innocence, exclaimed, what shall we do to clear ourselves of this great iniquity? History is full of evidence that human firmness fails in such times of trial. Men have been known to confess to crimes which had never been committed, to save themselves from being proved guilty and punished more severely than if they had not confessed. In a neighboring State, two brothers were indicted for the murder of a man whose body was not found; in the pressure of the hour, they both yielded – confessed themselves guilty, and were condemned on their confession, But the matter was published in the papers, and before the execution, the man supposed to be murdered came forward, from another State, and saved them from the consequences of their own weakness[3]. There was in this case public excitement; men went into the Dr's office to see him, without any pretense of business, as much as to say, you are a guilty man, and we come to see how a guilty man looks. What wonder that in this state of things he should resort of expedients not in accordance with truth, to be relieved from this painful position in which he was placed. The Jury has been told they are not to indulge sympathy. Mr. E. denied it. There is no case in

---

[3] In Vermont, Stephen and Jesse Boorn were convicted in 1819 for the murder of Russell Colvin, a brother-in-law, who had disappeared years earlier. They represent the earliest known case of wrongful conviction for murder in the United States.

which men are to shut out the kindly feelings of nature; to become automatons, things of wood and brass; to be wound up so as to run down like a machine. You cannot do it if you would. All that you called upon to do is, not to let your sympathies run away with your judgement.

The witnesses cannot speak of the most trivial events, without connecting them to this murder. When the deceased left Charles Mathews's store, the witness, instead of saying he went down Main Street, says he went towards Coolidge's office; true he went the way towards Coolidge's office; so it leads to the tavern, and to Bangor. So a witness saw him come on the platform at Williams's, and then turn and go back again; and says he came from the direction of his office, and returned in that direction. But the witness only saw him come on the platform, and go off again. We were told it would be proved that he was seen reconnoitering the river to see if he could throw the body in in; but it is only shown that he was seen walking leisurely in Water Street, without concealment, a little before 10.

The finding of the watch is relied on. It was found in Coolidge's sleigh. Would the prisoner have placed it there, or if guilty would he not have placed it where it would not be found on him. Some unknown person had been up there just before it was found; how easy for them to put the watch there! Is it not just the place where anyone would put it, who wished to throw suspicion on Dr. C.? The boy swears to the sleigh, although it has been pained since. But Mr. E. would discredit his testimony; he no doubt found the watch there.

The circumstance of Dr. C. rising early, at half past 4, when he directed that they should call him at 6, is relied on. Is the fact of his rising earlier than the hour he fixed, unusual or suspicious Have not other physicians done the same? Are they to be looked upon with suspicion? He rises not far from the hour, finds a messenger calling him away on professional business, goes, returns, gets his breakfast, and goes to Skowhegan. All this is natural in the ordinary course of business. As to the paper, in which the watch was found; it is sworn to, though there are no marks on it; it is like paper in Coolidge's office, but this proves nothing, for the same kind of paper was found in the bookstore for sale, and in the next store for use. The watch was not wrapped up when the blood was fresh; the paper is not stained; the blood was dry; the same person who changed the hatchets in the office may have taken paper from Coolidge's office and wrapped the watch in it, to throw suspicion on him. Why was this paper brought here? Why the carpet? Why the clothes? They have nothing. The cut on the pantaloons, was no cut at all. To Mr. E. it appears to be a tear; it was torn in two directions, all right angles. It must have been made by dragging the body on the wood. So might the marks on the neck. It will be argued that they show a gash. Why? For fear that he might shriek. And this well be argued, because dogs have been found, where brandy and prussic acid is given to them; sometimes to shriek and sometimes not. Is this evidence?

There is a great effort to get in improper testimony, Mr. Mathews examined some books, and turned down some leaves; what has that to do with the prisoner? Mathews had some business transactions, but they were not brought home to the prisoner. Mathews may have made false statements to get the money he wanted. But there was a letter inviting Mathews to his office that evening, and *not reveal it for his life.* The rest of the letter did not so impress the witness's mind as to lead him to remember it. He only knows the Dr.'s writing, by some hieroglyphics which he had seen, which are intelligible only to physicians and apothecaries; and by some unsigned letters thrown in at a fair, supposed to be the Dr's. "That evening," was what evening? No date is given. The witnesses say they saw the letter in the office Tuesday and Wednesday. – "That evening," then, cannot be Thursday evening. It was the evening of the date; the time had passed. They may have had business together; pursuits in common. Mathews was in the back office on Wednesday afternoon, and the door was shut. He may have been to drink brandy; that is motive enough. One witness says that after Mathews came out, Coolidge went out, and then returned, and called Mathews out in the entry, and when they opened the entry door again, Coolidge said, "Keep dark" or "all right," he cannot say which. Suppose this was so, it amounts to nothing. But it is all dispelled by another government witness; Dingley says Mathews went out first, and did not return. Here is witness against witness, and the whole must be given up. There is no proof of any plot or appointment between Mathews and Coolidge.

Another circumstance is relied on; a witness is questioned with great solemnity; at a particular time, the witness's dog set up an unearthly howl, left him in the direction of *Coolidge's office,* and only returned to him at the end of the street. The counsel has read Macbeth for more purposes than one. When the murder was committed by Macbeth, there were unearthly noises heard, and commotions in the elements. The nearest that he came to it here, is, one howling dog. Pray what does all this prove? Why this effort to strike the imagination? Why the clothes, the sleigh, the bottles brought here? Why does the gentleman try his case by this set of stage effects? One witness certifies that Dr. C. gave him a bottle, and produced the bottle. Does this make his testimony any more creditable? Does the fact of seeing these things make the crime any clearer, or strengthen the evidence of the prisoner's guilt? Is not the object to strike the senses, and thus read your minds, and lead to the conviction of the prisoner by outward impressions?

Mr. E. said some of the testimony has been so unimportant, that it made but little impression on his mind. One witness testifies only that he saw Mathews walking up and down the street in the afternoon. Another that he went into Dr. C's office to have an operation on his finger, and no one came in. What connection have these matters have with the murder perhaps the Attorney General may point out; also the connection of Mr. Hill's dog.

Some of the statements of prisoner before the inquest have been proved to be false. – This is admitted to some extent. It must be rested on the same ground with his declarations of Gray and Gilman; and his application to Leighton. The Dr. was suspected; he was striving to secure himself; anxious to avert the spirit of suspicion as soon as possible. Is not here an excuse for him to a certain degree? He had not firmness enough to stand up against the circumstances in which he was placed. Are not great allowances to be made for a man so situated?

Afternoon

Mr. E. said he had very nearly concluded his remarks. It was not his wish to amplify. He only wished the plainest and shortest form to present the facts in the case. Mr. E. said he may not, in all cases, have stated the evidence with entire accuracy. He had spoken this morning of the groundless reports of a business transaction between Dr. C. and Mathews. It will be said that Tobey testified to the Dr.'s statement that he was under obligation to convey his books and papers to Mathews. Tobey goes to him to get security for a note of $180; the Dr. is agitated and in trouble; he is in no condition to do business. Mr. E. argued

152

that there is no certainty that Tobey had not heard of the transfer elsewhere, and instead of the Dr. mentioning it to him, he mentioned it to the Dr. It is entitled to little reliance. Mr. E. also recollects that the witness who went into the office to have his finger operated on, thinks he saw Mathews there. What if he did? Mathews was seen everywhere that day. How many times his whereabouts is proved in various places. The proof is circumstantial. The value of circumstantial proof is that the circumstances -put together tend necessarily, conclusively and exclusively to establish the guilt of the prisoner.

After the great efforts made, to establish the facts, even down to minutes, where was this murder committed? Mathews was seen a quarter before 9; he then left the Parker House in the direction of Main Street; the persons in Shorey's shop left about 10 minutes after 9; five persons were there till 10 minutes after 9. Noises can be heard from one of these places to the other. They heard some one going up stairs about 8 – no one afterwards. The partitions and doors were thin. They speak here of blows and dragging the body – blood in the front office and the back office – the body behind the counter. At 15 minutes after 9, the hostler and Mr. Freeman say they saw the Dr. at Williams's House. Here is only 5 minutes. Add to that the great improbability that Dr. C. would at this hour commit this act in his own office. This is monstrously incredible. At half past 9, Flint finds the body in the office, with the limbs then rigid. Most improbable – impossible! Dead, and the limbs rigid, when 45 minutes before he was in full life! Can it be believed that in 45 minutes after he was in life all this had happened, and the prisoner was in the street seeking a confidant to whom to disclose his crime! No one was heard going up or down the steps after 8 – 10 minutes after 9, we have a right to presume the deceased was alive. Yet 15 minutes after 9, Dr. C. is going to the tavern, and again at half past 9. Can all this have happened in that time? The witnesses state the time; they know it; they tell here they know it. Mr. Shorey corroborates the boys; they got home a quarter past 9. The office was liable to be opened at any time; a person was actually at the tavern after the Dr. at a late hour. Every one of the circumstances proved seems easily to be accounted for. The obtaining of the acid bottles; the talking about a subject, belong to the Dr.'s course of life. Jurors are not to reason out guilt from circumstances; proof from these sources must be as strong and satisfactory as from other sources, in order to be relied on. It is absurd to say that circumstantial evidence can be as decisive as direct proof from credible sources. There may be direct proof which is not to be believed. But the value of circumstantial proof is that it all fits together. – The witness here is disjointed –it makes nothing consistent when put together. Mr. Evans stated a case of circumstantial proof, in which one testifies to one part, and another to another, and so on, until a chain of circumstances is made out which cannot be doubted. But he contended that it would be still more satisfactory if one or more of the witnesses had seen the act. Mr. E. would only ask that the jury should require that circumstances in this case to be as satisfactory as the testimony of one credible witness, which is the lowest testimony our law allows. He said circumstantial evidence must be conclusive in its character; it must exclude every other supposition. If it be possible that any other person may have committed this crime, the prisoner must be acquitted. He read from authorities to show what positive proof is required by our law, and argued that circumstantial evidence has been the cause of the conviction and execution of many innocent persons. The jury must be as fully convinced by circumstantial proof, as if direct proof had been brought.

Mr. E. inquired if all these circumstances proved in their cases, may not be consistent with the innocence of the prisoner? It is not enough that the evidence is the best the case will afford. The nature of a case may be seen, that sufficient proof cannot be had. – Yet before a conviction, there must be sufficient proof to convince the jury, The impression on the mind of the jury must not be, that the prisoner is probably guilty, but that he is guilty. Formerly, in England, criminals were not allowed counsel, but the proof was required to be frequently conclusive; counsel were unnecessary. Mr. E. read many authorities and cases to show that the law about circumstantial proofs, the danger of relying on sufficient proof. On one case two persons were going down to the sea shore with a living child, and to throw the child into the sea, and the body was never found. The Court charged their conviction could not be had, because the body might have floated ashore alive. In another case, a man was beaten and thrown overboard, and the body not found. The Court charged, that if the jury believed the man to have been dead before he was thrown overboard, they might find the prisoner guilty; otherwise not, because he might have been picked up alive. This is the humanity of the law.

Mr. E. argued at length, to impress upon the jury the necessity of caution when receiving circumstantial proofs. If there are 99 or 999 chances of the prisoner's guilt, and one of his innocence, he must be acquitted,

Mr. Evans now proceeded to speak of the testimony of Thomas Flint. This witness comes here with an unblushing face. He makes no apology for himself. Mr. E. wanted to hear his apology – his account of the persuasions, the implorations, the distress of his friend. But nothing of the kind. Immediately and readily he enters upon the iniquity which is proposed to him – becomes accessory to the murder after the fact, and follows it up by perjury. He has by his own confession committed two crimes. If he had been convicted by either, his testimony could not go to the jury – the law would not allow them to hear it. Not having been convicted, his testimony may be heard, but the law does not allow a conviction upon it, unless corroborated by other evidences. In all the important circumstances testified to by Flint, what happened in the office, and the scrutiny of the body, there is no pretense that his evidence is corroborated. Mr. E. read from various authorities to show that the testimony of an accomplice is to be received with great caution and allowance and requires confirmation; and where a witness has once sworn to a material fact, and on trial swears differently, his testimony is not to be received – that law does not allow the jury to give credit to such evidence – it would be unsafe to give it weight. – The whole confidence reposed in a witness, is overthrown the moment he is found to be capable of committing a perjury. These are not principles got up for this case – but settled principles to be applied to all cases. The jury are sworn to bring in their verdict according to the law and the evidence – a part of the law is the law of evidence telling the jury what they may and what they may not believe. The jury has a right to say to the government – the law requires them to do it – bring us testimony that is free from suspicion. Perjury has been committed on this occasion or on a former by this witness – which we do not know. He must be corroborated in material matters bearing on the guilt of the prisoner, or his testimony is of no weight. Instead of being corroborated, Flint's testimony is contradicted in some points. If Hill's testimony is correct, Flint's is not. Hill cannot have been mistaken in the evening – returning he met Hasty and Gray – they know what evening it was, for they were called for the next morning to account for their being out that night. Hill started from home at 20 minutes before 10, and after walking about 10 minutes, he met Coolidge; after walking a few minutes longer, the clock struck ten. The time therefore must be right. Flint's story therefore is not true. Flint testifies that about 11 o'clock on Friday he saw Dr. C., at Dr. Thayer's, and immediately he went to the office, and saw Dr. C. making the charge of $200 to Mathews. If the other witnesses tell the truth, this story is not true. Flint says Dr. C. had not then been in the hall – had not been examined. But the other witnesses say that Coolidge went into the hall with John Mathews about 11, and it was not till afternoon, and after he had nearly completed his testimony before the inquest, that he went to his office for the books, and brought a fresh charge on it. Flint is corroborated in a few minor unimportant particulars, but in no important matter connected with the crime. It is of little importance that Flint has made other false statements, after it is proved that he has committed perjury. The improbability of his statements as to getting the body down in the darkness – the narrowness of the passage, and the impossibility of its being done without moving the chairs, are all against his statement. His statement as to the blood and hair on the carpet, is contradicted. He says he picked up the hairs, and Dingley and the boy might have seen if they had looked. But Dingley says he saw no such thing. His creeping down the stairs, their narrowness – their going down in the dark – their nerves not the steadiest, it may be believed – climbing over the wood pile, only 2 ½ or 3 feet from the floor above, and depositing the body near the door, is totally incredible. That body never went over there – it was put into the door. It is possible that it was taken over the other way, but is not probable. It is said the boots were clean, as though a body could not have been carried along the street outside without dragging it. As to the cleanness of the boots, it is in evidence that deceased, after his boots were clean, crossed a muddy street twice – his boots must have been muddy to some degree. Mr. E. contended that the whole story was improbable – that to have taken the body down, and through that narrow passage without moving the cloth, was impracticable. It may be asked what motive the witness could have? That we cannot tell. Mr. E. would not say that he intended by his testimony to produce conviction, that he might reap some of the benefits he desired as the successor of Dr. C. But it is not for the jury to seek a motive – it is enough that the testimony of this witness is not corroborated – is not probable – not worthy of credence.

The testimony of a uniformly fair character is more than enough to outweigh the testimony of a person who confesses himself a felon. Any number from one to one thousand witnesses, might be brought to prove the unblemished character of the prisoner. Born in this State, and never having been abroad to receive contamination from vicious society – laboring till of age on his father's farm – educated in the public schools, aided by an uncle who was a literary man – with the fairest prospects, what could be expected but that he would have continued in a course of virtue. None but the most abandoned, or the most insane person could have done this crime under such circumstances leaving the evidences of guilt scattered all abroad. Mr. E. said if he believed the whole testimony of Flint, he should believe that Coolidge stated the truth to Flint – that this was not a case of murder, but of sudden death; and that these partied agreed to seize on the property of Mathews; and convert it to their own use – and this would be the crime committed, and not the one charged. Not believing either, Mr. E. asked at the hands of the jury an acquittal.

I tremble, said Mr. E., at the imperfection with which I have presented this case. I have aimed at no display – I am capable of none, least of all in such a case. He would not appeal to the sympathies of the jury, but would ask them to temper justice with mercy. We are not standing in an ordinary court – but in the temple of the Most High God, where His teachings are ministered suited to our condition. Mr. E. trusted that the verdict would be such as the truth demands. When your verdict shall be given this assembly will disperse to meet no more in this world; but to meet once more, where all will assemble, not to judge, but to be judged. God grant, that at the day, the blood of no man may be found on your hands.

Notice was here given that witnesses in the case were discharged from further attendance, and Hon Mr. Blake commenced his closing plea for the government.

Samuel H. Blake, the new Attorney General of Maine.

Blake's Closing Argument to the Jury

He said he had listened to the argument of the learned counsel for the prisoner with a great deal of pleasure - but that at present he must ask the jury to come down with him from the hazy atmosphere of doubt and conjecture, though lighted up by the flashes of genius, to the plain ground we stand upon, for we have here matters of reality and fact to deal with. I am overwhelmed, however, said Mr. Baker, at the very threshold of the case; for I dare not trust myself to an expression of the feelings that oppress me, and I have hardly physical strength enough left to grapple with this great mass of facts.

The charge of murder had been preferred by the government against the prisoner - the evidence to sustain that charge is now out. If it carries conviction in your minds, you will say so; if it does not, then restore the unfortunate man to the arms of his friends and to liberty. The burden of proof is upon the government; the charge must be affirmatively made out.

The first position necessary for me to establish is, that Edward Mathews is dead. The testimony on this point all concurs. The surviving brother saw him on Sunday, upon his arrival from Boston, in his coffin.

Next - was he murdered? The position of the body, when found - the wounds upon the head, inflicted by three separate blows, (the hat not broken, and upon the head,) causing wounds adjudged by the coroner's inquest to be sufficient to occasion death - the robbery committed upon the person, and the poison in the body - all conspire to place this point, also, beyond controversy.

If, then, the robbery speaks the language of violence, and if the wounds upon the body are too eloquent of the cause of death, who was the author - in whose ink was the pen dipped, and by whose hand was it held, when those letters of death were traced upon the head? Whose heart was so darkened to the light of all moral influences as to conceive, and whose hand had nerve enough to execute, a deed so bloody and so daring? If the charge of the government be true, the annals of crime hardly afford a parallel in atrocity. Let us look, then, carefully and doubtingly at the testimony.

The body was found on Friday morning, in a sitting posture, in the cellar connecting the prisoner's office and the tailor's shop underneath. It could have been carried there from *within* the building - from the tailor's shop or any of the offices above. Could it have been thrust in there, between the double doors of the cellar, from *without*? And if so, was it? The cellar doors were opened some 12 to 18 inches - the wood pressed down against them from within, so that they could not have been pushed open any wider. - There were no marks of blood upon the edges of the doors, to indicate that the body was crowded in from the outside. The body lay, the head inclining on the right shoulder, the left arm *raised up*, and the hand resting against the door. Mr. Hasty could not get the body out till the door was opened wider, because it was stiff. But the raised position of the left arm shows it was also stiff and rigid when placed there - the arm could not have lifted itself up after death; and muscular intractability ordinarily attends, I believe, death induced by the agency of prussic acid. It would have been as difficult, then, to get the body *in* as it was for Hasty to get it *out*, on account of the rigidity of the limbs.

The clothes of the deceased were not soiled - his boots, just blacked, were not dirtied, - thus negativing the idea that he could have been knocked downing the street or dragged on the ground at all · for the streets were *muddy* that night. There could to have been great danger in carrying the body there from Main street, as it must have been taken round through Williams's passage-way or past the other end of the block of brick stores · thus exposed to the view of passersby in those most frequented thoroughfares of the village · the houses on Water street too, as well as the back windows of this whole block, commanding a view of this wide area upon which the cellar opens. The murder was not committed by strangers, for then the watch and money would have been taken with them as they fled, and would not have been found secreted in the prisoner's sleigh and the back buildings of his boarding house. If committed by a citizen elsewhere than in this building, why run the risk of discovery in carrying it there through so public places? So far then the tracks all point inwards. We will go in to that den by and by.

Day Eight: Wednesday, March 22
Baker's Closing Argument to the Jury – Continued

How then, inquired Mr. B., was death effected? The indictment alleges by prussic acid. Was there, then, the presence of prussic acid in the body of the deceased on Friday morning?

The stomach was taken out on Friday afternoon by Dr. Coolidge, and the contents placed in a wash-basin. Mr. Williams takes the basin from the hall where the body then lay, and hides it behind a hogshead and a basket in his shed. Suspicion arises in the evening that the deceased was poisoned, and by light next morning Mr. Williams takes the basin and locks it up in his ice-house, where it remained a few hours, until it was delivered over to Prof. Loomis, that the contents might be analyzed. And there can be no reasonable doubt as to their identity. No one knew where the basin was concealed, even if any one knew the contents of the stomach were preserved. And what motive could have induced anyone to put poison into it, if they had found it? No, this suggestion of the learned counsel for the prisoner presupposes a depravity of heart, that I have yet to learn has ever disgraced poor frail humanity. The presumption against it is so violent, that you will reluctantly yield to it, only when affirmatively proved.

Prof. Loomis then takes the contents of the stomach and submits it to a chemical analysis. And of this learned Professor, permit me here to say, that by his scientific attainments and clear, accurate knowledge, he reflects credit upon the institution of which he is an ornament and upon the Professorship which he adorns. He first applies a test as directory merely, and not reliable, but it indicates the presence of prussic acids. He then applied the iron, the copper and the silver tests, and the results are satisfactory to his mind, establishing the fact to a moral certainty, as he says, of the presence of the acid. This species of evidence, the result of scientific knowledge, you may not be able, gentlemen, so well to judge of, but in all the pursuits of life, we must depend upon the knowledge of others, where we have no experience ourselves. Life is not vouchsafed to us long enough to learn everything. We are obliged, therefore, to risk our property, and trust our lives upon the knowledge of others. Dr. Hubbard, an eminent physician, of large experience, and of unquestionable integrity, says entire reliance may be placed upon the accuracy of these tests.

The post mortem examination of the next day, almost as decisively shows the presence of hydrocyanic acid in the body. The morbid appearances as well as the pungent odor of the acid emitted from the brain and stomach, and so distinctly noticed at the time, indicate with great certainty the presence of the acid. The suggestion that the brain in its natural state has sometimes the odor of prussic acid, does not seem to be well supported, and if it were, the other viscera here emitted it quite as distinctly. The other position of the learned counsel, that hydrocyanic acid may be generated by animal decomposition, is hardly applicable to the facts of this case, if true, and is not sustained by experience. The physicians and Prof. Loomis all concur to this effect, and Dr. Hill of this place, whose opinion is entitled to very great weight upon all questions within the range of his profession, has carefully examined this theory, and pronounces it unsustained by authority. We may then assume, with all the confidence of moral certainty, that the death of Edward Mathews was occasioned by the agency of this deadly poison. By whom, then, was it administered? In August the prisoner is proved to have in his possession a large phial half full of prussic acid - a quantity more than Drs. Hubbard and Hill have ever prescribed in their entire practice. On the 17th of Sept. he sends an order to Wales for an ounce more of the acid of the strongest kind. He has received it by the 19th, but it was only of the official strength. William M. Phillips saw it in the prisoner's office, in his safe, accidentally open, on the 19th. He sends still another order on the same, 19th September, to Burnett, of Boston, for an ounce of acid, "the strongest that is made." Why did he send for this? Was it that the Wales acid was not strong enough? But the Wales acid was the acid of the shops - the only kind physicians have any means of knowing how to prescribe. The concentrated acid is manufactured differently, and it's definite per cent strength is not known, and it cannot, therefore, safely be used, and is never prescribed. But Mr. Barnett happened to have the concentrated acid, having imported four ounces of it from London, for the Eye and Ear Infirmary, of Boston.

Now there was a notice for the purchase, all at once, of so much acid; and what was it? None is assigned. And why did he want the concentrated acid? Not to sell or experiment with. Was it then that it would kill quick as lightning, and with little if any danger of a death shriek? And was this the deadly purpose for which the prisoner ordered the strongest acid that is made?

And further, gentleman, said Mr. Baker, who else had prussic acid at Waterville? Is suspicion even whispered against any one else as having used it? On Friday evening, Samuel Doolittle asks the prisoner if the stomach had better not be analyzed. "Have the contents of the stomach been preserved?" he quick enquires, with surprise. No - "they had been kept too long to tell anything by." "Kept too long!" and how did he know it? Would prosaic acid evaporate quickly, and was it therefore too late, did he hope or know, to detect it? How did he know it was not arsenic or some other mineral poison, if any, that might be discovered for months or years after? He had told Williams in the hall to carry the basin out, "for it would scent the room." He had hoped they had not been preserved - he had an object in having them thrown away. Yet Williams, not then suspecting poison, but impelled as if the hand of God moved him, disposes of the "contents" as he has stated - showing how true it is always that "murder will out" - a truth that the experience of the world has stereotyped, and is now again, for the thousandth time, illustrated in the case.

Pausing for a moment here, said Mr. B., bear in mind, gentleman, that the prisoner has enquired of Robinson when Mathews would return from Brighton, and how much money his drove of cattle would bring - that he had heard of this return, and invited him to his office that evening - that he admits before the coroner's inquest that he was on there between 8 and 9 o'clock, with $1800 in his possession; and this is the last that is *seen or heard* of Edward Mathews, until he is found dead the next morning, on the prisoner's premises - his money, his watch and his papers gone, and the body in a position indicating that it was deposited there from within.

Now I submit, said Mr. Baker, if here is not a train of circumstances making up, link by link, a chain that binds down the prisoner to the dead body of Edward Mathews - too strong to be broken, and grappled too closely to be severed.

But we have been told by the learned counsel, in a running commentary on all the cases that can be gleaned from the books, that this is circumstantial evidence. True, but not therefore the less to be depended upon - the death being admitted. It is the ordinary evidence of crime. Abandoned men do not take witnesses with them to bear testimony to their turpitude. A man steals in secret, robs in the dark, and murders when no eye is upon him. Let the secrecy of crime, therefore, secure impunity, and you have no protection to your property or safety to your lives.

No, gentlemen, circumstances are soulless, passionless and objectless, and will not, therefore, lie. You act upon them every day of your lives. You depend upon them here, and you trust upon them as to an hereafter, There once lived in Judea a man illustrating in himself the purity of divinity and the perfection of humanity. It is your faith in him that buoys you up through life, and upon which you trust for life beyond the grave. And yet it is circumstantial evidence, the history of the times in which he lived, the authenticity of the record, as they have floated down to us upon the current of eighteen hundred years, that this faith is based. And it rests securely upon it, and may rest on it as upon a rock. The learned counsel had not closed his argument, even, before he invoked the aid of this very circumstantial evidence to wield it, with what of strength he could, against the positive testimony of Flint.

No, gentlemen, said Mr. Baker, you can have but little evidence of crime except as inference from circumstances. You can know of your own knowledge but little to aid in its discovery. You do not know that Edward Mathews ever lived, for you never saw him - you do not know that he is dead, for you did not see him in his coffin. But as sure as he lived he is dead - as sure as he is dead he was murdered, and as sure as he was murdered, there sits his murderer.

We come now, gentlemen, to the positive testimony of Thomas Flint. This is enough alone, the fact of death by violent means having been proved. And the testimony of Flint is to be depended upon. It is horrible but it is truthful. He is asked to go into the office as stated; the prisoner locks the door behind him; the scarlet curtains are down at the windows; the dim spirit lamp but makes the darkness apparent; the prisoner stands up before him in the earnestness of life at stake, and appeals to him to save him. "I am going to reveal to you a secret that involves my life. That cursed little Ed Mathews came in here, went to take a glass of brandy, and fell down dead, and is now lying in the other room. I have thumped him on the head, to make folks think he was murdered." Overwhelmed at the announcement, Flint sinks down into a chair. Too much overcome to reason, he does not realize that murder has been committed. He had not known that Mathews had money about him the evening before;

he did not now know of the robbery; he refuses to assist in carrying the body to the river or to the street. The prisoner had taken out of his mouth the suggestion to call in the neighbors, for he "had thumped him the head." A student, taken by surprise - astounded at what he saw - having confidence in his master - he aids in carrying the body into the cellar. It was a great offense, but this was no time for reason. You would not have done so; but then it might not have been quite safe for Flint to turn and run; the door was locked and the prisoner prepared. A second murder would have deterred but little when the discovery of the first was inevitable.

Now, gentlemen, why should not Flint be credited - all the facts narrated here by sixty odd witnesses tend more or less to corroborate him. And if this story be not true, where was Mathews after he was in the prisoner's office with $1800, and where was the prisoner?

And what inducement has Flint now to perjure himself? They were friends - and Flint was not suspected at the time, and is now proved to have been innocent. Edward Mathews was alive at the Parker House after Flint was in Williams's sitting room, where he remained till called by the Dr. to the office, at half past 9 o'clock, and then he returns at half past 10 o'clock from the office, where all admit he was, and goes to bed with Baker. By his oath here, then, he jeopards the life of his friend, not to save himself, for an alibi is established in his behalf, during the whole time in which the murder can possibly have been committed.

Again, gentlemen, Flint denies any knowledge of the murder as Mr. Paine testifies, before the Coroner's Inquest. He was then under oath. He made no admissions till Thursday of the next week, after he had seen his father, to whose good advice, perhaps, we owe this whole disclosure. If his object, then, now is, or was then, to ruin Coolidge, why has he not done it without implicating himself in the transaction, and without confessing his perjury, by simply swearing to a confession of the prisoner, made subsequent to his testimony before the inquest? He is a young man of intelligence, sustaining always before an unblemished character; no motive to tell an untruth about it is now attributed to him, and why, therefore, should you not yield credence to his story?

But one remark more in this connection of but little moment itself, it may be - but a chip will show the current of the stream, or a feather the direction of the wind. On Friday night Coolidge wishes to sleep with Flint, and on Saturday a sham sale of his property, as proved by Baker, is made to him. Had Coolidge confidence in Flint? Undoubtedly. But it may show more- the prisoner had entrusted his life to him - does he not entrust his property to him, to hug him the closer to his breast, to fasten himself upon him, if not to implicate him, as with hooks of steel?

Now, gentlemen, let us take a stand-point, from which we can look down upon the theatre of this sad drama, and some of the actors in it.

On the morning of Thursday the 30th Sept. a letter is lying on the table of the prisoner, in his office, directed to the deceased. His students all saw it and Flint recollects that it was on Thursday, and mentioned the circumstances in Mr. Boutelle's office the next morning. Charles K. Mathews saw the deceased between 10 and 11 o'clock A.M. Thursday, in his store, and heard him read a note from the prisoner, requesting the deceased to call "to his office that evening, and to reveal it not for his life," and this injunction of secrecy was deeply underscored. He saw the note. Upon the same day Edward Mathews, the deceased, made a note of $1500, which his uncle, John Mathews, signs with him, as principal, and his cousin, Charles, as surety, and the Ticonic Bank discounts it, and pays the money out to Edward about 3 o'clock P.M. He then returns to the store of Charles, takes a book of forms, and turns to a form for giving a lien on notes and demands - takes a blank mortgage of personal property, and sits down and fills it up, stating at the same time his object - to whom the $1500 was to be paid, and for whom the securities were to be assigned to him. But that declaration has been excluded by the Court. He came from Clinton that morning with the same object in view, so far as can be inferred from his there getting a book of forms, called the "Business Man's Assistant," and turning to a precent for the conveyance of personal property. His declaration there, too, as to his object, and the individual to whom he was intending to loan money, is excluded. You can only infer it.

John Mathews comes into the village next morning and hears of the murder. The guilt of Coolidge flashes on his mind - he rushes to him, overtakes him, seizes him by the arm, and takes him into the hall, where committees of vigilance were being organized, and puts to him three questions, the answers to which you will recollect - when an objection was interposed to any further enquiries at that time. He admitted to him that Edward was at his office twice the evening before - denied that he had borrowed any money of him but pretended that he had lent deceased $200, to be repaid the next morning - charging it at the time on his book - the very charge itself, besides not being posted, while those before it and after it are, carrying on its face a most suspicious appearance, - and it is now proved the charge was made the next day, and after prisoner had been examined before the inquest under oath, and that when made, the prisoner asked Nudd whether he had better say to the inquest it was made that day or the evening before. This charge was the idlest pretence in the world.

But let us look again at the parties the evening before. The deceased dresses for a party at the Parker House. He has a business engagement with some one, but still accompanies his cousin Charles to the party. They are standing on the steps of the parker House at eight o'clock in the evening, - Edward leaves, saying he is "going to Dr. Coolidge's office." He goes out, but returns in a moment. It was he who knocked at Coolidge's door before Flint left the office. The prisoner was waiting for him in his lair, but did not dare let him in, for then Flint would have seen him. He had locked his door, that no one other than he might come in, and gives Flint a hint to leave, under a pretense of an engagement about a *subject*. Upon his return to the Parker House - his cousin still in the entry way - they go up stairs to the party, remain a while, and then Edward leaves the room, saying again, he is going to Dr. Coolidge's office. He is seen on his way, toward 9 o'clock, by Simpson, in the middle of Silver street, crossing over to the prisoner's office. He finds him in - Flint had left him there waiting - and the prisoner admits, in his examination before the Coroner's inquest, that deceased was in his office after 8 o'clock, with $1800 in his pocket. And that is the last that is seen of him or heard of him on earth, until he is found the next morning, a mangled corpse in the cellar, on the premises of the prisoner - his clothes shrugged up on his shoulders, just as they naturally would be, if the body had slipped forward in their carrying it down stairs, as Flint says it did, his hold of it partly giving way.

The prisoner had prepared his way. He had beckoned to him from this carriage on Wednesday, and spoken a word in his ear - he had inspired him with his confidence - he had induced him to raise a large sum of money for him, and invited him to call that evening. He decoyed him within his reach - lured him within his grasp · coiled himself round him like a serpent, and then struck his fangs into him with the poison of an adder's sting; and there was no warning hiss in that dreadful sting, for it was done with a serpent's cunning. In a moment, quick as the flash of lightening, the poison does its deed of death · Edward Mathews is no more · his spirit has gone, and his body falls lifeless on the floor. There was danger of a death-shriek · hyena-like, the prisoner seizes him by the throat, and hence those marks the witnesses have described. The prisoner then attempts to put the body in the cask in the closet, and hence the blood upon it · the cask is not large enough; he then takes it to the window · the window was raised clear up when Flint when into the office, and the body lay half concealed by it behind the counter near it. But, upon a moment's thought, it would not do to throw the body down outdoors from the window. His strength, too, may have failed him · his nerve may have been unstrung. And then it is he goes down, and passes up by Williams's sitting-room, and looks in to see if Flint is there · but the curtains are down. Howe then sees him in the passage-way, and Hill meets him reconnoitering in Water St. He hurries back for Flint · meets him in the entry-way, with a lamp in his hand, going to bed · takes the lamp from him, blows it out, and in an agitated tone requests him to go to the office. They enter the office. And then was acted that dreadful scene in this sad drama, that I need not describe if I could · for that dim spirit-lamp on the iron safe, the deep curtained windows, the dead body on the floor, its passage down the back-stairs in the dark, are objects that the plain narrative of Flint so impressed on your minds that you will carry them with you to your graves.

This, gentlemen, is a general view of the tragedy that was acted at Waterville on the evening of the 30th Sept. It was too strange for life · and yet too real for fiction.

The testimony of Dingley throws a ray of light upon the case. In the early part of the week the prisoner observed that a person was sick in Clinton, of fits, and would die soon, and make a good "subject." Upon being asked where a subject could be kept, the prisoner replied, in a cask in the closet · saying that it would not scent the office if well covered with spirits. On the afternoon of Thursday, he said to Dingley that the "subject" before referred to had died, and made the same remark to Flint after tea. What did all this mean? Had anybody been sick of fits, in Clinton? · Had anyone died of fits in Clinton? Or was he preparing the way that a subject in the office might not create surprise? "He was hell on subjects," and needed no aid. No aid, indeed! The subject in life, so soon to be a shadow, was coming itself into his office.

Further: he refused to secure Tobey with his notes, for "he had agreed to make them over to Mathews, and was liable to be called upon at any moment." What Mathews? What Mathews was in his mind? Not Edward, for he was dead. John, was it then, who had aided in raising the $1500? Aye. Had he then got the $1500, and therefore liable to turn out his notes to secure it? And how did he get it? Why of Edward, who had it in his pocket. Aye, how? The poison in his stomach and the blows on his heads tell too plainly how. This was a dreadful declaration. He was guilty and suspected - it overcomes him - his mind loses for a moment its balance, and he tells the truth. It was an acknowledgment that he had got the $1500 - a confession therefore of the crime - a confession of his guilt.

It is said, and is it is conceded, said Mr. Blake, that the general reputation of the prisoner has been good. But there may be a false reputation, and a bad state of moral feeling - a whited sepulcher without, and dead men's bones within. The deep embarrassment of the prisoner, and his urgency for money, indicate an indulgence in vice or crime that we were precluded from proving. It appears, however, in evidence that he was guilty of perjury before the Coroner's Inquest, and of three unsuccessful attempts at subornation of perjury. It may be the ordinary history of crime, that a man should first steal, then rob, and then murder. - But men have suddenly fallen from light to darkness. Benedict Arnold had sustained an unblemished character and was entrusted with an important position by one of the best judges of character the world ever saw, at the very time of his treason. The disciples of Christ were not only of good repute, but illustrated in their lives great moral worth up to the time of the last supper; and then, when told that one of them would betray his Master, they, confiding one in another, enquired doubtingly who it was. And yet Judas betrayed his master, to suffer an ignominious death at the hands of the populace. A good reputation does not constitute a defense against the charge of a crime.

It is then said, gentlemen, that the prisoner had no motive to commit so aggravated a crime. I do not know what motive he had, nor do I care what motive he had - it is enough for me to prove the commission of the crime upon him. And if he would excuse it, then and then only, will I inquire why and wherefore he did it.

I do not know whether he wished to get money to go abroad, as he once intimated to Prof. Champlin, enjoining secrecy. And he did, I do not know whether it was to pursue his studies or to gratify his desires - to travel for information or to riot in crime - whether he was going alone, or going to take with him a *compagnon de voyage* - nor to I care. Enough, and quite enough it is for me to know, that the Grand Jury on a tithe of the evidence here, have preferred a charge against him, and that that evidence is such as to carry conviction to an impartial mind. That the prisoner was in great want of money is proved. He borrowed in all the adjoining towns, wherever he could, and at any interest that was exacted of him. His necessities, too, at this time, were surely approaching a crisis, for he offers Gray $500 for the use of $1000 six months, and Gilman $500 for $2000 three or four months. And yet I concede this could not have been an adequate cause for the commission of the crime charged - less inducement, however, has often before led to murder. - There never was, and never can be, good reason for the commission of crime - a sound mind, anchored on correct moral principle, like a staunch well moored ship, rides out the storm of life in safety, unhurt and uninjured. But a mind rotten to the core, its moral energies impaired by indulgence in vice or crime, yields to the pressure of temptation - its fastenings lose their hold, its moorings give way, and it swings from its place, to go to pieces on the shore, or to go to the bottom of the deep. Whether the desire for the $1800 was a pressure upon the prisoner he had not moral strength to resist, or what other motive influenced him, I do not know.

The learned counsel, said Mr. B., refers to a passage in Roman history familiar to us all - to ridicule the introduction here of the clothes of the deceased. The clothes were exhibited to explain the testimony, and not to move you to indignation or excite your sympathy. But was the allusion quite happy? For Brutus was a murderer, and confessed his guilt - excusing it "Not that he loved Caesar less, but Rome More." The murderers of Mathews appear to have had no ill-will against him. It was not that he loved Mathews less, but that he loved money more. And to my apprehension the learned counsel's allusion to Macbeth was not more fortunate. For Macbeth was a murderer, and having stained his hands in the blood of his sovereign, he tries to arrest suspicion by accusing the innocent sons of the king.

> We here our bloody cousins are bestowed,
> In England and Ireland, not confessing
> Their cruel parricide, filling their hearers
> With strange inventions.

And a dreadful retribution was visited upon his devoted *head*.

The learned counsel has appealed to your sympathies, entreating you not be mere machines, to be wound up and run down again. Oh, no, said Mr. B., have for the prisoner all the sympathy you can, for a man stained with his guilt. But remember you are under oath to give a verdict according to the law and the evidence. The ancients well illustrated the idea of justice by a marble statue with its eyes closed, holding an even balanced scale. I do not ask you to be cold as marble, but your oaths require you to be blind to results. All pity the prisoner - none but regret his condition - sympathize with him, then if you can- but remember, also, *for once*, the agony of that dying man on the night of the 30th of September, - remember, for once, the bereaved mother, disconsolate, inconsolable - and think for once, of the afflicted brother, who survives to watch with painful interest, the progress of this trial.

A fearful responsibility, gentlemen, said Mr. B., now rests upon you. The public hold you to that responsibility now, and will hold you to it always. Give expression, then to the conviction the evidence has induced in your minds, fearless of consequences - that you may return to your homes with the approval of your consciences and the world.

In addressing the punishment for murder, he could only say that should a verdict of guilty be returned, the prisoner would await in confinement, his sentence one year, and that execution would then follow or not, something as the public mind should dictate.[1]

I have now, said Mr. Baker, done my duty, and I cannot close better than by invoking Him to whom this House is dedicated to give you courage to do yours.

---

[1] Omitted in the report in the Maine Farmer, which is otherwise fullest account of Baker's address.

Afternoon Session

Charge to the Jury by Chief Justice Whitman

Gentlemen of the Jury; - I congratulate you that your labors are about to be closed. That you are likely to be liberated from your unpleasant condition which we have found it necessary to impose upon you. In cases of this kind it is customary to separate the jurors from their fellow citizens so that there may be no possible chance for them to be interfered with by those who might be interested to make erroneous impressions upon their minds.

This is more necessarily the case in times of great excitement, and you will be satisfied by the great concourses which have assembled here day by day in the progress of the session, greater than ever assembled before to my knowledge, that with reference to this trial there must be a great excitement. It is the right of the prisoner and of the government to have the trial decided by a jury which is as impartial and unbiased as the frailty of humanity would admit of.

The crime is that of murder; a crime only committed by those whose hearts are utterly devoid of social duty, and fatally bent on mischief. All the jury have to do is do their duty as they would in any other case. If the testimony is such as to produce conviction as to the correctness of the charge they must find the prisoner guilty. But if on the other hand they entertain reasonable doubts of his guilt they should find him not guilty. It is usual for the Atty. General to insert as many counts in his indictment as may ultimately turn out from the evidence in the case to be necessary. You may acquit generally on all the counts or you may convict one some one or more and acquit on others.

In this case there are four counts. The first count is for killing the deceased by striking him with a billet of wood.

With regard to this count, I believe the gov't do not press for a conviction, and you will have no difficulty in rendering a verdict of not guilty. The other three counts only contain a description of a murder committed by poison. You have therefore only to inquire whether the prisoner killed the deceased by means of poison. The evidence with regard to this is circumstantial. No man commits crime openly; therefore circumstantial evidence must be relied upon in almost every case. If conviction could not take place upon such evidence, there should be no safety for the community. You must first be satisfied that the person is dead; and second, that he came to his death by violence, and did not die a natural death,

The third point of which you must be satisfied, is that the crime was committed with malice aforethought. It will be necessary for me here to define to you what is understood by malice, in law. It is not exactly what we mean by malice in common parlance; but a murder is considered as malicious when committed by one perpetrating some crime, whether he intended to kill or not. For instance, if a man in a scuffle took up a deadly weapon, on slight provocation, and death ensued, he would be guilty of murder. Or if a burglar, in entering a house with an intent to steal, accidentally kills those opposing him, although he may have no ill will against the victim, he is still guilty of murder. So in riots, where there is no particular malice against the persons killed, the perpetrators are considered guilty of murder.

By a law of this state, which I think is contained in the Revised Statutes, the jury, if they find the prisoner guilty, shall consider whether the murder committed by of the first or second degree.

A murder of the first degree is where the murder is committed with express malice aforethought, or in the commission of some other crime punishable with death or confinement in state prison for life. All other murders are considered to be of the second degree. The first is punishable with death, and the second with confinement in the state prison for life. If you convict the prisoner, it will be necessary therefore to consider whether this be a murder of the first or second degree. But if you are satisfied that the murder was by poisoning, deliberately administered it can be no other than murder in the first degree.

As I before remarked, the evidence is circumstantial. If you are satisfied that every circumstance which is considered necessary for proof is established beyond a reasonable doubt, your duty is to convict the prisoner. These circumstances must be such that they cannot be explained in any other way. There are many cases which might illustrate this; as in a robbery, in which the articles stolen are found upon a person. This is evidence beyond a reasonable doubt that the prisoner is guilty, unless he can show how he came by it, consistently with his innocence.

It is very important, however, that you should be satisfied beyond a reasonable doubt of the existence of these circumstances. The evidence with regard to this must be direct and positive. You have an instance of this in the case of the prisoner before you. If you are satisfied from the evidence presented, that the last that was seen of the deceased he was going into the office of the prisoner, and when next found he was dead, with prussic acid in his stomach; and if no other person in the vicinity had prussic aid, or could have given it to him, but the prisoner – if, I say, you are satisfied of all of these things from the evidence offered you, you must decide that he was murdered by the prisoner.

Here I think it proper to allude to the testimony of Thomas Flint. He is a competent witness, but his testimony comes to the jury under disadvantages, consequent upon his previous conduct. His credibility has been assailed by his having given different accounts of the transaction before, and by his having been concerned in an attempt to conceal the murder. However this may be, still he may speak the truth, and you are to consider the probability of this being the case. Men do not perform wicked acts without a motive. – Much less is it probable that they would do so contrary to the natural feelings, and against their own interest. It is true he has been guilty of aiding the prisoner in concealing the body, according to his own confession, thus making himself accessory after the act. In the second place he went before a coroner's jury, and under solemn oath before God he denied all knowledge of the affair, and made statements respecting his actions which were false, thus committing perjury. In all this there is indication of a very loose moral sense. But you are to consider whether, if he had persisted in the statements first made, there was any prospect of injury accruing to himself. No suspicion rested upon him, and he was able to account for his conduct in a manner inconsistent with the supposition of his guilt. On the other hand, by what he has disclosed he has brought a stain upon his character, from which he can never recover. A man like him, in the prime of life, with a reputation fair and unspotted, probably had expectations of future success in his profession. We cannot imagine that such a man could have acted in such a way without a strong motive. You are to judge, then, whether there was any such impelling motive. If there had been any evidence of personal enmity existing between the witness and the accused, this might have been a motive. It remains for you to judge whether he felt any hatred for his former master and friend. If he did not, but if on the other hand he shew every evidence of the kindest feelings towards the prisoner at the bar, you are to judge whether it would be natural for him to make a statement which would cost the prisoner his life. But if you find, upon examination of the facts, that he was impelled by conscience thus to criminate himself and implicate the prisoner, you are to give his testimony the weight which in this case it ought to have. If you are afraid to convict from such a witness, you must judge if the other circumstances are not enough to substantiate his testimony. And while you do this, you must inquire whether there is any possibility for all these things to be true and the prisoner still be innocent.

Crimes are not usually committed without a motive. You are to see if the evidence given has made it probable that this prisoner had a sufficient motive for the commission of this awful crime. The government have endeavored to show you that the prisoner was in pressing want of money, that he had made repeated applications for it at various times and places. If you are satisfied, from the testimony adduced, that this had created a craving in his mind which would be enough to induce him to commit this act, you must so decide. With regard to this point in the evidence, the prisoner's counsel have argued that the prisoner had plenty of money and was in no need of such as effort to obtain it. You are to judge how for the prisoner's repeated application for money at exorbitant interest, is compatible with such a state of things.

You are to judge whether the counsel for the government have fully established the existence of an arrangement with the deceased, by the prisoner, to obtain a large sum of money, You have the testimony of Dingley and the office boy, that there was a letter directed to Edward Mathews on the prisoner's table; that the prisoner denied on oath, having written such a letter; that this letter called upon the deceased to come to his office on peril of his life. You have the evidence of Mr. Tobey, that the prisoner excused himself from giving security, on the ground that he expected to be called upon to make an assignment of his notes to Mathews. That the deceased was seen to be preparing a bill of sale, which he put in his pocket, but which was not found with him after his death. It now appears, that, instead of acknowledging that he was trying to obtain money in various ways, he swore before the jury that he had lent Mathews two hundred dollars – [His Honor here repeated the story of Coolidge's making a charge against Mathews, after he was sent for his books.] After the examination of his testimony, if you are satisfied that he was strongly impelled by a desire to obtain money, you must let it have its weight in the decision.

It is shown, by the evidence, that he had on hand two vials of the strongest kind of poison, when the murder was committed. You are to judge whether he could have had any other motive for procuring a vial of this description, and whether this is not also a circumstance in favor of the position of the government.

Your next duty will be to consider if there is any reason to suppose that there was any more of this kind of acid any where else in Waterville.

A question has been raised whether it is morally certain that the contents of the stomach were in the same condition when placed in the hands of Professor Loomis as they were when taken from the stomach. You have the testimony of Mr. Williams, that he took the bowl and secreted it; that he thinks no person knew where he put it, and before sunrise on the following morning he carried it and locked it up in his ice house; from this place it was taken when delivered to Prof. Loomis. The counsel for the defense have admitted that these must be the same, unless they were tampered with by some person during that night. In such cases, if the evidence does not afford an absolute certainty, you must be guided by a *moral* certainty. You are to consider whether any other person could have had the acid to insert. Dr. Plaisted tells you that he had a small vial left with him some years ago, but it had never been opened. There is no evidence that any other physicians used it, or that any other person was in possession of it besides the prisoner, - But when the prisoner was asked if the contents had been examined, he did not know they had been preserved. It is for you to judge then, gentlemen, whether the poison was likely to have been inserted by the prisoner, of, if not by him, by any one else.

The next subject for your consideration is, whether these contents of the stomach contained the acid. You are told that they were carried from Williams's to the laboratory by Prof. Loomis, and then analyzed. He has given you an account of his mode of proceeding. It seems he applied to them three tests, all of which gave evidence of the existence of prussic acid in the stomach. Relying on these, he tells you there is moral certainty of its existence, and that in a quantity of about two grains. In confirmation of this, you have the testimony of other skillful physicians, who concur with Prof. Loomis in his opinion. Doctor Hubbard states that these tests are unerring, and are equal to the testimony of three reliable witnesses. This is a strong expression, but I do not know that it is too much so. I am not acquainted with the science of chemistry myself, but I rely with confidence upon those who are skilled in it. They did not see the acid with their own eyes, but consider the proof by these tests as impossible to be mistaken. This is a kind of evidence necessarily introduced, because in the course of events we are compelled to deal with many things which we do not understand, and must depend upon the knowledge of those who are conversant with such subjects. We have, accordingly, in this case, resorted to a Professor of Chemistry, and to Dr. Hubbard and others, who agree with him. You are to judge, from these facts, whether you can have any reasonable doubt that the acid existed in the body when it was found.

If you decide that it did, then you may take into account the other circumstances of finding the body; that it was found in the cellar of the prisoner's office, and that the boots and clothes were not soiled. He *could* have been poisoned at some other place, and conveyed there; but if you are satisfied as to the cause of his death, and that the *means used* could only have been obtained at the office of the prisoner, you will judge whether or not the body must have been carried to the place where it was found from the office of the prisoner.

These are the more important circumstances of the case, and it is for you to judge whether they do or do not confirm the testimony of Flint. If you cannot come to a conclusion, beyond reasonable doubt, that the deceased was poisoned, and that the poison was administered by the prisoner, you will bring a verdict of acquittal; but if you are satisfied on these points, and the others which I have named, you will convict him.

I am here reminded that Flint is said to have been contradicted in two respects. First, with regard to time. He states that he went to the office of the prisoner at one quarter past 9, and remained there with the prisoner one hour. But Hill testifies that he met the prisoner after 20 minutes of ten, and before ten, in Water street, the same evening. But you must be aware how uncertain is this matter of time. Hill must be mistaken, for the prisoner himself admits that he left the house of Mr. Williams at a quarter past 9, in company with Flint, and went directly to his office. Again Flint testifies that the prisoner made his charge upon his books against Mathews, before he went to the jury of inquest. You will judge whether Flint was mistaken, or willfully stated what he know to be false.

Gentlemen of the Jury; - with these remarks, I leave the case for your decision. It is our custom, always to instruct the jury that the prisoner at the bar is to be presumed innocent until he is proved guilty. You are not, however, to permit your sympathies to influence your decision. If, upon a careful and deliberate consideration of each part of this testimony, taking up the case point by point, you are not satisfied of his guilt, beyond a reasonable doubt, you will acquit him; but if, on the other hand, you are satisfied, then it is your duty to convict.

After His Honor closed, the jury retired and the Court adjourned to half past five o'clock. As they passed by the prisoner, he was observed to look each one of them full in the face, as if to read their decision in their countenances.

At half past five, the Court again assembled, but the jury had not agreed upon a verdict, and they were adjourned to nine o'clock tomorrow morning.

Day Nine: Thursday, March 23, 1848

The Court met according to adjournment at 9 o'clock. The jury, upon enquiry being made, returned for answer, that they had not agreed, but that there was no certainty but they might agree; whereupon the Court adjourned to meet at half past 11 o'clock.

The Court met at on half past 11 A.M. The jury being enquired of, replied that they were not able to agree; whereupon an officer was directed to call the jury into Court. Having interrogated as to the probability of their agreement, the foreman stated that there was none whatever - that they differed as to their judgement of the law and fact, and in respect to the amount and weight of testimony; whereupon they were sent out again, and the Court adjourned until 3 o'clock P.M.

The Court met at 3 o'clock. Upon enquiry made, the jury returned for answer that they had not agreed, but probably should agree in half an hour.

The jury returned into Court at 4 o'clock this afternoon to discharge their credit, and the prisoner was brought in.

The Clerk then called the prisoner and the jurors, who answered to their names.

Clerk. - Gentlemen of the jury, have you agreed upon a verdict?

Jury. - We have.

Clerk. - Who shall speak for you?

Jury. - Our foreman.

Clerk. - Valorus P. Coolidge, stand up and hold up your right hand. Mr. Foreman, look upon the prisoner - prisoner, look upon the foreman. What say you, Mr. Foreman, is the prisoner at the bar guilty or not guilty?

Foreman. Guilty of Murder in the First Degree, upon the 2d, 3d and 4th counts - not guilty upon the 1st count.

Clerk. Gentlemen of the jury, hearken to your verdict as the Court have recorded it. You, upon your oaths do say, that

Valorus P. Coolidge, the prisoner at the bar, is guilty of, &c., &c. So you say, Mr. Foreman, so say you all, gentlemen?

The jury assented.

The Attorney General having moved for sentence, the Chief Justice enquired of the prisoner if he had any thing to say why sentence would not be pronounced again him. He then rose slowly, and with the utmost calmness addressed the Court substantially as follows:

I have nothing more to say, than that you are about to pronounce sentence upon an innocent man. My counsel have done all that they can do in my behalf. I believe the Court and the Jury have intended to do right, but they have been misled by false testimony. I will not go into a detail of that evidence here; but may leave it, perhaps, on paper. [Then slowly raising his eyes to Heaven, he added with the utmost solemnity,] Thank God, there is another and a higher Court to which I may appear; and I await with patience the award of that tribunal. There the truth will be seen and known. I choose rather my situation, than that of one, who may now be within the sound of my voice. And now, I bid you all, enemies and friends, an affectionate farewell, and am ready to receive my sentence.

Mr. Evans asked for a postponement. He had learned, since the case had gone to jury, that important letters from Dr. Potter to the prisoner had been improperly taken from the prisoner, and suppressed by the government – letters relative to experiments with prussic acid, and understood to account for the fact of Dr. Coolidge sending for acid of the strongest kind. Mr. E. before moving an arrest of judgement, said he wish to ask the Attorney General if such letters were in his possession. Mr. Blake said he thought there were among the papers some letters from a Mr. Potter, but he was not aware that they contained any such thing as represented. He was not aware that there was any thing among the papers which he might not consistently with his duty submit to prisoner's counsel.

Mr. Evans proceeded to remark with considerable earnestness on the impropriety of withholding from prisoner the personal papers necessary to his own defense, and intimating that there were such papers in the possession of the Attorney General.

Mr. Blake said that after the imputation, cruel and underserved as he considered, upon his predecessor, he should withdraw his offer to submit the papers to the prisoner's counsel.

Day Nine: Thursday, March 23, 1848

After further consultation by Counsel and Court as to what time was wanted, Mr. Evans asked that he might have till tomorrow. The Court suggested that if his witnesses were present he might take them to a room below, see what they would testify to, and make up his motion, After some time he returned and made his motion for an arrest of sentence with the affidavit of J. B. Norris, that when he arrested Coolidge he took the papers on his person, and among them was one treating to a remedy for diseased eyes.

Mr. Evans now asked for a longer time than tomorrow. The testimony of Dr. Hill, who had seen these letters, might be obtained tomorrow perhaps but he wished to hear from Dr. Potter himself.

After numerous remarks between the Court and Counsel, the Court finally gave notice that the sentence would be deferred till to-morrow, (Friday) morning at 9 o'clock.

While this discussion was going on, the Attorney General rose and stated to the Court that he held in his hand a letter, addressed to the foreman of the jury, which had been found in such a situation that led him to suppose it was placed there to influence the jury. He placed it in the hands of the Court, that they might do with it as they judged best. The Chief Justice handed it to the foreman, remaking that the letter was addressed to him, that he could open it, and if of a private nature he need not communicate the contents. The foreman, having unsealed and read the letter, stated to the Court that it was not of a private character, but addressed to the jury, anonymously - he returned it to the Court. The Chief Justice then handed the letter to their Attorney General, and directed him to do with it as the law required. Justice Shepley advised the Attorney General not to permit the letter to pass out of his hands without fixing a mark upon it by which it might be identified.

This letter was apparently in the hand writing of a lady, and contained in substance an appeal to the Jury to acquit the prisoner, with sundry quotations from Scripture in favor of the appeal. It is but justice to the Jury, to remark, that the Foreman stated that they had never seen the letter, and of consequence had not been influenced by its contents.

Day Ten: Friday, March 24, 1848.

The Court met at 9 o'clock.

Mr. Evans was asked if he had anything further to say in regard to his motion. He replied that he had not. He had not been able to procure definite proof as to the contents of the letters. Dr. Hill's recollection was not sufficiently distinct[1].

The Attorney General said he had supposed the letters were taken from the office of the prisoner; but he now understood that they were taken from his person by the officer; and of course he had always been acquainted with their contents, and his counsel could have had notice of them at any time. He now held them in his hand; he had not been able to examine them fully, but was advised that their contents had little bearing upon the case. He was also advised that they did contain reflections upon some of the most respectable people of Waterville, and by giving publicity to them much injury might be done. He would however place them in the hands of the prisoner's counsel, to be used as they saw fit.

[He then laid the letters upon the table before Messrs. Evans and Noyes, by whom, however, they were not taken up.]

Mr. Evans said they had hoped to be placed in possession of them in season for a careful examination. They preferred their own judgement as to the weight of the evidence the letters might contained. They had hoped for a postponement of sentence until the next court; but as the wish would probably be of little avail, they should decline any further proceedings upon the letters at the present time.

The Court. Then the motion is withdrawn?

Mr. Evans. Not so; we place it on file.

The Court then said that as the motion was unsupported, it must be overruled.

The three Judges then rose - and the prisoner also rose - when the Chief Justice, in the most solemn and impressive manner,

---

[1] This account is from the Eastern Mail and the Portland Advertiser. Other accounts are less informative: 'Evans, upon being enquired of whether he had any thing further to say, replied that the evidence of Dr. Hill did not amount to what he expected, and that he had nothing further to say.'

and apparently deeply affected himself, addressed the prisoner as follows:

Valorus P. Coolidge - You have been indicted for the crime of murder, and have been put upon your trial for that offense, and have been defended by eminent counsel, who have done all that could be expected from human effort and ingenuity in your behalf. Yet a jury, believed to have been as impartial as the lot of humanity would admit of, after a patient and lengthy investigation, have pronounced against you a verdict of Guilty; and the Court are not aware of any reason why they should not have so done. We must, therefore, deem your guilt to be legally established; the duty, therefore, devolves upon us to award against you the sentence which the law has prescribed.

We have understood that you have been duly admitted a member of one of the learned professions - that, for a few years, you have been a practicing physician, and in that profession that you have been successful beyond what has often fallen to the lot of men of your age - that the charges upon your book have, in the space of about four years, amounted to the sum of eight thousand dollars. We have understood further, that you are unencumbered with a family to support; and so far as appears, could not have been under any pressing necessity to become indebted for borrowed money to any considerable amount. Yet, at the time of the fatal catastrophe, you had, in the course of three or four years, become so indebted to the amount of nearly or quite three thousand dollars, and were still pressing for further large loans.

And we cannot see reason to doubt, that on the evening of the thirtieth of September last, you had made arrangements with Edward Mathews, the deceased, whereby he was to procure for you a considerable sum of money; and for the purpose of furnishing you with it, and taking security therefore, he had entered your office, not many moments before the fatal deal was done And for what was it done? We are constrained to believe that it was done to afford you an opportunity to rifle him of whatever of value you could find upon his person. How inadequate the temptation! How awful the deed. And how astonishing it is, that you, with the flattering prospects before you, should have perpetrated it! It is a case unparalleled in the history of crime, and affords us a woeful instance of the frailty of human nature.

But our statute, in reference to those so convicted, is conceived in mercy. You are not to be hurried at once from time into eternity. You cannot be executed short of a year from this time; and that space, it may be hoped, will be devoted to the contemplation of your forlorn condition. And may contrition and sincere repentance make you a fit subject for the mercy of an offended God; and render it consistent with His eternal goodness, at last to admit you to the society of just men made perfect.

The sentence we are compelled to pronounce is, *that YOU BE HANGED BY THE NECK UNTIL YOU BE DEAD; and for this purpose, that you be conveyed to the State Prison, situate in Thomaston, in the County of Lincoln. And until this sentence of death shall be inflicted upon you, that you there be put to hard labor, in solitary confinement.*

The prisoner was then remanded to jail and the Court adjourned *sine die.*

Scenes from the Trial

From all accounts, the trial was a mob scene, or, at least, a carnival; none of the transcripts of the trial mention any particular issues - there is no report of the Chief Justice pounding his gavel and saying "I will have order here!". But if reports are to be believed that may have been necessary. This was a period when a strong temperance movement had developed in response to wide-spread drunkeness, but had not yet gotten laws in place forbidding the sale of alcohol.

The "Ladies" came in for a lot of the attention.

The Eastern Mail March 30, 1848
The Hallowell Gazette, in speaking of the trial of Dr Coolidge, says —
    'Crowds have attended, and the large meeting house of Dr. Tappan has been crowded to overflowing. Many ladies have attended, and, we are sorry to say it, some of them have exhibited not the most lady-like demeanor. The ladies will probably not be again admitted as spectators at a trial for murder in this county'

The Portland Advertiser March 28, 1848
The interest excited in this trial has been probably without a parallel in this State. Judge Whitman stated in his charge that he had never witnessed its equal. Through the whole long course of the trial, the large house was crowded to overflowing — the galleries being reserved for and filled by the ladies.
We witnessed many scenes which we should be glad not to have witnessed. We witnessed more drinking and rowdiness than we have seen before for years. During the whole progress of the trial, liquor was dealt out openly and unblushingly at Augusta as freely as water, to crowds of young men in fine clothes, expensive gold watches and chains, loud, profane and obscene conversation, and flushed if not bloated countenance. From all we can learn, we fear that Augusta and some other places on the Kennebec River are behind the times in the cause of temperance. Perhaps we are mistaken. But if not, does it not become the men of influence in that region to inquire into the cause, and put forth strenuous efforts to check this flood of evil?
The great multitude attending the trial caused a great scramble for seats, especially for those near the stand, where the proceedings could be heard and understood. When the doors of the house were

opened, the multitude would rush up the aisles at full speed, with loud yells. some with hats off and coats streaming behind to secure their seats - a most disgraceful scene on such an occasion. There was some scuffling, too, we believe, among the ladies in the galleries to secure the best seats. These things viewed upon the surface might lead one to believe that the effects of public trials are highly injurious. But

"This partial view of human kind
Is surely not the *last*."

We have no doubt that many, who in the excitement of the moment may have joined in those scenes and been guilty of light and trifling conduct as if in no way seriously impressed with what was passing before them, did, nevertheless, reflect upon it with seriousness, and especially when alone and after they had retired to their respective homes.

No one could have witnessed the scene during Flint's testimony, - heard the recital of that terrible scene in the office, in which he became so deeply implicated, thought of the position which those two young men then and a few days after, occupied towards each other, and that in which they then stood, without feeling the full force of the truth that "the way of transgressors is hard."

The verdict we believe is a righteous one, and increases our confidence in the value of jury trials. The greatest care and caution was used, by the prisoner in selecting this jury, and from the fact that opportunity had been given for acquiring a thorough knowledge of the habits, mind, character, &c. of the jurors, many anticipated that, there would be no verdict - that the jury would not agree. We know that sometimes juries make what may appear to be strange decisions. So do Courts and other tribunals. But it is more the habit to ridicule any supposed error in the decisions of juries than of other tribunals - hence we fear that there has been a somewhat too prevalent and growing disposition to throw ridicule on the trial by jury, and thereby create a distrust and weaken the confidence of the people in this important provision of our constitution.

Waterville's own newspaper begins by being very coy about the female attendees, and ends with a few digs at Coolidge, strongly implying that his troubles came from dealings with women. It is revealing, however, to read that the women of Waterville, among whom he practiced, remained strongly on his side.

The Eastern Mail April 6, 1848
THE TRIAL AND THE LADIES - Webster has given no definition of the word 'lady,' that enables us to decide precisely what demeanor

should characterize a genuine lady in a court of justice. A lady in a ball-room is one who moves with the least noise, whirls longest on one toe, and exhibits the greatest economy of cloth in the upper portion of her dress. A lady at home, is one who fondles a lapdog, keeps a nursery-maid, and addresses her husband, 'my love.' A lady in the street, carries her purse across her hand, talks louder than when at home, and 'cuts' all gentlemen who have not a ring on the little finger and a tuft on the upper lift, So everywhere there is some means of distinguishing the lady from the mere woman - always excepting places where propriety seems to forbid their appearance. Here is probably the ground of disagreement in regard to those ladies who attended the late trial of the 'lovely,' 'beautiful,' 'charming,' murderer at Augusta. The Rev, Editor of the Banner thinks their conduct was not too lady-like; while Dr. Mann - (and who shall decide when doctors disagree, though one may be a doctor of divinity, and the other a doctor of 'strippings and molasses.') who knows as much of symptoms as anybody, says the charge is all a sham, and that the ladies were grossly abused. We confess an inclination to favor the 'strippings' Doctor's side of the question; not from any home-interest in it - for, thank fortune, we had not so much as a tenth cousin in the whole mess - but because the weight of argument is there. It has but to be shown that the wearers of all those bonnets were ladies, and it follows that their conduct must have been lady-like. Taking our definition above as correct, we should agree that no mother could leave her home at daylight and reman till dark, unless she kept a nursery-maid; that no one would trust her toes in such a press for fifteen consecutive hours, unless they had been well toughened in the giddy dance; and lastly, that no wife would venture to cast sheeps-eyes, bouquets and billet-doux to a handsome young murderer and libertine, unless they said 'my love' by way of sweetening. So the ladies - ladies - have the argument.

But the Banner must have designed only the good of his own near neighbors, for the towns beyond Augusta are said to have been sparsely represented in that 'lady-like' audience. Waterville had only a few rare stars there. Sure, others might have gone but Waterville husbands are prudent, careful men. So the Banner may throw stones as he will, but not this way. Hear him:

 "The arrangement, also tempted the ladies to come out - the whole gallery being expressly reserved for them, and this, perhaps, was, after all, an unfortunate feature in the general arrangements; for it drew forth largely the female population, took many from their families and children, to the neglect of all domestic cares - some of them even repairing to the meeting-house at or before daylight so as to obtain a seat, and remaining there all the live-long day - and this, day after day, for nearly a fortnight; the conduct of some too was highly unbecoming - thinking to be looked upon as ladies because occupying the most conspicuous seats, and yet forfeiting their claims to ladyship by scratching, kicking and fighting off every other and less selfish woman who dared to venture towards the same pew. There were a few such women, and their conduct has given them a notoriety all over the State that no real lady would covet, and that will not soon be forgotten. These and some others so sympathized with the prisoner, on account of his beauty, that they would look first on him and cry, and then upon the government attorneys and frown; and even their glances at the Court and Jury were far from being respectful. They knew the prisoner's character, nor were they ignorant of the probable motive which led to the murder - a motive by no means honorable to their own sex; and yet they manifested their zealous interest in his behalf, and would almost have taken him out of the custody of the Court given him his liberty, and made the 'dear man' their own 'second husband.'"

But the Banner is not alone in this. We think every reporter for the press has noticed the same impropriety. Even the kind and gallant editor of the Farmer says -

"Another trait developed in some, but which was, we believe, more particularly confined to the 'softer sex,' was a sickly sort of sentimental sympathy for the person arraigned, merely from the fact of his being 'good looking,' and totally regardless of any evidence of guilt, or respect for justice, and an impartial administration of the laws of the land."

Well - the fault must be forgiven and in the course of time forgotten, if the ladies of Kennebec would not become a proverb. They were always on the Doctor's side; it was peculiarly so here, and it was so there; and it is more than surmised that an effort to reciprocate the favor was what ruined him. We shall not quote Solomon, for there are but few in the same danger. We have not a handsome doctor left in Waterville, and hope never to have another.

Harsh criticism of the whole proceeding comes from a Belfast Maine newspaper.

The Republican Journal, April 21, 1848
CASE OF DOCTOR COOLIDGE. It is evident there has never been in this State so much excitement among all classes of people as there has been on account of the trial of Doct. Coolidge. It appears by some newspaper accounts, that great preparations were made for the trial, in order to accommodate a vast concourse of people; and of every shade of character, from the candid, sober, reflecting and honest - down through every gradation of depravity, to the basest of the base, and the vilest of the vile, of both sexes. The meeting-house

of Dr. Tappan was fitted up with much care and expense expressly for the purpose of the trial; and after this internal transformation of the house, it seems that it must have more resembled the Areopagus of the Heathen Greeks, or the Triumphal arch of the blood-thirsty Romans, than a Christian temple of worship, or a civilized hall of candid, sober Justice. If the conduct in the house was as bad as strangers say it was, it certainly shows a low state of morals in Augusta and vicinity. It seems that drinking was indulged in even to intoxication. For this no doubt the people of Augusta were in the fault, by furnishing the poison. What method Doct. Tappan and the church will adopt in order to clean their sanctuary from sin and defilement, by its late desecration, we know not. Most defiled things under the law of Moses, were purged, or cleansed with blood · but as it is yet in doubt, whether Doct. Tappan's sanctuary has not in fact been defiled with blood, and as it would be unreasonable to attempt to cleanse blood with blood, it would perhaps be the better way to burn incense in the cool of the morning, and at eventide sprinkle all the inside of the house · and especially where the inebriated males congregated and lewd females had their station in the sanctuary · with pure water.

Views of the Trial

The Republican Journal

At the conclusion of the trial, most newspaper editors agreed with the verdict. A few - notably the Waterville paper, the *Eastern Mail,* seemed to find an explanation of the Doctor's actions in gambling or womanizing - two vices that were nowhere mentioned at the trial, and, since the prosecution did not hesitate to put on testimony of the most trivial actions that might tell against the doctor - declining Prof. Champlin's request for a donation to the college comes to mind - that does not seem very convincing.

A writer who signed his name 'Howard, Hancock County' in the Belfast newspaper wrote the only sustained criticism of the process that I have encountered in a Maine newspaper. The extract below follows his criticism of the atmosphere of the trial, which is printed at the end of the previous chapter.

We have read with much care and close attention all the evidence in the trial of Doct. Coolidge, have viewed it separately in all its parts, have examined the whole, over and over, not only once or twice but three times - and this without partiality, prejudice, favor or affection - never having heard of either Doct. Coolidge or Mathews until after the death of the latter - and have come to the following decision, i.e. that Doct V. Coolidge sustained a good character as a citizen and as a good, humane doctor, until after the death of E. Mathews. This was proved at the trial. While we do not say but that Doctor. Coolidge may be guilty; *we do say that it has not been proved against him;* and hence in the language of the law he is innocent. We will look at this long protracted trial once more and give our opinion in a different light, yet equally tending to show that Doct. Coolidge has been rather vindictively treated and wrongfully judged. And first, we ask, is it in accordance with law, justice, and humanity, to hunt a fellow down, because he borrowed or rather hired money - and what connection can there be, between hiring money three or four years ago and the death of Mathews. It will be said, no doubt, that Dr. C was a borrower of money up to the time of Mathews death - granted - and that shows that what he received for his practice (some pay down, others must be dunned hard) was not sufficient to support his extensive humane business in the healing art.

Views of the Trial

Dr. Coolidge has been condemned, it appears, for poisoning Edward Mathews with prussic acid. That Dr. C had prussic acid in his possession is proved - and that he had an ounce of the purest, or as it is generally expressed, strongest kind, which he had received from Boston a short time previous to the death of Mathews, is also proved. Now if Dr. Coolidge was wicked enough to procure prussic acid for the purpose of taking the life of E. Mathews, or any one else, is it possible that he should have spoken of it openly, freely, and universally as he did - telling people what a deadly poison he had - that one drop of it on the tongue of a man, would kill him as quick as if struct by a bolt of lightning. He must be a very weak, simple, foolish man, to conduct as he did, provided, we mean, that he had murder in his heart, and prussic acid was intended to be his death agent. Upon no other hypothesis can his conduct be accounted for - but, that he is a weak simpleton, was deranged, or was innocent, and had no design of murder in his heart. Prussic acid in its pure state, is a deadly poison; but that it will destroy life as quickly as electricity, is not correct. It is extremely volatile, and when exposed to air is resolved in a short time, and loses its odor, together with a great part of its poisonous quality. Prussic acid, when in its pure state, has quite a strong odor, much resembling that of peach-tree flowers, or of bruised bitter almonds. Its taste is sweetish, but acrid.

Many intelligent people are of the opinion, that in the trial of Dr. Coolidge, too much confidence was placed in the *sense* of smelling; or in other words, to place more confidence in one single pair of nerves, i.e., the *olfactory*, than in all the other nine pairs, among which are the optics, auditory, &c., was going beyond what law and justice required; and at which, calm sober reason, philanthropy, and the true spirit of Christianity, revolts. We hope Dr. Coolidge will be treated with that degree of kindness which every human being is entitled to while he lives, whether under the condemnation of an earthly tribunal or not. All condemned criminals, though in chains, and dangerous, have their rights - and the more rights a man is deprived of, the more valuable to him are those which he still retains. That Dr. Coolidge had the right to speak for himself before sentence was pronounced, is a fact - and it is also a fact that what he said, was to all appearance, spoken with moderation, candor and solemnity. It has made an impression on the public mind in his favor, deeper than is at present manifested. Dr. C. still has rights; and we hope that he will retain them, and give to his enemies no new weapons wherewith they may torture him. In all this tragical scene, there is nothing which has appeared to us more out of place than the treatment which Dr. Coolidge received from the Rev. Wm. A. Drew. It seems that the Dr. was in great distress both mentally and physically - he had spent the night in weeping - the reflection that the news of his situation, would bring his father, his only surviving parent, with sorrow and anguish to the grave - the Dr.'s heart was swollen and near bursting with grief, his eyes were red, and bedimmed with tears · when Mr. Drew entered the gloomy cell. What was the duty of the messenger of the gospel of Christ? What! why to have spoken to him sympathetically the soothing words of consolation · told him what the Son of God suffered for a lost world, when, but the will of God the Father he tasted death for every man. He ought to have told the poor distressed man, that God required nothing of him, but true, sincere repentance, and though his sins were like scarlet and ever so numerous, yet for his Son's sake God would forgive him all, and give him comfort and divine consolation in his own soul, and cause his mind to be calm and happy, though his corporeal body might be confined in a gloomy cell, &c., &c. Those who wish to know to what we have referred, can consult the Gospel Banner of April the 8th, 1848.

We will close this communication by giving our opinion of this case which has terminated in the ruin, as far as this life is concerned, of a young physician of much promise, and of good repute up to the time of the death of E. Mathews, and in fact for some days after. We say *ruin*, as Dr. C is ruined in all his future prospects in regard to popularity, &c. unless some new things relating to this case shall come to light, and put a different face on the whole concern. We will now state that it is our candid, deliberate opinion, that soon after the death of Edward Mathews, a conspiracy was formed against Dr. Valorus Coolidge (We have said in this communication that Dr. Coolidge may be guilty; we intended at the time to have qualified it thus · *but if he is, he is not alone;* we have added this in a parenthesis, as we wish to be understood correctly in every sentence we have written upon this painful subject.) This conspiracy at its commencement consisted of but two, or, at most, three, managed by one master spirit of depravity. Should any wish to know why we are so confident upon this point, we only say now, *wait and see what time will bring forth.*

Howard.

Hancock Co., April 13, 1848

The Monthly Law Reporter

A second criticism, published in a Boston legal journal, Volume 11 (or New Series Volume 1) of *The Monthly Law Reporter,* for May, 1848, contains a seven-page article, "Trial of Dr. Coolidge." Authorship is attributed to Peleg W. Chandler, the founder and editor of the publication. The first pages are a summary of the case. The remainder discusses various legal issues. The author was critical of the case on three points: (1) the failure of the Chief Justice, in his charge to the jury, to give sufficient weight to motive, even after the judge had acknowledged that the government had failed to adequately show motive; (2) in the heavy reliance on the testimony of Flint, an acknowledged perjurer; here the author's criticism is quite harsh; and (3) in the refusal of the judges to allow the reading of medical reference works.

Pages four through seven are given below.

We say this case was *supported* by numerous witnesses. It can hardly be said to have been *established*, for although there was direct evidence to almost every point, part of it was contradicted, and part of it was of doubtful credibility. The prisoner was convicted, and the jurors undoubtedly considered the evidence irresistible, or they could never have overcome the powerful antipathy to capital punishment, which is now so general. Besides, we do not think that it falls within the province of a legal review to criticize the abstract questions of fact contained in the verdict of a jury. But the construction put upon certain facts becomes important as establishing a new rule in regard to presumptions. In this connection we take the liberty of doubting whether the government were held quite strictly enough to the proof of a *motive*.

In a charge of murder, the first great duty of the prosecutors is to prove the *corpus delicti*. This may be proved by direct or indirect evidence. If proved indirectly, the connection between the known acts of the prisoner and the death of the deceased must be proved so as to establish the fact of *malicious killing*, and under such circumstances, the existence of an adequate motive becomes a most essential element of the case. In regard to malice, the supreme court of Maine, in this instance, appear to have coincided with the dissenting opinion of Mr. Justice Wilde in *Commonwealth v. York* (9 Met. 93); S. C. 7 Law Rep. 497, 571; that the presumption of malice does not arise from the mere fact of killing, but that the malicious killing, as a single proposition, must be proved to the satisfaction of the jury. Thus, Chief Justice Whitman says, "It is incumbent on the government to satisfy you beyond a doubt that the person alleged to be murdered is dead. That being made out, the next point is, did he come to his death by artificial means, inflicted by some other hand; and *next, was the crime or the death occasioned with what the law denominates malice prepense, or malice aforethought?*"

How was it with Dr. Coolidge? It appeared, by the evidence of certain witnesses, that the prisoner had offered most exorbitant sums for the use of money even for a short time, and the general idea intended to be conveyed appears to have been that his immediate necessities were so pressing that he was willing to risk his life and reputation, and to commit one of the grossest crimes known in the statute books for the sum of $1800. Villains value human life at different rates. A common highwayman would require but a small reward for any act of violence to which he may have been stimulated by the necessity of starvation, or by a long life of crime. But the very strongest motives should have been proved to justify a charge of murder against a physician, high respected, enjoying a large practice, and whose professional prospects were so eminently encouraging, - of murder, too, committed in a cowardly manner, but, at the same time, a manner most easy of detection. The government entirely failed of showing what use the prisoner intended to have made of the money, and it was clearly shown, on the other hand, that he could easily have collected the money from his patients who were indebted to him, or that he could have borrowed it from friends. Ought not *character* to have had some weight? The following extract from the charge of the chief justice, contains his statement of general principles, and, considering that the presumption is always so strongly in favor of innocence, it seems that more attention should have been called to this very weak point in the case of the government.

"Crimes are not expected to be committed without a motive; and when you are to convict upon circumstantial evidence it is proper to see if there is one for the crime. The motive set up on the part of the government is that the prisoner was extremely embarrassed, and was pressing to being more so, for money in much larger amounts than he was accustomed to obtain. If you should be satisfied that he was in this state - that his wants were so urgent as to pervert his moral sense and to induce him to look to this source for relief - then the government have succeeded in showing a motive. Here, however, it is said, he was in a large practice - that he was prosperous - that the charges on his book amounted to a large sum - that he could have availed himself of collections and relieved his necessities so far as to have no occasion for pressing for more as he did. This you must consider for yourselves, and whether this accounts for the solicitude to obtain considerable sums."

The most indispensable witness to the government, was a medical student in the office of the prisoner, who not only denied any knowledge of the transaction, immediately after its occurrence, but fabricated a false account of the matter before a coroner's jury. Afterwards, becoming alarmed, and having taken the advice of his father, he was induced to come forward and state that he had perjured himself, that he had seen the body of the murdered man in the prisoner's office, and that having been told that he had died in a fit, he and the prisoner acted in concert in removing the body, and in destroying all evidence of the crime. The testimony of an accomplice is always odious; still more so, when the oath by which it is supported is proved to be worthless by the open acknowledgment

194

of the violation of a previous one. A person convicted of the *crimen falsi* in any shape, is forbidden to testify; and during the present season we have witnessed in this commonwealth the gross case of an individual, who having in early life submitted to a judgement in a justice's court merely as the cheapest and most expeditious way of getting rid of a charge of which he always asserted and afterwards established his innocence, was, after a long life of usefulness and respectability, refused the privilege of swearing to a simple book-account. Yet this medical student, whose previous perjury was the indispensable condition of his credibility, was relied upon to procure the conviction of the very man whose crimes he acknowledged that he had shared. What a mockery of justice under the name of law!

One other point of professional interest arose in this case, in regard to the reading of medical treatises. We have not seen any accurate report of the course adopted by the court upon this point, but some of the newspapers state that Mr. Evans having expressed a wish to read from some leading medical works, he was stopped by the court, and although he referred to the practice in Massachusetts and New York, the court adhered to their position. We cannot learn whether the court adopted a sweeping rule, denying the authority of all medical works, or whether they refused only in particular instances. If the former, the rule is a very hard one, and of doubtful propriety. It is laid down in *Collier v. Simpson*, (5 C. & P. 73), that professional and scientific works are inadmissible in evidence, although professional witnesses may explain the grounds of their judgment, which may be founded partly upon the opinions contained in such works. We know of no other authority for so broad a rule. On the contrary, the practice in this commonwealth is otherwise. In the case of Abner Rogers, tried in 1844, Mr. Bemis, of counsel for the prisoner, read, without any objection by the court, from Esquirol, Marc, and the official reports of Dr. Woodward, Dr. Bell and Dr. Brigham, and we believe the other counsel took similar liberties. In that case the defense of insanity was relied on, but insanity is no more a part of medical jurisprudence than the operation of poisons; and the opinions of medical men are not only useful, but indispensable to the salutary administration of justice. If the rule be enforced that nothing that can be stated orally and under oath shall be admitted, then we shall always lose the benefit of the opinions of professional experts in other countries and of other times. With equal justice might the treatises of Coke and Blackstone, of Story and Kent, of Pothier and Emerson, be banished from the courts, because their authors cannot be produced to swear to the correctness of their own writings. According to the rule in *Collier v. Simpson*, the contents of such works may be elicited from professional witnesses, but is it not far better for judges and jurors to use their own eyes, than to rely upon some ignorant practitioner to explain what, perhaps, they understand quite as well themselves?

Trial of Dr. Valorus P. Coolidge

We have examined some points in this case, because it has attracted more than the usual interest which attaches to all capital trials, and because a remarkable degree of professional skill was exhibited in conducting it. Besides, at such times, the practical operation of the law, especially of the rules of evidence, is more fully impressed upon all, and we desired to call attention to some of the most striking instances of it.

The Piscataquis Observer

Another note about the trial, excerpted from the Piscataquis Observer, April 20, 1848. They have several column inches about Coolidge and his background, and end with a paragraph which, I think, is intended to point out a moralistic lesson from the case, but in fact – or in addition – points out one of the most interesting features of the trial – that in spite of all the inuendo and cliched speculations that appeared *after* the trial, there was not one person who could be found to testify, under oath, during the trial, anything against Coolidge's character.

It is said by residents of Waterville, that in addition to the expenses of costly clothing, elegant furniture[1], fine horses, carriages, &c., he had latterly contracted the habit of playing for considerable sums, and not being very expert at games of skill, was generally a loser. Of course, what with his expensive habits of living and occasional indulgences in gaming, his two thousand a year was quite insufficient for his uses, yet he was considered an honest, upright person, and not a man could be found who would testify on the stand in opposition to his invariably good character up to the time of the murder of Mathews.

The Cold Water Fountain and Gardiner News-Letter

This article, published in the April 14, 1848 issue, describes the general concerns about the opportunities for jury tampering, and gives a supposed instance of it. They seem to be suggesting corruption in the handling of the jury. From the language of the article, it appears to be commonly thought there were three jurors who held out against acquittal.

TRIAL OF COOLIDGE · A CIRCUMSTANCE

---

[1] What furniture? He lived in a room in Williams's hotel.

We have already remarked, that considerable excitement was produced by the fact, that the jury men returned for the trial were drawn so long in advance, the supposed reason for which was to afford opportunity for the defendant's counsel to tamper with them before the trial, &c. Under such circumstances, it would be very natural for a look out to be continued, and notice and remark upon whatever bearing upon the case occurred. Among the many known to have *particularly* interested themselves to promote the discharge of the accused, one *distinguished* personage is known to have been very active. · Mr. Ephraim Foss, of Leeds, who was, not long since, himself, tried for the murder of a female, under very revolting circumstances[2], is reported, not only to have been repeatedly seen conversing with one gentleman of his own town, who actually sat upon the jury, but he is known to have extended his officiousness so far as to have carried said gentleman to Augusta to attend the trial, both in January and March! After this man had been subjected to the moral lectures of *such* a man as Foss, it is not very surprising that the Dr.'s counsel concluded that he *must* be one of the jury, so far as they could determine. It has since been credibly reported that this very juror was one of the three who delayed a verdict of conviction. When men whose former acquittal on a charge of murder fails to wipe from them suspicions of foul play, are even allowed to thus proceed regarding a jury in such a case as that of the Waterville murder, is it to be wondered at that honest, high-minded people complain that the return of venira[3] in a manner so suspicious is a high handed outrage. It is well worthy of the consideration of the people, whether such laws ought not be immediately passed, as will hereafter prevent a similar occurrence.

---

[2] I can find no reference to any trial of an Ephraim Foss. There was an Ephraim W. Foss, of Leeds, born Sept 6, 1791, died Aug 15, 1877. One of the jurors, Harrison Gould, was from Leeds.

[3] A panel of prospective jurors.

The Gospel Banner and Transfer to the State Prison

After the trial, Dr. Coolidge was held in Augusta a few days before being sent to Thomaston. He received various visitors, among then the publisher of a religious newspaper, the *Gospel Banner*. We reprint a portion copied by the Cold Water Fountain (Gardiner, Maine) April 14, 1848. The entire piece, under the title 'A Prison Scene', was reported by the Eastern Mail to take up six newspaper columns. We have only found extracts quoted in other newspapers.

DR. COOLIDGE. In the Gospel Banner of last week we find a lengthy article, describing the situation of Dr. Coolidge and the state of mind exhibited by him after receiving his sentence, and during his temporary confinement in the Jail at Augusta. We make the following extract: —
* * * We approached his bedside, and, with words of mournful salutation, paced our hand upon his brow, and gently stroked his glossy hair aside. At so simple a token of sympathy, he burst into tears - the *thought* of friendship, in a condition so forlorn, greatly affecting him; and he exclaimed - Oh! Mr. Drew, what *shall* I do, - what *have* I to live for now? and with these and other words of grief, he gave way to his feelings. We thought it was a pity that a young man, of talents and attainments so far, of prospects so good, should thus, in the very beauty of early manhood, be brought to such a fate. He spoke of his venerated father, whose death he feared would be hastened by *his* misfortunes; of his sainted mother, now in heaven; of his affectionate sister - his only one - in a distant State; of his two brothers, and of his other relatives, — all, we know, of the highest respectability, because of the best characters; and as he spoke of them, he wept aloud. He should see and enjoy them no more, in consequence of a fate infinitely worse than death. We inquired respecting his early education, literary and religious. He said that his opportunities were not great. His education was such as the free school system in our state enabled him to obtain; he had taught school some; had pursued his literary studies with his uncle, with whom he also studied the medical profession. His religious culture in youth, he said, was slight; he had heard preachers of different denominations preach, but never attended a meeting regularly, and never belong to a religious society. We marveled some at this, because we knew he *had* such opportunities in Waterville. He said that for the last year he had attended meeting but twice, both times

at the Baptist church; but his reason for not attending oftener was, that, as a physician, his business would not allow him. We inquired for his religious opinions. He replied, that he believed in a day of judgement in eternity, when men would be rewarded or punished according to the deeds done in the body; he never professed religion, other than to do as he would be done by. He wanted to make friends of all · his business required this; and therefore he chose not to attach himself to any particular sect, lest he should offend some; but respected all according as they lived up to the Golden Rule.

With regard to his moral notions (on which we pressed him with some solicitude,) he remarked, that it was unfortunate for him that, entering the world young and inexperienced, and knowing little of the temptations of life, he first established himself in business where he did; for there the moral atmosphere was bad, and he fell into certain companionships which were willing to take advantage of his confidence and of his necessities: had he commenced business in some other place, surrounded by different influence, he thought he never should have been where he now was. 'There are cases behind a poor fellow,' said he, 'which are really as blameworthy as is he who is made the victim of them.' He denied, however, that he had been an habitual gambler or drinker; nor did he confess that he had been guilty of the crime for which he was sentenced. He seemed to admit that he *knew* how it occurred, but gave us to understand that there was a mystery about it of which the public yet know nothing. We advised him to disclose the whole truth · to tell all he knew · assuring him that he was going to the State prison, probably for life, and the *only* and the *best* companion he would have there would be a *clear conscience*. He had better make a clean breast of the whole matter; and if he had sinned, confess it frankly before God and man; which confession would be evidence of repentance · of a repentance *always* necessary to forgiveness and pardon. he thought our terms were one-sided; he said we did not ask him so much to confess the truth as to confess that he was the murderer, and the sole murderer, of Mathews: if he did not do this, he would not be believed; and if it was necessary to tell a story prepared for him, in order to be believed, he chose not to say anything. He wanted to criminate nobody; and this was a further reason for keeping his own counsels. He did, however, tell *us* what he said he knew: · he told us how Mathews came to his death · accounted for the body being found in the cellar, and for various other facts that appeared on trial · such as the brandy and acid in the stomach, &c., but we were satisfied that *that* story was not all true and, as we did not believe it in his presence, we shall not relate it in his absence. We believe he knows more than he told us, and that some time, perhaps before long, we shall know it all.

Before we left the cell, Hon. George Evans, of Gardiner, his legal counsellor, who so ably defended him on trial, came in to see the prisoner. It was an affecting meeting. It was the first time they had met since the trial. We stood at the head of the bed as Mr. Evans approached the doctor: with an earnest grasp, he seized him by the hand. · may, by his whole arm, · and bending over his prostrate and weeping client, pressed his fevered cheek with a kiss, and we thought we saw a generous tear drop from his lustrous eye upon the aching brow before him. The embrace was as honorable to Mr. Evan's generous sympathies, as it was creditable to his fidelity as a lawyer. We spake not. The silence and weeping of the parties were the eloquent language of soul with soul. We chose to leave them to a private interview, which they had for some time: after which we had a free conversation with Mr. Evans in relation to the prisoner. Mr. E. has been, and will be, faithful to that client. It was the first *capital* case in which he was ever engaged, and he felt the weight of its vast responsibilities. His whole management of the case from first to last exhibited great skill and industry, and his argument before the jury was one of the ablest defensive efforts ever made in this country. Mr. Evans has talents of the highest order, that every day qualify him for the highest office in the Nation, which (unless prevented by one thing) we shall not be surprised yet to see him occupy.

Howard, the contributor to the Republican Journal (see the section "Views of the Trial") wrote:

In all this tragical scene, there is nothing which has appeared to us more out of place than the treatment which Dr. Coolidge received from the Rev. Wm. A. Drew.

From Thomaston State Prison itself, Coolidge wrote a long refutation of this account, citing several witnesses to the conversation not mentioned by Drew, and denying much of it We include it here as it was copied by the *Eastern Mail* · a strongly anti-Coolidge paper.

Coolidge's Letter in Response to the Gospel Banner

From the *Eastern Mail* April 27, 1848

LETTER FROM DR. COOLIDGE

We have received the following letter, postmarked Thomaston, April 19, which we are urgently requested by Dr. Coolidge to publish. We hesitated about giving place in our columns to any such controversy as the publication might lead to, believing that most of our readers have read as much as they desire to see. But on the whole we conclude to publish it, not from a conviction that he has suffered any injustice at the hands of our neighbor of the Banner, but that the public may see what sort of a letter he wishes to send forth to the world, for he requests other papers to copy it [Ken. Journal]

"A Prison Scene"

Yes, a Prison Scene, and to that scene has been pictured to you by my friend Rev. W. A. Drew, in his paper bearing date of the 8th inst. in colors of a deep and aggravated hue, and I have no doubt with the intent, as he says, "to excite a horror for crime through the terrible consequences to which it leads, and thus be instrumental of promoting the cause of virtue amongst men." It is with deep regret that I deem it a duty which I owe to myself, to the public, and to God, that I attempt to make some corrections in his statements.

At the time of my trial the excitement was intense, the very air we breathed was impregnated with all kinds of stories that could fall from the lips of men, and it is not to be expected that one can account from whence all came. Having no doubt that he heard such statements as he published, but not from my lips, and believing that he made them from feelings of friendship towards me, and from pure and honest motives · believing such to have been his sentiments, it is with a great deal of satisfaction that I seat myself to write this article with the same feelings towards him · trusting and believing that he will receive it as such, and as coming from one whose mind is as calm and unruffled as the gentle breeze that fans itself o'er the bosom of a peaceful lake.

During the time of my trial, my system was excited far, far above the natural standard, and when my trial was over, and my fate sealed, so great and powerful was the change that it produced sickness. Friday night I was taken with vomiting, and that vomiting continued more or less frequent until the Monday night following, notwithstanding all that my skillful physician, Dr. Hill, could do. I was visited by my friend, Rev. Mr. Drew, on Saturday, the 25th ult.; my physician, and L.D. Moor, Esq. were present. The first things that meets my eye, that I will notice, though it is of but little importance. It is in relation to my early education. I have no recollection of anything being said in regard to my teaching school, or in relation to my early education, literary or religious. All that there was said in relation to religion was the following. Rev. Mr. Drew says, "I see by your remarks in the Court House yesterday, that you believe in future punishment." I said in answer that I believed we should be punished or rewarded according to the deeds done in the body. The above was all that was said; and it may be well for me to remark that the Rev., Mr. Drew visited me last Fall, sometime in the month of November I think. It was on Saturday, and he then made the inquiry what meetings I had attended and who I had heard preach. I answered that I had usually attended the

Universal meetings, and had heard Mr. Case and Mr. Quimby, when they formerly preached in Livermore, Mr. Bates of Turner, Mr. Thomas of Buckfield, and when I went to Waterville, being a stranger, I attended meeting at the Baptist Church, with my predecessor, (Dr. J. F. Potter,) and after he left me I attended Mr. Gardiner's meetings, but for the last year I had not attended but two half days, and assigned my reason, which was that my professional business would not allow me to. To refresh his memory, I will say that I spoke of Mr. Gardiner in terms of the highest praise, and he agreed with me, and said that Mr. G. was to preach in town to-morrow. I say I believe in a date of judgement in eternity; that belief I have formed since my misfortune, by a careful study of the bible. That belief causes me to cherish, to sweetly cherish, *truth*. My friends belief, I believe, causes him to do the same; and I believe him to be one of *the* noblest fountains of truth.

I positively deny being interrogated in regard to my moral notions. I deny of anything being said about my being a gambler or accustomed to drinking. All that there was said in regard to gambling or drinking was connected with the deceased (Edward Mathews,) and which appeared in the testimony at the time of my trial.

I do not positively deny of saying anything in relation to causes behind me, or anything as being blameworthy, or anything that could possibly be construed in the language that my friend as wrote it, or into any language that could possibly bear the least similarity. I might have said that if I had not gone to Waterville I should not have been where I then was; if I did say so, I said so not from any particular cause or causes, except the one cause that I *did* settle in Waterville. All that was said in relation to the moral atmosphere in Waterville was said on Tuesday morning, the day I left Augusta. I was sitting by the stove, and Rev. Mr. Drew and Dr. Hill was also sitting there, and Mr. Drew says,'it is a pity that you did not settle in some quiet village, where the moral atmosphere was purer than in Waterville. · It would have been much better for you.' I said in answer that the standard of morality in Waterville was far below what it should be, and that there were some persons there than was perhaps more demoralizing than could be found in other villages of that size. I will say that the *general* standard of morality is as good in Waterville as in other villages of that size.

The greater part of this conversation was in regard to my revealing what he supposed I knew in regard to the murder. I had told Dr. Hill and Mr. Moor something in relation to it, and feeling not able to tell it, I asked Dr. Hill to relate it to Mr. Drew. I think he commenced, and as I was taken vomiting he stopped, and about the time I got through, the Hon. George Evans came in, my legal counsellor · one who, in so eloquent and able manner defended me at the time of my trial, one who done all for me that as in the power of man to do, one in whom I am so abundantly satisfied with, yea, there is not even the least glimmer of dissatisfaction, and thank God that I am permitted to make known to the public that degree of *satisfaction*. The same unbounded satisfaction am I happy to express in regard to my junior counsel.

But to return; being more dearly attached to Mr. Evans than to any other person on earth except my aged father, brothers and dear sister, I requested to be left along with him, which request was kindly granted.

No one called upon me Sunday except my physician and Mr. Moor, the jailor. I will say in this connection, and, too, with feelings of friendship and of gratitude to L.D. Moor, Esq. that no language can express, both in sickness and in health he done all that was in his power, consistent with his duty as a jailor, to render me comfortable and happy; every wish of mine was gratified, that the law would allow of, and, too, with a kindness that will be long cherished in my memory. I trust to *God* that my friends will remember him in all coming time. Monday, Rev. Mr. Drew visited me again in company with Dr. Hill and Mr. Moore. The most of the conversation at this time was in the form of advice for me to reveal what I knew. Mr. Drew began to make further inquiry in regard to their story alluded to, but as I was disposed to believe it to be fabricated, and had requested Dr. Hill and Mr. Moor to let it sleep in silence, and as no one responded to his enquiry, it there ended. · There is but one thing more that I will allude to, and not to that in the form of a correction, · I have reference to his saying that I am guilty. If that is his opinion, why not let it slumber in silence, and not publish it to the world so as to wound more mortally those that are so near and dearly related to me? Because my trial is over, and all, all, far and near, have had by the publication of it a fair opportunity to form their own individual opinions. I should not allude to this were it not for the sympathy that I have for my friends. My heart can still feel. So far as I am concerned it matters but little; for I am, as it were, not of this world, a this comes as from one in his *grave*.

I will say that I received no love ditties, nor any other ditties at the time of my trial, and if my friend has done the ladies injustice, he really is to be pitied.

I send this to the editor of the Kennebec Journal, leaving my friend, through the columns of his own paper, to substantiate what he has wrote, provided he can do it by the testimony of Dr. Hiram H. Hill and Lewis D. Moor, Esq. who was there during all the time, and heard all that was said.

If they substantiate him, the, with my arms and eyes raised to *Heaven*, will I humbly ask his forgiveness. Then I shall be compelled to believe that a shade of insanity had showered itself over the surface of my brain.

Trial of Dr. Valorus P. Coolidge

It is with deep and solemn regret that I send this for publication, because it places my friend a minister of the Gospel, in a situation that is not becoming. But alas! his own good sense will soon spread a picture before the public eye in its true color. Very respectfully,

Your obed't servant

V. P. Coolidge

Thomaston, April 19th, 1848

We are as willing as the Journal that Dr. Coolidge would be heard in self defense, especially when his communications tend to quiet the alarm existing in certain sections for the morals of Waterville. As this matter, however, seems to be in a way for adjustment by the discussion between the Doctor and the Banner, we shall await the issue with commendable patience; confident that the Doctor's appear to witnesses will bring out the whole truth in the next Banner. When it comes our readers shall have it.

Eastern Mail May 4th 1848

Coolidge continued to general a lot of column space. Following a long article basically favoring capital punishment for "one who murders sentiment and the Queen's English with quite as much *sang froid* as he has his fellowman", the paper follows up on the controversy between the Rev. Drew and Coolidge. The Banner had printed a notice in their column that they were not going to enter into a controversy on veracity with a convicted murderer, and that what they had said was true · just that it had been improved upon for the reader.

MORALS OF WATERVILLE

We made an oversight when we promised our readers that they should know what reply the Banner made to Dr. Coolidge. But this is only the Banner's fault, as it is also his bad luck; for how could we suppose he would impose a task involving us in such an act of cruelty? So we offer him the only apology we can · our readers have our word, and we inflict the injury because our veracity must not be put where he suffers his to remain.

The Journal's New Correspondent.· Our neighbor, the Kennebec Journal, has a new correspondent, and from a new place: it is no less a personage than the famous, or rather infamous Dr. Coolidge, writing to that paper from the State Prison in Thomaston. We notice, too, that he corresponds for other papers · for the Thomason Recorder, the Prisoner's Friend, in Boston, as well as for the Kennebec Journal. Is he under pay for these services? We doubt very much the policy of allowing convicts to appear in the newspapers, to create a public sympathy in their behalf and thus defeat the ends of justice. He sent us a letter the first week after he reached his cell: we suppose he expected us to publish it - but we did not think we should be in the way of our duty to do so. Perhaps this disappointed him for his last, long letter to the Journal is a sort of review of our "Prison Scene," in which he would like to be understood as contradicting us in many points therein stated, but each of which he virtually admits to be true, before he gets through. We wrote that article, not indeed in the form in which our conversation with him took place, for that was dialogistic; but in a form that would be more descriptive; and what we said was true We can have no controversy on a point of veracity with a convicted murderer. The Journal's apprehensions, therefore, that the publication of Coolidge's letter might lead to a controversy, are groundless. - The Doctor had better keep to his cell at present and not set up as editor-general for half the newspapers of New England.

Was it before or since the Banner compelled the Doctor to be the subject of six columns of "dialogistic" details - in which an effort is made to transfer his guilt from where "the ends of justice" have placed it, to the bad moral atmosphere of Waterville, and the associates he there betrayed - that he began to "doubt the policy of allowing convicts to appear in the newspapers?" Does justice claim anything in this case for the prisoner, as well as for the injured public? - or shall he rest under the imputation of falsehood, when "in the mouth of two or three witnesses," whose names he offers, the question could be settled? There are those in Waterville who would be glad to know whether the malicious and ungentlemanly thrusts at the morals of our village were made by an imported malefactor, or by him who judged them of sufficient importance to be thrown before the public. Is it less dignified to "hold controversy" with a convicted murder, than to be made the medium of retailing his scandal? We should judge not; and if nothing more is due to the slandered, they should at least be allowed to inquire "whence came the ungrateful blow." This question is not answered till the Doctor's self-imposed sanity is credited. When the public shall do this, the veracity of the Banner and the morals of Waterville may be acquitted together. Till then, let them both suffer together.

Coolidge's transfer to Thomaston also generated controversy, specifically charges of cruelty from sending Coolidge, very ill at the time, in an open carriage for a trip that took an entire day.

The prison officer in charge to transmitting Coolidge, Alexander Young, took offense at this, and Coolidge wrote another long letter, partially in defense of Young, in florid mid-nineteenth century prose.

Lewiston Falls Journal Apr 28, 1848
A week or two since we condemned the removal of Dr. Coolidge from Augusta to Thomaston on an inclement day while suffering from disease, and charged the officer of the prisoner with cruelty for removing him then. Our remarks have called forth an exceedingly coarse, abusive and passionate communication from the officer, Alex. Young, published in the Thomaston Recorder[1].

If we said anything in that article condemning the treatment of the prisoner by Mr. Young during the journey, we willingly correct it, for we are satisfied he was kindly treated by that officer after leaving the jail. But we did say that his removal, under the circumstance, against the advice of his physician, was cruelty worthy of a barbarous age and a disgrace to the State. We say so still. Let the responsibility rest where it belongs.

The character of Mr. Young's communication precludes its publication in our columns, but we are now convinced that his *orders for removal were positive*, and our imputation of cowardice, and of cruelty so far as Mr. Young is concerned was not deserved. A narrative of the circumstances of his removal as related by Dr. Coolidge appears in the Thomaston Recorder, elicited from him by Mr. Young and which, while it reflects credit upon that officer for his kindness as an individual, confirms our charge of cruelty upon the *authority*, whether it came from the Court or the Prison, by which he was removed at that time. — *Hallowell Cultivator*

[From the Thomaston Recorder]

STATEMENT OF DR. COOLIDGE

Sir: · By the request of Mr. Young, I will here give a statement of his treatment towards me a week ago to-day on my journey from Augusta to this place. I make this statement not merely by request of Mr. Young, but because I deem it a duty which I own to myself, to Mr. Young and to the public · and taking that view of it, it may be well to state all the circumstances connected with it.

Saturday morning, the 25th of march, *I was unable to rise from my bed, having been vomiting all the previous night*, that vomiting continued more or less frequent until the Monday following · *during that time I took nothing into my stomach, except gruel and some medicine directed by Dr. Hill.*

---

[1] All sources indicate that the Thomaston Recorder ceased publication in 1846.

The Gospel Banner and Transfer to the State Prison

Monday evening I was informed by Mr. Moore that I should have to leave for Thomaston on the next morning at an early hour. Dr. Hill was present, and I said that I did not feel as though I could ride there, and asked Dr. Hill if he thought it would be prudent; and *he said it would not unless it was a very pleasant day.* I then requested him to say the same to the man who came after me · he said he had so stated to him, but he and Mr. Moore would go and see him again and come and let me know the result. They went and returned saying that all they could do was to get him to say that he would lay over one day, provided it rained in the morning. That night was one of anxiety · in the morning I was able to rise from bed, though feeling extremely week · took for my breakfast a little sponge cake and custard sent to me the day before by the kindness of Mrs. Nichols. At about 9 o'clock A. M. I was informed by Mr. Moore that I should have to go. Rev. Mr. Drew and Dr. Hill was present, Mr. Moore then made all necessary arrangement, for my comfort, and it is due me to say that during my confinement there he treated me with the kindest feelings that can ever flow from a human bosom · every wish of mine was gratified that was consistent with his duty, his name will long be remembered in my heaving bosom and I trust to *God* it will be in the hands of my friends. After getting ready, I was then chained by Mr. Young, (that being his duty,) stepped into the carriage, and bid farewell to Rev. Mr. Drew, Dr. Hill, and others who were standing by, and lastly and most heart rending did I bid farewell to Mr. Moore. We then started, having a span of horses, good carriage, buffaloes and umbrella. The weather was somewhat unpleasant, though not cold nor neither did it rain at that time, but misty. Having the buffalo robes wrapped around me well, and the umbrella spread when necessary, I rode very comfortably to the town of Jefferson. We then stopped at Mrs. Weeks' hotel about two hours. Mr. Young then took of the chains that were on my wrists · went into the parlor before a good fire, and in the course of an hour we were called to dinner · went into the dining room with a number of others, and was seated before a table that was decorated with everything that a human heart could ask for.

Though my journey to my last abiding on earth, yes, to that place where I was going to bid farewell to earth, and bury the last ties as it were to humanity in a solitary cell. Oh how solemn was the scene, one in the bloom of life, and stored with knowledge sufficient to render himself useful to his fellow creatures should be on his journey to that place to experience as it were, *death in life.* But alas! it was so, and believing it to be a *Dispensation of Providence*, I sat and partook of the bounty sat before me as my last social meal on *earth*. After getting well rested, we then started, and it this time, and all afternoon, if rained hard, but my friend, Mr. Young, took all means in his power to keep the raging storm from me and to exposing himself. I rode quite comfortably all the way, though I got exceedingly fatigue before we reached Thomaston, which was 5 P.M.

It is due me to say that Mr. Young treated me with all the sympathy and with all the kindness that was in his power - such sympathy and kindness as can only spring from a noble and generous heart; his conversation was of such a character as tended directly to remove the gulf of distress and sorrow that my heart was beating in. Not only that day did he treat me as a kind and affectionate brother, but since my stay here he has visited me with the same affectionate feelings, and made me presents which has contributed to my comfort and *happiness*.

If this short sketch, made here in this lonely cell will be of any service to you for a publication to the world, it is at your command.

Very respectfully,
Your Obt. Servt.
(Signed) V. P. Coolidge

Mr. Young.

Commutation

In 1848, the sentence for first degree murder was death by hanging after one year in solitary confinement at Thomaston.

The Prisoner's Friend, a prison reform publication printed a brief description of Coolidge's situation. (They had also published a letter from him, and noted that some ladies had subscribed to the journal on his behalf.)

> The *Prisoner's Friend* Vol 1 No. 3, Nov, 1848.
> Dr. V. P. Coolidge · This unhappy man is now confined in a cell of which the ground dimensions do not exceed eight feet by four. A part of this narrow room is occupied by his bed. The cell has no window, the light and air being admitted through an aperture in the door. His friends say he cannot survive the winter. Gov. Dana called the attention of the Legislature to the case last summer, and requested that body to say whether they wished to have the convict executed or not at the end of the year. The Warden of the prison also requested that some enlargement or change of treatment might be ordered; but the legislature declined to take action in the matter. A brother of Coolidge has lately been from Ohio to see him. A sister, whose home is in Mississippi, is now in Maine, and will there spend the winter. · *Maine Paper.*
> The Maine legislature *did* act on this case, and he is *probably* now enjoying all the room and comforts which any judicious friend of humanity could desire. · *Age.*

The journal printed a substantial portion of the Governor's communication, which provides an excellent summary of the legal situation,

> To the Honorable Council.
> Valorus P. Coolidge was in March, 1848, convicted of a capital offense, and the time (one year from the date of sentence,) within which the statute prohibits an execution, has nearly expired. In view of its expiration, I have endeavored, with all the care which would characterize an investigation and conclusion on which the life of a fellow creature is suspended, to give a just construction to the laws under which he was convicted and sentenced, that I might rightly determine what duty devolves upon the executive in the premises.
> The law under which he was sentenced is the law of the Revised Statutes, with a slight, but (so far as it bears upon the question,) immaterial amendment. This law is nearly a transcript of the law

passed in A. D. 1837. For some years previous to the passage of the law if 1837, a very general effort was made for the abolition of capital punishment, by arguments presented and appeals made through the press, by the presentation of petitions and by discussions in the legislature. The agitation finally resulted in the law of 1837, which was claimed as having accomplished the object, by making the issuing of a warrant for an execution, a mere discretionary act, instead of imperative, as under former laws. After the passage of this law the efforts of the advocates of the abolition of capital punishment ceased, and the public mind, with but slight indications of dissent, concurred in their construction · that the duty was no longer imperative on the executive to order an execution; and in their opinion, (though with less unanimity,) that the discretionary power should never be exercised. The evidence that such was the state of public opinion cannot have escaped the attention of those who are the least observing of its indications. But if doubts exist on this point, they must be removed by a review of the case of Thorn, the only conviction had since the law of 1837, except the of Coolidge. In 1844, Thorn was convicted of a capital offense, aggravated in its nature and circumstances. When the proper time arrive for inflicting upon him the penalty of death, if at all, the then executive withheld his warrant. I am not advised, whether he adopted the construction that the duty was discretionary, or only refrained to act because copies of the case had not been certified to him; but this question is not material to the present purpose. The fact is one of universal notoriety that the punishment of death has not been inflicted upon Thorn, though convicted of a capital offense, unattended by any extenuating circumstances. Thus the knowledge is brought home to every one that our laws have failed to inflict the penalty of death, and yet not an effort has been made through the legislature or otherwise to ascertain and remove the cause of such as result in this instance, or to prevent its recurrence in future. The conclusion is therefore irresistible, of the general believe and acquiescence that therein, the penalty of death will not again be inflicted. This position was assumed by the Attorney General in the trial of Coolidge and the consideration was urged by him upon the jury, that his conviction would not result in this execution.

The Governor next proceeds to show that, notwithstanding all these circumstances in favor of the idea that he may or may not order an execution, at his discretion, still such an opinion is not warranted by a just construction of the statutes, and then concludes as follows: ·

It follows then that my action on this subject must conflict with the popular construction of the law, with all the indications of public sentiment to which I have alluded, sustaining and acquiescing in that construction, and with the opinion of the government officer urged upon the jury when the conviction of Coolidge was procured, or I must take for my guide the opinions of others, entirely abandoning my own convictions. But the Executive is bound to discharge the duties of the office, "according to the constitution and laws of the State." Not as constructed by others, but by himself. True, he may borrow light from other minds to aid in in forming a conclusion, but his own mind must be the ultimate tribunal.

The one way of escaping this difficulty is by the exercise of the power of commutation. The duty of issuing a warrant for an execution devolves upon the Executive alone, the power of commutation is vested in the Executive, with the advice of council. After the expiration of the year, I shall feel impelled, under the construction which I am forced to give of the law, to issue a warrant for the execution of Coolidge, unless a commutation of his sentence to imprisonment for life, is interposed. For the reasons indicated in this communication, I would readily concur with the council in such commutation, and would invite your consideration of the subject.

Dr Coolidge has since been sent to the State Prison for life. Ed.

I do not myself see, in Attorney General Blake's closing arguments to the jury, any explicit expression that no execution will ever be carried out. There is a vague statement that whatever is done with the sentence will be the will of the people.

In addressing the punishment for murder, he could only say that should a verdict of guilty be returned, the prisoner would await in confinement, his sentence one year, and that execution would then follow or not, something as the public mind should dictate.

The commutation was announced in February, 1849.

The Age (Augusta), February 15, 1849

VALORUS P. COOLIDGE. The Governor, by advice of Council, has commuted the punishment of Coolidge (now in the State Prison at Thomaston under sentence of death for the murder of Edward Mathews,) to "*confinement to hard labor in the State Prison during his natural life.*"

The Case of Thomas Flint

On May 18, 1848 — which was coincidentally the date of Coolidge's death, and the announcement of Coolidge's plot for the murder of Flint - the *Eastern Mail* reprinted, on page one, which usually contained no local matters or even anything that could properly be called news - a long extract from the *Yankee Blade* written by William Mathews, Edward Mathews's brother, the Yankee Blade's editor. From it we find the most explicit statement that (a) Thomas Flint had spent the winter of 1847-1848 at medical school in Philadelphia by virtue of being on bail, funded by his father, (b) Flint was widely suspected of being either the murderer or of being an accomplice to the murder itself, and (c) it had been commonly expected that he would skip bail and not return to Waterville for the trial.

THE CASE OF THOMAS FLINT

We find in the last Yankee Blade, under the above head, an able article from the pen of Wm. Mathews, brother of the murdered Edward Mathews, which is designed to defend Mr. Flint against the suspicion of participation in the murder. We have not room for the article entire, but publish the following, which embraces the entire argument. Though it fully meets our own views, we are aware that a large portion of the public think differently. - As they can have no interest beyond arriving at the truth, and as the writer cannot be suspected of any motive but the protection of an innocent man from the most blaring suspicions, they will examine with interest, and we doubt not with candor, an argument coming from such a source. The article is at least honorable to the writer, whatever may be the effect of this reasoning.

———

We say, we believe him innocent. We will give our reasons. In the first place, it is too monstrous to believe he was accessory before the fact, unless there is the strongest evidence. It is hard enough to believe *one* man so depraved as to plot such a crime, without supposing another also to have the same diabolical disposition. But where is the *proof?* - We have searched all the testimony through and through with the utmost care and scrutiny; and not a single fact have we been able to discover, out of all the circumstances testified to by some sixty or seventy witnesses, that goes, in the slightest degree, to connect Flint with the murder *before its commission.* There is not a particle of evidence to show that he knew, or had any suspicion of, what was to be done on the fatal night. It was Coolidge · and Coolidge only · who took all the preparatory steps in the affair; who inquired when the deceased would return from Brighton, had all the conversation with him, wrote the letter, &c. Would *he* have consented thus to be Flint's "cat's-paw," or tool · to expose himself in various ways to the chance of detection, in case suspicion should point to his office · while Flint was standing back in the dark, directing what was to be done only, and not committing himself in any way? We think not. He was too proud-spirited · if a sufficient blunderhead · for that. It is, certainly, a little singular, if Flint aided in planning the murder, that, after a lapse of six months or more, not one suspicious circumstance has been discovered in his conduct, prior to the crime.

But we are told that Flint, when called in by the Doctor to aid in secreting the body, did not, according to his own testimony, express the slightest horror or surprise · that he gave full credence to Coolidge's strange and improbable story, that Mathews "had fallen dead suddenly, and he had thumped him on the head to make it appear that he had been murdered in the street." All the circumstances, it is said, in the scene that presented itself when he was first locked in by Coolidge, were such as would inevitably have excited in any innocent mind the most violent suspicions of foul plan · yet, if we may credit his own statement, though neither intimidated by threats, nor moreover by entreaties, he made no objections to the Dr.'s request, but went about the removal of the body with as much coolness, nonchalance, and *sang froid*, as if such scenes were of daily occurrence, · His extraordinary calmness and self-possession on the stand, while telling his dreadful tale, are also pointed to as proof of a hard-heartedness sufficient for any crime. In answer to all this, we reply, that it was Flint's business, as a witness in court, to state *facts* only, not to explain his *feelings*. Had he attempted to tell the whole story there as he would tell it in private, he would have been stopped at once. Besides, before appearing on the stand, he was counseled by his wisest friends, to confine himself to the naked facts alone · stating all the circumstances of the affair, from beginning to end, in the clearest and most succinct manner possible. The reason of this is too evident to need comment. It requires too metaphysical a turn of mind, for an extraordinary witness to enter into any exact statement of his feelings on a particular occasion · any one who attempts to do so, however honest or truthful, usually involves himself in much perplexity and confusion, if not contradiction. It was to the facts, therefore ·

what he *saw*, *heard* and *said*, that Flint restricted his testimony; and the fact that he gives no long elaborate account of his emotions on hearing Coolidge's statement about the manner of Mathews's death, is to our mind one of the most convincing proofs of his veracity. · Had he been originally implicated in the murder, would he not naturally have manufactured a good deal of mock pathos for the witness's stand? Would he not have given a long, cut-and-dried, raw-head-and-bloody-bones account of his feelings on the occasion · showing how horror-struck he was on being locked in with the dead body, how he nearly fainted at Coolidge's elevations, and that it was long before he recovered self-possession enough to act? · Would he not have declared that it was only after the most earnest and pressing entreaties, mingled with threats, that he consented, though most reluctantly, to assist? Such, it strikes us, would have been his course. Instead of giving a simple, unvarnished statement of the affair, he would have painted all the incidents in the most glowing colors possible. It is not strictly true, however, that Flint expressed no horror on hearing from Coolidge's lips of Mathews's death. One little circumstance which drops out, evidently without design, in this story · the fact he states explanative of his feeling · speaks volumes for his veracity. He said that, on hearing Coolidge's story, he *"sank down into a rocking-chair, and for a few moments nothing was said on either side."* This little incident, so true to nature, and which could not have been manufactured for the occasion, outweighs in our mind volumes of affected horror or sentimentality. Again, Flint says that on the night after the affair he lodged with Coolidge at his request, and add, *"I guess neither of us slept much that night."* · Such straws as these, let fall accidentally and without premeditation, tell more with us than more highly-wrought, striking statements that are open to the suspicion of having been conned and prepared beforehand.

That no suspicion of murder flashed upon Flint's mind, upon listening to Coolidge's statement, is not very marvelous. Why should he have suspected foul play? He knew not that the deceased had a large sum of money about his person, of which he might have been robbed. He knew of no grudge or ill-feeling cherished by Coolidge again the latter, which might have led to murder. Nor was it possible to conceive of any other motive for such a diabolical deed. On the contrary, all the facts within his knowledge negatived such a theory. The deceased and Coolidge were friends · or, at least, companions to some extent · on the best of terms. The latter had shown no inhumanity in his practice, but bore a good

214

character, and was generally esteemed. What reason, then, could his student, who had always placed implicit confidence in him · who, during two long years, had been conceiving a stronger and stronger attachment for him · have for changing, in the most abrupt and violent manner, his opinion of the Doctor's character, and charging him suddenly with the foulest and most atrocious of crimes · that of *murder*? It is strange, that, if he did harbor a fleeting suspicion of something wrong, that he at once rejected it as too monstrous for belief · that he believed, as the doctor had said that Mathews died in a fit, and, through excessive fear, the former was led into the ill-judged measures he had described? Recollect if it was weeks before Coolidge's other friends could believe him guilty, though having double the evidence that Flint *then* had. The story of Coolidge was not so outrageously improbable as some have supposed. Innocent men have done things equally as foolish to screen themselves from an apprehended charge of crime. But it is unnecessary for Flint's innocence, to imagine that he fully credited Coolidge's statement. He nowhere says that he did. It is enough to suppose that, in the excitement and astonishment of the moment, he was utterly at a loss what *to* conjecture about the matter, but believed, at all events, Coolidge to be innocent, till on Friday night he was told of the hidden money, when he had gone so far in the latter's service that he dared not divulge the truth.

We see no force, therefore, in the remark that Flint was, apparently, a willing tool · lending himself at once to Coolidge's purposes, as if he did no violence to his senses right, nothing repugnant to his feelings. We believe he had no suspicion of foul play, or, at all events, that if he did, it was at once scouted from his breast: and we believe, too, that he *was* nevertheless greatly shocked at the scene he beheld, though he was not permitted to tell just how he felt, on the stand.

But, it is asked, why did the doctor call in the aid of Flint, unless the latter had *previous knowledge* of the crime that was to be perpetrated? Does not this argue the grossest folly in Coolidge · a degree if imprudence wholly incredible? Would he have dared to call in such a witness · to run such a risk of exposure · unless that witness were already in the secret? In answer to this, we say, that none but egregious fools ever commit murder, under any circumstances; and it is only the wildest calculation of changes that induces the plotter of such a deed to believe he can long escape detection. Nothing less than the possession, for the time being, of omniscience and omnipotence, would justify a man in flattering himself with such an idea. "Murder", says Shakespeare, "though it have no tongue, will speak with most miraculous organ." There is not a truth in the universe that may not furnish a clue to the "secret'st man of blood;" that is not at war with, and mocks at, every false theory he would have set up. That one, therefore, who is so lacking in brains, or, at least, in common sense, as to premeditate murder at all, should commit the grossest blunders in its execution, is what we should expect, as the merest matter of course. Doubtless Coolidge, in pre- planning the disposition of his victim's body, concluded finally to be governed by circumstances, such as the darkness of the night, the probability of meeting people in his way to the river, and so forth. That he *did* try to get rid of the body without assistance, is quite certain; for, just before calling in Flint, he was met by James Hill on Water street - doubtless exploring the way to see if it were safe to lug the body to the river. It was that encounter, probably, that deterred him from pursuing this scheme. It is true there is some little discrepancy in the testimony about the time when this must have occurred; but every one knows that it is impossible, in the nature of things, for such testimony to be very precise or exact. - Great latitude is always expected from witnesses, about time, and no arguments can be based upon slight disagreements. But suppose Coolidge had made no such attempt as supposed - was it marvelously strange that he should seek the aid and counsel of Flint, even at the expense of divulging his secret? We see nothing so unnatural in this. The whole history of crime shows that when once the murderer has perpetrated his horrid deed, he is a changed being - he is another man. He is no longer swayed by the same impulses - new feelings and emotions take possession of his bosom - he loses, in a degree the control of himself and his actions. In the ardor of pursuit, blinded to truth by avarice or revenge, he sees all things in a false coloring; but no sooner is his horrible purpose accomplished, than a new light bursts upon the horror-stricken man, and all things wear a different aspect from before. A myriad of eyes seem staring at him in every direction - even inanimate objects seem to have a tongue to speak - and his nerves, which were braced so easily to do the fearful deed, suddenly become weaker than a child's. Is such a man in a situation to drag away a long distance the dead body of his victim? - a body which under the most favorable circumstances, he could hardly carry at all? Or is it strange that, in his terror and perplexity, he should seek for sympathy, counsel, and support? We think not. It is precisely what we should expect. At all events, if this *was* a piece of stupid blundering on the part of Coolidge, that affords no argument against the theory · for he evinced a more egregious folly in other matters. After reading his absurd story before the coroner's jury, to say nothing of numberless other false steps he took, it requires no great stretch of the imagination to suppose him guilty of any imprudence. But it will be said, that Coolidge's calling on Flint, trusting that he would not divulge, was at least no compliment to the latter's honesty or strength of intellect. This would all be true enough, were the scene to which Flint was introduced, proof positive, in itself alone, of murder. But as such, all the circumstances being considered, was not the case, the fact in question casts no suspicion on Flint's character, but was, in reality, a compliment to the strength, sincerity, and devotedness of his friendship, which would suspect no ill of the Doctor, much less deem him guilty of the most atrocious of crimes, without overwhelming proof.

In conclusion, we have a few questions to ask of those who believe Flint to have been originally implicated in the murder · to which we wish for a distinct answer. First · Why is it that Flint, in all his accounts of the affair, has never once pretended that Coolidge every *confessed* to him that he was the murderer? If he were fabricating a long tissue of falsehoods to screen himself would not this plan have suggested itself at once? Would it not have added much to the apparent plausibility of his story? Yet this confession, which, at first blush, one would have expected Coolidge to make as a matter of course, Flint admits was never made to him; and thus the guilt of the former is left to be wholly *deduced* and *inferred*. Next · How happens it that during three hours of the closest and most searching cross-examination, after Flint had made already a long, minute, and circumstantial statement of two hours in length, Messrs. Evans and Noyes were unable to draw out any material statement, where in they could contradict him by his own testimony or that of other witnesses? Thirdly · is it not remarkable, if he has sworn to a long catalogue of lies, that his story before the Grand Jury, and as written out shortly after on paper at the request of the Attorney General · a document which he has never since seen · should chord in in every particular with that told at the trial? Fourthly · If Flint was guilty, equally with Coolidge, is it not singular that he dared return to the trial? What assurance had he of safety, if he came back from Philadelphia? Might not *new* facts, affording the most damning proof of his guilt, have been discovered and kept secret during his long absence of 5 months or more · ready to be drawn out in terrible array against him, on his return? Had he no fears of convicting himself by his answers on cross-examination? Hundreds predicted last fall that he would never appear as a witness against Coolidge - that he would let his father, who was abundantly able, pay his bail, and strike for the South, or some foreign country. On the supposition of this guilt, as an original accomplice in the murder it is a marvel that he did not.

In 1848 Flint was not awarded a medical degree by Jefferson College due to his involvement with the case. But by 1849 any clouds hanging over his legal situation seem to have been dispersed. He was awarded his medical degree with the class of 1849, and the *Eastern Mail,* took notice.

Eastern Mail April 12, 1849
Jefferson Med College. – We have received a copy of Prof. Huston's Charge to the Graduates of this institution, at the late Commencement 19th ult. The pamphlet also contains a list of the graduates, 188 in number. We are gratified to notice among them the name of Thomas Flint. Dr. Flint was entitled to his diploma at the previous anniversary, but in consequence of his connection with the Coolidge affair, the honor was deferred for further consideration. In conferring it now, we must understand the authorities of the College to say, that they discover nothing in Dr. Flint's connection with that affair which should exclude him from the confidence of the public, as a physician or a citizen. We believe the sentiments of this community will sustain the College in this opinion.

Death and the Plot Against Flint

On May 24th, 1849, the Lime Rock Gazette, of East Thomaston, announced both that Coolidge had died, and that a plot had been discovered whereby Coolidge was intending to arrange the murder of Thomas Flint, to be masked as suicide, and frame Flint for the murder of Edward Mathews, by placing a letter of confession next to Flint's body. The suddenness of this; the simultaneity of the discovery of the plot and Coolidge's death; and the vagueness of the supposed cause of death, all no doubt contributed to the subsequent skepticism about Coolidge's death.

The story was widely printed throughout the United States - most accounts follow the Lime Rock Gazette account verbatim - 'The Only Full and Authentic Account Published'; the best-printed account I have seen was printed June 21, 1849, in Burlington, Iowa, by the Burlington Hawk-Eye. The Portland Advertiser printed on May 29th an abbreviated that it copied from the Boston Herald.

Coolidge's death was Friday, May 18.

A history of his proceedings and deep-laid plot for the murder of Thomas Flint, with a correct copy of all the documents relating thereto, taken from his own hand-writing.
THE ONLY FULL AND AUTHENTIC ACCOUNT PUBLISHED.

Knowing that great interest is everywhere felt to learn the facts connected with the plot of Coolidge for the murder of Thomas Flint, just brought to light through the vigilance of the officers of the State Prison, - and that many conflicting reports are in circulation relating to it; we have taken much pains to gather all the facts, and lay them before the public in full. In thus laying open one of the darkest and most artful[1] plots that ever held a place in the records of crime, the officers of the Prison have all due regard for the feelings of the friends of the late Dr. Coolidge, but justice to the public seems to demand its publication.

We are indebted to Mr. Carr, the Warden, for the particulars in regard to obtaining the writings, and for copies of the same. We are also under obligations to Dr. Rose, the physician of the Prison, and

---

[1] Artful?

Dr. Buxton, one of the inspectors, for other important facts in relation to the affair.

After the commutation of the sentence of Coolidge, it is generally known that he was allowed the liberty of the yard, and some light duties put upon him such as sweeping out the Prison, supplying the cells with water, etc. which gave him decided advantages. For many weeks previous to the discovery of the present affair, the Warden had just grounds for suspicion that Coolidge was exerting an injurious influence among the prisoners; and that he was endeavoring to communicate through the wall outside. This put him on the alert, and orders were given to watch Coolidge's movements closely. At this time a young prisoner (whose name is withheld) was confined to his cell by sickness, and as Coolidge was passing and re-passing, a fine opportunity was afforded for conversing with him from time to time; when Coolidge, being convinced he could make a confidant of the sick man, revealed to him his whole plot, and the name of the person whom he intended to employ to consummate it; the person was a prisoner whose term of confinement expires in a few months, but as there is no available evidence against him as yet, his name is not given. So confident was Coolidge of having enlisted the sympathy of the young man on his behalf, that he entrusted to him the papers he had prepared, for the purpose of reading. Upon obtaining possession them he refused to give them back, stating as a reason that he had not finished reading them. Coolidge became impatient, and gave some threats; but the sick man succeeded in retaining the documents until a week ago last Friday, when he handed them over to the officers, whereupon Coolidge was placed at work in the shoe shop, where more vigilant watch could be kept over him.

When it was first intimated to Coolidge that he had been writing certain papers, and holding unlawful correspondence, he stoutly denied it. On Wednesday following he complained of being unwell, and went to his cell. This was probably done, with the hope that his papers were still in the hands of the person with whom he left them, and he might possibly have an opportunity to obtain them back.

At this state of the affair, the Warden consulted with the Inspectors upon the best course to pursue in regard to the writings found; and it was thought most advisable to re-commit Coolidge to close confinement, and make his foul designs public.

The plot being thus revealed to the Warden, he went to Coolidge, together with Dr. Baxter of Warren, and reproached him for the deed, the truth of which, however, Coolidge immediately and strongly denied. The Warden then told him that denial was vain, since his hat was half filled with the proofs of it. Coolidge burst into a passion of tears, and confessed that he was guilt, and expressed sorrow for his crime.

This was on Wednesday the 16th, and on the morning of the Thursday he was removed to a solitary cell, and every precaution taken to isolate him as completely as possible. Thursday evening he sent for Dr. Rose, of Thomaston, physician to the prison, and complained of being unwell, and manifested some slight symptoms of indisposition, vomiting a little &c. He also appeared extremely depressed, and spoke of having lost all the sympathy which had heretofore been entertained for him; expressed a disregard of life, and enquired as to the disposition made of convicts after death. He also very earnestly requested pens and paper, and on being refused, begged for a slate, saying that he might wish to write some poetry, and he would rub it out again. This also was denied him.[2]

The next morning between 7 and 8 o'clock, when breakfast was taken to the prisoners, Coolidge did not answer to his call. The Clerk was immediately called, and upon entering the cell, he was found upon the floor, having apparently rolled from this bed, with his head partly in a bucket; when shaken he exhibited slight signs of life, but soon after expired. A post mortem examination was held on Saturday morning and Dr.'s Rose and Buxton inform us that no signs of poison was discovered in his stomach; his lungs were slightly effected, but not sufficiently to cause death; his brain was perfectly sound and healthy; his heart was very small, weighing only 9 1/4 ounces. It is the general opinion that he "died in a fit, brought on by extreme mental depression, and the general prostration of the whole nervous system, caused by the sudden frustration of his long fostered hope."

The principal papers found we have copied entire. The first is a pretended 'letter of confession,' which was to be copied in Flint's handwriting by the person employed to carry out these designs, and placed about Flint's person where it might be easily discovered after his death. Then follow very minute directions how to proceed to obtain a knowledge of Flint's writing, and perpetrate the murder without exciting suspicion. These directions are, many of them, most ingeniously conceived, and prove him to possess cunning and art, without depth or capacity. It appears that he used all precaution of which he was capable, to avoid even the possibility of detection: for among the papers was one sheet containing the most important names, words and sentence, written out very plainly, intended as a reference or guide for the person who was to copy the letters, &c., that no error might be committed in this respect. But there is, upon the whole, a general shallowness running through the plot which a mind of ordinary capacity would soon detect.

Those papers are written in an uncommonly fine but legible hand, and we should judge him to be very rapid and easy in the use of the pen; but he was sadly deficient in language and orthography,

---

[2] This is an embellishment not present in the Lime Rock Gazette account,

and seemed entirely ignorant of the philosophy of condensation. We introduce the papers without further comment; the reader must do his own moralizing, · the subject is a fruitful one!

Letter of Confession

Dr. Coolidge ever treated me as a dear and only brother; I treated him with all the cruelty of a *pirate*. His treatment to me and mine to him is ever before me, and so great is my misery that I cannot live. I make the following confession and take my life.

I, Thomas Flint, murdered Edward Mathews. Dr. V. P. Coolidge is as innocent as a lamb. I was connected with two Physicians and they are virtually guilty in the murder of Edward Mathews. Dr. Coolidge mistrusted that others were connected with me and asked me the names of a number of physicians; · some of which I told him had nothing to do with it: and it will be in his power alone to free them of the suspicion that must otherwise rest upon them. From what I told him I think he must know which two physicians were connected with me. We made Mathews believe that we had bought out Dr. Coolidge, and he agreed to get us $2000 and bring into Dr. Coolidge's office the night on which he was murdered; where we agreed to meet him. Mathews kept himself concealed during the evening in the Alley-way that leads up to Carter's office. I went to bed, and as soon as Baker got to sleep, I got up and went into the office where Mathews life was quickly taken. He was first tried to be put into a cask, so as to head up and leave in the cellar, but as he could not be, he was let out the back window and placed where he was found. All that Dr. Coolidge said that I told him is true. I told of two different ways in which I murdered him so that he would not be believed when he told of it. All that Mathews told those who assisted in getting the money out of the Bank was told to him by us, to tell them so as to have it appear against Dr. Coolidge and make it really appear that he was getting the money for Dr. Coolidge. We agreed to give him a forged note and assignment of accounts on Dr. Coolidge's books in Dr. Coolidge's name, so he could show them to those who helped him get the money and thereby carry out his falsehood and make his promise good. Mathews said he hired $200 of Dr. Coolidge and there was a one hundred dollar Bill in the money that was taken from him. I saw a man pay Dr. Coolidge a one hundred dollar bill a few days before the murder. It was for secret practice. I know Coolidge did not know what he said or done half of the time that the inquest was in session. I even made him believe that it was best for him to say that Mathews was getting the money for him, and am quite sure that he so told his council[*sic*]. Dr. Coolidge charged Mathews with two hundred dollars as soon as he got home from Skowhegan, and did not carry his Book into the Hall

222

till some three hours afterwards. It was through Dr. C.'s influence alone that the stomach of Mathews was taken out. I forged the letter in Dr. Coolidge's name, that Mathews took from the office and showed to his cousin. Dr. Coolidge sent and got the acid for me, I told him that I wanted to experiment with on animals up to my father's, so as to write my dissertation to graduate with. A cat was killed with the acid and her body thrown into the river. Dr. Coolidge's conversation with George Gilman was all ideal; he told me about it at the time. James F. Gray told me that Dr. Coolidge never applied to him for money; but he would swear so, as Dr. Coolidge tried to throw it on him; it was through my influence that Dr. Coolidge said anything about Gray. Some two months before the murder a man came to Dr. Coolidge's office, accustomed to have fits. Three or four days before the murder, I told Dr. Coolidge that that man was dead, though I never heard so; but as we was calculating to put Mathews into a cask, we hoped by my saying that, he would say something to Dingley about getting him. When Dingley asked him about a subject, he gave him the answer he did, though he had no idea about getting *him*, for he was calculating to send and buy one for him.

Dr. Coolidge was on Water street that night and met Mr. Hill. He went to make a friendly call on Mrs. Eldon She had been a patient of his. When he got most to the house, he see that there was no light except in the second story, and thought it later perhaps than he was aware of, and would not go in, but returned to Maine Street again by way of the common, for the purpose of going into Miss Hall's shop. That being closed, he went to his office, and soon after called me in for the purpose as I testified before the jury of inquest. Dr. Coolidge once exchanged notes with Mathews; he gave him a note that he held against a man in Clinton, at the time he gave it to him, Mathews had to the note with him which he agreed to give for it, but said it was at his mother's and he would get it. It was to get that note that Dr. Coolidge requested to see Mathews as soon as he got home from Brighton and before he went to Clinton. It was through my intriguing influence that Dr. Coolidge gave Prof. Champlin the answer he did; he mourned much about it afterwards.

The story that the young man told at the Hallowell House is false; he was hired by us to make it appear that Dr. C. slept with Mrs. Bates[3], and to tell the story he did. We thought at first that we would ruin Dr. Coolidge by getting out bad stories, but afterwards fearing of success, concluded to connect it with the murder; we thought it would be brought at the time of his trial, to appear against his character. When Dr. Coolidge went to Boston, I found out where he was to stop over night, down river. The young man was seen, and the bargain made. When Dr. Coolidge came home from Boston, he

---

[3] Where did this come from?

was sent to Hallowell House by me, to see on what day that Mrs. Bates was expected to come from Boston, so as to make it appear that he was to meet her there. The young man was instructed to tell Dr. Coolidge when he came that; —— and they had left ten dollars for his visit. I told Dr. Coolidge that the man lived in Windsor, and was ill with disease of the heart. He charged the man with the visit, and so it stands on the Day Book. My motive for telling a different story than I told first, was, that I was afraid of being arrested.

Dr. Coolidge's superior skill · lofty reputation · love of profession, and fervent friends was the cause of his ruin. Had he have had less love of his profession, he would have had less confidence in his friend. I should not have known so much about this business. I know more about his pecuniary affairs than he did himself. Persons that came there to pay money, I took it, and some I payed to Dr. Coolidge and some I did not. When they wished for their bills, he always asked me to look over and see how much was charged. I sometimes told him that there was a number of dollars more than what was charged.

A plot was going on to ruin him before his downfall. It was for Dr. Coolidge's interest to hire money and pay the interest he did, for soon after he went to Waterville, he made up his mind not to stay there but five years before going to France, and it was necessary for him to do all the business he could, and get all the friends he could. He had an opportunity of seeing that very many who were able to pay their bills, were his predecessors friends until he called upon them to pay; then they became otherwise. Dr Coolidge was calculating to leave for France in about a year from the time of the murder. He would have had an abundance to pay all, carried him to France, spend two years there and home again. He would have charged on his books, and in notes $11,000, and the value of his other property with what he could have sold his right of practice for, would have made his property worth $15,000. I helped prize his property, and took all the advantage I could. He had every thing that could possibly aid him in his practice and all of the very best kind. We was the author of many minor things that was calculated to injure Dr. Coolidge. I will say that a purer and nobler being, in motive never lived than Dr. Coolidge. He had but one failing, and that was an overwhelming love for his profession. It was all he thought of.

As for Dr. Coolidge having a disposition to seduce young females, and to seek the society of Immoral women, it is as false as false can be. No person ever had so bitter an indignation against such things as he had. He was as pure as an angel; as to any improper conduct towards female, or even having a desire for any. Dr. Coolidge never played cards but very little. He never played for money. His motive for playing was to become more intimate with men of influence. He had sworn off entirely from playing, months before his down-fall,

224

and told me at the time to never play, and as he spoke, great tears rolled down his cheeks.

I have wrote perhaps more than is necessary, but I wish to free my conscience and restore to Dr. Coolidge the glory and honor that belonged to him. I need not speak of his professional skill. His practice stands without a parallel in our country. Well did one of the physicians connected with me say, "that Dr. C's appearance in a sick room was enough, without his saying one word, to gain the eternal confidence of the sick. He has no failings by which we can injure him, and if we do not injure him in this way, the time is not far distant when he will take all of the praise, and we must ever be in the ditch." Oh! When I think if his age · his *beauty of person* · his *lovely countenance* and his *sweet voice* · his *noble* heart · his amiable *disposition* · his superior skill, and the fair prospect that was before him, at the time we ruined him it seems as if I could not endure life for a moment. Could I see him again at Waterville as he once was, I could almost die without a *regret.* I pray that he may be restored without delay. I now take my life with the same kind of poison that Mathews was poisoned with, and bid farewell to this world.

(Signed)   Thomas Flint.

July 24, 1849

P.S. This letter I wrote a long time ago, and have kept it concealed with the acid, for it has seemed at times as if I could not live. I wrote an anonymous letter at Anson, and left it in the bar-room, and then took it up again, so as to have it for an excuse to my folks for leaving home. I started with the idea of running away, but I feel as if I cannot. Therefore, I take my life.

(Signed)   Thomas Flint.

Now the last part of the postscript is written as if you got him to go to Bath. If you take his life elsewhere you will put into it according to circumstances.

Directions How to Proceed

Go direct to Bangor, buy a pair of green specks. Then go to an Apothecary's shop and buy one ounce of Prussic acid, of common strength. Then go to another shop and buy a similar ground glass stopple viol as the one you buy the acid in. Then go and buy a rod of iron eight inches long, and bigness of one of the bars of our cell door; · go to a blacksmith's shop. Then go from Bangor to Waterville. There you can inquire about Drs. Boutelle, Noyes, and other physicians &c., &c., (See if I have not stated the facts.) Go from there to North Anson. You will find out at Waterville, probably, where Flint is. You stop at Williams's Hotel, in Waterville. If Flint is at home, go to Anson: stop at the tavern, and the next morning feign sickness and send for Flint to see you; after he has come and prescribed, you have pen and ink and paper on the table, and ask him to give you a list of the best kind of books for a student to buy, to study medicine; and make him carry out the prices, so as to get figures. After he has given you the list for a student to buy, you ask him to add such other books as would make a good library. Then that you have an uncle that you are to purchase a library for. You will, in that way, get all the capital letters, and a large quantity of his writing. Well, you will tell him to come and see you again in four or five days; when he comes, you say his medicine has done you great good, &c., &c.

Then make him make out his bill; if he says he shall charge nothing; then say make it out and receipt it by gift, that it is a rule of yours, and you cannot break it. Call and register your name as Cathew E.I. Moolidge, in that way you will get my name and Mathews, almost in full, of which you will need very much; and also the capital I. My name he has written hundreds of times, and is in the hands of many, and it will be the one now likely to detect forgery - Moolidge, Coolidge - Cathew, Mathew. In his bill you will get his name written twice. At this time you will get him to give you a letter of introduction to the family where he boards in Philadelphia; that you are going there to attend medical lectures.

At this time you will have made up your mind whether you can take his life here. You must get alone with him without any previous appointment, and where the letter to C———, will not be concealed. If his friends get hold of it first, here is the end of it. All is lost! If there is no chance there to do it, you will write the following anonymous letter, and leave it in the barroom, in such a manner as no one can say but what Flint left it there when he came in to see you, and then took it again. If he should not notice it, you must carefully call his attention to it before he goes out: —

"Augusta, July 10, 1849

Dear Sir: — Being interested in your welfare, as well as in Dr. Coolidge's, I have sought means to communicate with him. He has promised me that he will free you from all suspicion and blame connected with the murder of Edward Mathews, provided you will promise to do so and so after he has made a public statement, to free you from all. His requests are reasonable, and which you can comply with, with great honor to yourself. I shall be at the Elliot House in Bath on the evening of the 25th of this month, and if you will meet me there, I will make known to you his proposals. You must come alone, or I will have nothing to do with it, for I have run great risks as well as others in getting a chance to communicate with Dr. Coolidge. My responsibility is tremendous. I shall not sign my name to this, for my correspondence is unlawful, and it will lay myself liable, as well as others. You know me and I am well acquainted up and down the Kennebec. I will mention such things as must prove I have had recent correspondence with Dr. Coolidge. Dr. Bowtell received Dr. Coolidge cool in Philadelphia, and you and Dr. C. talked about it, and thought it was in consequence of a Miss Mussey that was there. You and Dr. C. attended the Museum in Chestnut street, near the Washington Hotel, where Dr. C. stopped. He gave you a ticket. It was very cold in the Museum, and you went to the stove and warmed you; once you put up some medicine wrong in the office, and it killed a child. You asked Dr. C. to let you have $30, and he let you have a $50 bill. He gave it to you in the office; you was setting by the rails of the table. he thinks you wanted it to pay Noyes; you told Dr. C. that you would take that anatomical head of his that Noyes wanted to buy back. Friday night after the murder you slept with Dr. Coolidge, you laid on the back side of the bed, you told him that Philander Soule was in No. 6, and you must be careful, or he would hear you talk. Dr. C. asked you at the time if your father was to Waterville at the time of the murder, what he was doing. Once you said he was abed, once you said he was writing a letter. Dr. C. requested you to find out when you went up home, whether your father was willing for you to buy him out; and you told him after you came back that he was. You told Dr. C. that your friends did not wish you to be with him, that being the day you went to Augusta. You must now know that there is no hoax about this matter. Now if you will come at Bath at that time, and register your name and the No. of your room, I will call to see you during the evening. You must come alone, or I will have nothing to do with it for the above reason. I have no objections to your consulting your father about it, after you return; I send you this by a true friend, and he will leave it where you will find it in due time. Come and your once unblemished character, and fair prospects will be restored to you, with everlasting honor.

A Friend of Humanity and Justice."

If you cannot take his life at home, you will then write and leave the anonymous letter in the bar-room, in such a manner as no one can say but what Flint left it himself. At that time you will tell him that you are going down the river to be gone a few days, and then you think you will return to Anson, to stop till the medical letters commence in Philadelphia. — By telling him that, he will not think strange of seeing you at Bath, and then if the anonymous letter does not fetch him to Bath you can return to Anson, to give him HELL. In the anonymous letter you will set the time for him to be at Bath one day after you get there, You will then get the hang of the house. Register your name something else there, and keep in your room, so as not to be seen by those that know you. Not wear your specks till you go to his room; you will say that you have a private difficulty that you wish to consult him about. * * * * * Well, when he is examining you, strike him a heavy blow just at the edge of his hair in the back of the neck; that will knock him stiff without noise or sound. — You will immediately lay him on his back, and pour the vial of acid into his mouth, and be sure and get as much down his throat as possible — *be sure, now*. That will take his life in an instant. You will lay him just as if he fell with the back of his neck against the rounds of the bottom of a chair that stands side of the partition, so it cannot slip. That will account for the bruise on his neck. Lay on one side of him, some foot or two from his lips, the vial with a little acid in it. Take the vial that you buy with nothing in it, similar to the one you buy with the acid in it, and then they cannot identify the vial. Pour the acid into it just before you wish to use it, and keep it stopped tight, or it will lose its strength. Lay the stopple upon the opposite side of him. Have the acid in your vest pocket when you wish to use it. If his nose bleeds, be sure to wipe every speck off clean. Have your handkerchief out at the time you strike him, so as to slap it instantly over his mouth and nose, to prevent the blood from escaping, if any. It will be best to have something soft wound around the iron, so as not to cut through the skin. If he should object to seeing you that evening, you will then have to tell him you was the man who wrote the anonymous letter, &c., &c.,— Then say I am a phrenologist, and I want to examine your head, so I can feel satisfied your promised can be relied on, before making known Dr. C.'s propositions; then, while you are examine his head, you will give him *hell*. After doing it you will leave, and go a put the rod of iron in the back-house — have nothing around it when you throw it away. Destroy your handkerchief if you get it bloody. Take the cars the next morning, and be off where no one can find you.

After I am set at liberty, you will write me a letter, and date it at the place where I shall find you, so as to pay over the $1000 and make such other arrangements as may be necessary. Sign your name John Howard, and direct it to North Livermore, Maine.

You see you can take his life in that way without noise, wound, or any thing by which you can possible be mistrusted. If one should go into his room in three minutes after you leave it, it would amount to nothing; for he could take his own life the instant you left the room. If he has the anonymous letter with him, you destroy it. You see in his postscript, he says he wrote the anonymous letter so as to have it for an excuse if needed, Be sure and have the hotel understood right, that you are to meet at. Look at the papers to see advertisements. There is now a noted house there by the name of Elliott's.

Now be sure and get every thing written right. If the "doing business at the rate of $5000 per year," is not in the letter of confession, you will put it in that place. Perhaps it will be well to put it in the postscript that he wrote the anonymous letter, all but dating it sometime before he left it in the bar room, so they cannot make any thing out of the paper.

Buy your paper at Bangor, and have that which you write the letter of confession, long enough so as not to have more than one sheet of it. Anonymous are on common paper.   Call your name Cathew E.I. Moolidge. He has written my name hundreds of times, and it is in the possession of as many persons, and it will be the most likely one to detect forgery. You see if you can get him to Bath, you will be away from all his friends, and before they can get there, it will be lauded to the skies, and the sympathy will be so tremendous for me, that his friends would not dare mention that there had been foul play, even if they thought so. Unto your hands I commit my life, liberty, and all on earth. Farewell, dear friend!!

I think you had better buy two phials of the Acid, at Bangor, for fear that you might break one of them. If Flint does not practice, you will go to his house, to get him to give you a list of books so as to get his writing, Oh! to God, could I know that you will prove true, I should be the happiest being in this world. Your sincerity I shall test before you leave here, if I have an opportunity.

This letter reads more like a juvenile prank than a genuine plan to murder a man, make it look like suicide, and then transfer the blame for the murder of another person to that murdered man.

The Boston Herald account, as reprinted by the Portland advertiser, has more details on the autopsy.

The next day (Saturday) a post mortem examination was had by Drs. Buxton and Rose, but without finding any lesions or indications of disease sufficiently grave to account for his death; and they entirely agreed that it was probably occasioned by the extreme mental depression and loss of energy which the sudden exposure of his schemes had occasioned. His brain was perfectly sound and healthy in every respect, and his lungs though affording some slight proof of former disease, presented no appearance worthy of notice. His heart was excessively small, weighing but nine and a quarter ounces, two thirds of which weight was appropriated by the left ventricle, the walls of the right ventricle not exceeding a sixteenth of an inch in thickness, and the auricles being so small as to render it astonishing how such an organ could perform its necessary functions. The stomach was almost empty, containing nothing but a little gruel, and the walls were very much corrugated or thickened midway between the cordiac and pyloric orifices. Internally it was throughout of a uniform bright scarlet color, presenting no indications of active inflammation; neither were the vessels belonging to it in any degree turgid.

The publication of the plot and letters by Coolidge seems to have erased any remaining suspicions of Thomas Flint's role in Mathews's death. The prison reform journal, the *Prisoner's Friend,* published what seems to be the general view of the affair.

The Prisoner's Friend, vol. 1 No 11, 1 July 1849, p. 507.
DR. COOLIDGE

Since our last publication, the news of the death of this individual has reached us. We thought at first of inserting the letters that reveal his plot, but we cannot see any great good to be obtained, and therefore we omit them for the present. The whole matter reveals great depravity. And the opponents of the death-penalty have thought that they found in this a new argument against imprisonment for life, inasmuch as here they find an individual laying out an infernal plot after his sentence is commuted. We have only to say now that the whole matter reveals very distinctly three facts that would not have been obtained if he had been executed: -
1. The absolute, positive guilt of Coolidge.
2. The equally positive innocence of Flint, his student.
3. The awful consequences of crime.
True, it may be said, that there was but little doubt of his guilt in most minds. But then the evidence was chiefly circumstantial. Then, very many had strong suspicions that the student was somewhat involved in the crime. Now his character is cleared entirely. Then we learn a great moral truth. Here is a man laying out a plan, and its very development causes his death. Here is a great lesson given to the world. It shows the intense suffering through which the culprit must have passed. Then again, no law can provide for every case. The victim was in prison, and certain privileges were allowed him, and he abused them. Does it follow, therefore, that prisoners are never to be allowed these privileges? Or is every man to suffer because one has turned out to be a greatly-depraved being? Or are we to hang every murderer because forsooth, Coolidge has abused his privileges? Or because hereafter some one in prison may be guilty in plotting the death of an innocent? We now have eight men in our State prison[4] whose sentences have been commuted to prison for life. Should we take them out and hang them

---

[4] Massachusetts

because they may be guilty of laying out some infernal plot? This idea of hanging men because they may do wrong, is based on a very slender foundation. On this ground we might hang every man in the community. The law of Capital Punishment still remains on the statute book of Maine, though one year must elapse between the sentence and the execution. Maine has gone so far towards abolishing the death penalty. Let her remain firm, and not be moved by this occurrence in her prison. Let the advocates of the death punishment show any case where the death penalty has done any good, and we will gladly insert their communications.

The story of this plot was reported not just throughout the United States, but also in Great Britain.

Piscataquis Observer August 9, 1849
The London Times pronounces "the last schema of Dr. Coolidge, one of the most cool-blooded and atrocious schemes every suggested to the mind of man," and publishes the whole account.

Is Coolidge Dead?

In its issue of June 16th, 1849, *Scientific American* journal, which perhaps was not then what it became later, published the following brief notice.

A paper published in Maine, entitled Mann's Physician, states there is reason to believe that the body found in the cell where Coolidge should have been, may have been the corpse of some stranger resembling Coolidge, and that Coolidge had been restored to liberty. We do not assert it with the fullest confidence but we have many very strong reasons to believe that Valorus P. Coolidge is not dead – which we could give to the public, were we called upon. On the other hand, the Hallowell Cultivator says the body of Coolidge was given up to his relatives by the state prison officers on Monday, and was taken to North Livermore by his brother on Tuesday.

[The above first report will find many believers, those who were not satisfied with the report of Coolidge's death. The name and examination of the prisoner who was the alleged cause of detection has not publicly been known.]

Mann's Physician [and Down East Screamer] was the latest publication of Amos Angier Mann[1] (1810-1884), of Norridgwock, a dispenser of his own blend of herbs, strippings and molasses, which were reported to be still consumed as late as the 1920's. He was well known over much of the state for his profane views and controversies with traditional physicians, and it is generally assumed that he used the issue of Coolidge's death as a good vehicle to push sales of his medicines and his new publication, which began in May of 1849, a vehicle to advertise his *cream of life*, and keep himself before the public. *Scientific American* was

---

[1] See "The Down East Screamer", by Alan S. Downer, The New England Quarterly Vol 42 No 2, June, 1960, for a very entertaining account of Mann, and his controversies with the physicians of the day. An example: A physician in Anson mistook pregnancy for dropsy, tapped his patient, drew blood instead of water, and killed a seven-months fetus. He acted, said Mann, from "ignorance and dishonesty, cruelty and avarice." Of all men the Anson Doctor should have recognized a seven-months' pregnancy since his wife (his second) had just produced a baby after seven months of marriage, and it must have been premature since his first wife had been dead only eight months.

The standards of medicine of the day were such that someone who basically dispensed a mild laxative that tasted good could frequently produce better results than physicians with medical degrees practicing in his part of the state.

After the trial a letter was printed that purported to be a letter from Coolidge to Mann requesting a meeting to discuss business matters.

correct to point out the questions raised by authorities not identifying either the prisoner who revealed the plot, or the prisoner who was to be his accomplice. The population of the state prison in 1849 was just 67[2]; there were only a handful who were due to be released that summer. And the young prisoner who revealed the plot – there were only a half dozen prisoners at Thomaston younger than 20 – anyone present in the prison would have known who was laid up ill at the time of the discovery.

The controversy was taken seriously enough that a government inquiry was called for.

Piscataquis Observer July 5, 1849
DR. COOLIDGE. A foolish story is going the rounds in the papers, that Dr. Coolidge, the murderer of Mathews, is in existence. It emanated first in "Mann's Family Physician and Down East Screamer," a paper published in Skowhegan by the celebrated and eccentric Dr. Mann of 'Strippings and Molasses' memory. The Dr. is always getting up an 'excitement,' if not with the Regulars and Steam Doctors, and Politicians, he will in some other way. He is a droll fellow, and you had better believe it.

The latest news respecting Coolidge is, that Dr. Mann of Skowhegan, states that the body brought from Thomaston and buried as Dr. Coolidge was disinterred a few days since and examined in the presence of sixteen persons, including Mann himself and Coolidge's father, and they agreed it was NOT his body. Coolidge's father testified that his son had lost the end of one thumb, and had no scar on this cheek, whereas the corpse had a scar on the cheek and both thumbs were whole.

This is the latest intelligence from Skowhegan via Portland and Boston.

Dr. how comes on the Libel trials?

Piscataquis Observer July 12, 1849
Dr. Coolidge. · The last Thomaston Gazette says · A letter has been received by the officers of the State Prison, from N. Livermore, the place where Coolidge's friends now reside, stating that the excitement in that town was so intense, that hundreds of citizens assembled for the purpose of disinterring his body, a committee of seven were chosen to examine it, among whom were two physicians

---

[2] The *Annual Report of the Warden of the State Prison* each year listed the names, dates of birth, crime, sentence, and date of committal of each prisoner,

intimately acquainted with the subject in his lifetime, and they UNANIMOUSLY PRONOUNCED IT THAT OF VALORUS P. COOLIDGE!

An official statement of the whole affair is being prepared (says the Gaz) as we go to press. The full particulars will then be given, which will relieve the public mind and set this foolish matter at rest, and the authors of those malicious reports will probably receive their just desserts!

The Maine Farmer published a much fuller account, with the second disinternment and the depositions of the prison warden and other officials. The account of the second disinternment will be later be questioned by one of the physicians present.

> *Maine Farmer July 19, 1849*
> ### "IS COOLIDGE DEAD?"
>
> Last week we gave our readers to understand that a letter had been received from North Livermore, by the officers of the State Prison, disapproving the report put in circulation by one Mann, and so extensively copied by the press, that the body purporting to be that of Coolidge, had been ascertained, upon disinternment to be that of some other person! We have since been favored with this letter for publication, and also the depositions of the Warden, and several other gentlemen of veracity, which must prove conclusively that Valorus P. Coolidge is actually dead! And he who doubts it after reading this evidence, might with equal propriety doubt his own existence!
>
> When this fabulous announcement first made its appearance, it was supposed by those most interested that the author was too well known, and the story too ridiculous, to enlist the belief of even the most credulous. But a large portion of community are ever ready to seize upon anything which savors of the marvelous, and the more improbability there may be attached to a story, the more willingly they believe it. What motives could actuate any individual in putting forth this silly report we are at a loss to divine, but since it has become so wide-spread, it is thought advisable to treat it seriously, and let the pubic have a plain statement of facts; we therefore submit what evidence we have in our possession, without deeming it necessary to assure our readers of the integrity of the gentlemen who give their names below; and here we shall drop the matter, trusting that the remains of Coolidge will be suffered to repose in peace for decency's sake.
>
> LETTER
>
> North Livermore, June 27, 1849
> Benjamin Carr, Esq.
> Dear Sir, - I write you at this time, thinking it might be a source of satisfaction to you to learn what I am about to

communicate. I suppose you have ere this learned the report of Dr. Mann, respecting the remains of Dr. Coolidge. * * I will write you respecting Dr. Mann's course, which if you have learned before will explain my letter, and if not, my explanation will show why I write the following.

Dr. Mann, on the 25th inst., together with three gentlemen from Jay, I think, went into the vicinity where Dr. Coolidge's remains were deposited, and raised some twelve or fourteen persons, and took up and examined the remains, and retired reporting that they were not the remains of Coolidge, being much larger, an of very different features. He reports the remains to weight about 180 lbs., hands and feet large, having a thick head of hair.

Dr Mann's source caused so much excitement that we have this day taken up what we have good reasons to suppose are the remains of Dr. Coolidge, and have examined weighed and measured them: a committee of seven were selected to examine and report facts. Two physicians, who were acquainted with Coolidge before his imprisonment, constituted a part of the committee. We found the length of the body to be about five feet ten inches, the foot ten inches or less, (the boot he last wore was eleven inches long) and the corpse to weight 133 lbs. We found the features rather small, somewhat swollen, which changes the appearance of the corpse at first sight, more so than they prove to be on a close examination.

There were, I should judge, more than one hundred persons present, and various opinions expressed; but the committee have made a report, and are of opinion that the remains are those of Coolidge, *and none other*, and have signed for it for any use you or the public may wish to make with it.

If you wish, we will send you the report of the committee, signed by them; and any other information we can give you will be given with pleasure. Yours in much haste.

Isaac Strickland.

[We expected to receive the official Report of the Committee in season for this week's paper, but as it has not come to hand we are obliged to go to press without it.]

DEPOSITIONS

"Whereas certain rumors are in circulation in many of the newspapers of the day, respecting the certainty or uncertainty of the death of Dr. Valorus P. Coolidge, late a convict of the State Prison in Maine. And whereas great excitement seems to prevail amongst the people on account of those statements, I have thought proper to publish a few certificates toughing the same; believing the public are entitled to know at all times what their servants are doing. I have had charge of the Maine State Prison nearly ten years and feel perfectly willing to render an account of my stewardship.

Maine State Prison

Thomaston, July 2, 1849.

I Benjamin Carr, as Warden, on my oath do testify and say that on the 28th day of March 1848, Alexander Young, Esq., of Thomaston, and Deputy Sheriff in Lincoln County, by my order brought to the State Prison and delivered to me a person by the name and calling himself 'Valorus P. Coolidge,' convicted at the Supreme Judicial Court Kennebec County for the crime of murder of one Mathews of Waterville.

I further state I received said Coolidge into Prison, he always answered to that name, persons called on him frequently while I Prison, stating they were his brothers and sister and always addressed him as brother.

I further state that this was the same man who was arraigned at the Supreme Court in August for the murder of Mathews, as I was present and saw him.

I further state I was called to the said Coolidge's cell on the morning of the 18th of May 1849, at 8 o'clock, where I, in company with several others, saw said Coolidge's dead body, who had but a few moments previous drawn his last breath, as I was told by the Deputy Warden, he witnessing the same.

The corpse was then warm. I ordered and assisted in taking the dead body to the Prison Hospital, where it was taken care of, locked up until the next day Saturday, the 19th of May, when a post-mortem examination took place which I witnessed in company with many others. The remains were as usual interred decently at 5 o'clock P. M. the same day,

I notified the Father of the decease of his son within a few moments after his death by a hasty, ill-written letter, handed the stage driver to be mailed on the way to Bath, informing him he could have the remains if he would call for them.

I further testify and say, on Monday May 21st, about 2 o'clock P.M., E. P. Coolidge, in company with his friend, a Mr. Simmons, called on me for the remains of V. P. Coolidge; I accordingly went to the grave with some others, disinterred, and brought into the highway the said remains; when the lid of the coffin was removed, the corpse exposed to public view in the presence of, and by request of the brother of the deceased who readily recognized them and said he was satisfied. Many witnesses were present. I then aided in putting the coffin into a box, and bound it on the carriage, when the brother and Mr., Simmons left Thomaston, with what I swear was sent me to be V. P. Coolidge, and I know he is dead.

Benjamin Carr

Lincoln, ss. July 2, 1849.

Is Coolidge Dead?

Personally appeared Benjamin Carr, above subscribed, and made oath to the forgoing statement by him subscribed.

Before me, J. D. Barnard,
Justice of the Peace.

I Asa Persons, Clerk and Commissary of the Maine State Prison on oath testify and say, that a person under the sentence of death for the crime of murder, calling himself Valorus P. Coolidge, was brought to this prison by A. Young, Esq., March 28th, 1848; that on the next morning I took his height and description and put the usual questions of where he was born, where he resided, &c. &c.; and recorded it in a book kept for that purpose, that Ezra P. Coolidge and Mrs. Sabin always addressed him as brother, and other friends as Dr. V. P. Coolidge; that on the morning of the 18th of May, 1849, I found this same individual insensible on the bottom of his cell; that I immediately called assistance and lifted him to his bed and sent for the physician, but he ceased to breath before his arrival; that the morning after his death a post mortem examination was had at which I was present; and that the body was then decently interred in the place of burial for the prisoners, at about 5 o'clock P. M.

Asa Perkins.

Lincoln, ss July 2, 1849.

Personally appeared the above named Asa Perkins, and made oath that the above certificate by him subscribed is true.

Before me, J. D. Barnard, Justice of the Peace.

I hereby testify that I was at the Maine State Prison, when Alexander Young delivered to the Warden a person whom he said was V. P. Coolidge, that I saw him as often as every other week during his confinement, that on the morning of the 18th of May last, being informed that the said Coolidge had died about 8 o'clock in the morning I visited the prison about 11 o'clock of the same day, found the body in the hospital of the prison and new it to be the body of V. P. Coolidge as known while in prison, that said body was warm, blood fluid in the veins, but little rigidity of the muscles, and with every appearance of having but very recently expired.

I further certify that on the 19th of May, in company with Dr. Rose, physician to the Prison, in presence of the Warden and Clerk of the Prison, Edwin Smith, Jr, John W Smith of Warren; Capt. George Crawford; Alexander Young of Thomaston, and Mr. Jackson of East Thomaston, made a post-mortem examination of the same body, and then advised the Warden to have the remains buried in the course of the day.

B. Buxton, Inspector of Maine State Prison.

Lincoln, ss. July 2, 1848

Then personally appeared the above B. Buxton before me and made oath to the truth of the above statement.

Trial of Dr. Valorus P. Coolidge

Emerson Smith, Justice of the Peace.

I, Daniel Rose, Physician of the Maine State Prison, make the following statement on oath: - On the morning of March 29th, A. D. 1848, I was made acquainted with V. P. Coolidge, and afterwards saw him as often as *twice* a week while he was in Prison. I saw him *alive* in said Prison on the 17th of May last at 5 o'clock P.M. and on the 18th of *said May I saw the body of the said Coolidge dead* at said Prison. When I first saw him after his death, he could not have been dead more than 15 or 20 minutes; and on the 19th of said May, I made a post-mortem examination with Dr. Buxton, (in presence of Captain George Crawford, John W. Smith, Edwin Smith, Mr. Jackson, Alexander Young, and others) on the body of said Coolidge.
Thomaston, July 2, 1849,
Daniel Rose
Lincoln, ss. July 2, A.D. 1849
Personally appeared Daniel Rose and made oath that the above statement by him signed, is true. Before me, George Abbott, Justice of the Peace.

I, Alexander Young, on oath make the following statement: - On the 28th, March 1848, I brought the late Dr. V. P. Coolidge from the Augusta Jail to the State Prison, that I saw said Coolidge as often as once a week while he was in prison, and that said Coolidge died on the 18th of May last.
That I saw his dead body on the same day, very soon after his death, and knows that it was the dead body of V. P. Coolidge, and I was present at the post-mortem examination of the same.
Thomaston, June 30, 1849
Lincoln, ss. June 30, 1849.
Signed and sworn to, by the said A. Young.
Before me, G. Abbott, Justice of the Peace.

Camden, July 3, 1849, Being requested to state what I know in reference to Dr. V. P. Coolidge, both before and after his death, I very willingly comply.
I hereby certify that I saw and conversed with Dr. V. P. Coolidge, as Chaplain from week to week after he arrived at the State Prison in Thomaston until the last of October 1948 – at which time another Chaplain was appointed. I have also seen him eight or ten times since, and the last time but a few days before his death.
Being in Thomaston the day he was buried, I called at the Prison, saw him in his coffin, put my hand on his forehead, and had not *then*, or *now* the least shadow of doubt that it was Coolidge, and that he was dead, any more than I doubt any others who have died in Prison during the 24 years that I officiated as Chaplain.
His looks were uncommonly natural for a corpse.

238

Is Coolidge Dead?

J. Washburn

Waldo, ss. July 3rd, 1849. Personally appeared Rev. Job. Washburn and made oath to the truth of the foregoing statement by him subscribed.

Before me, Nath, R. Talbot, Just. Peace.

I hereby certify that I saw the dead body of Dr. V. P. Coolidge in the Hospital of the State Prisons of Maine, that I attended his funeral, and that I saw him interred in the burying ground without the prison.

Edward Freeman, Chaplain of Maine State Prison

Lincoln, ss. July 2nd, 1849. Then appeared personally before me the above named Edward Freeman and made oath to the truth of the above certificate by him subscribed.

Joel Miller, Justice of the Peace.

Dr. Mann had his own depositions.

Kennebec Journal August 23, 1849

Dr. Mann still persists that the body carried to Livermore from Thomaston to be buried was not that of Dr. Coolidge, but that of another man, and has a large number of depositions to prove the same opinion. He calls for the publication of the report of the committee appointed by the Governor and Council in June last.

Piscataquis Observer August 23 1849

We have received No. 2 of Dr. Mann's Family Physician and Down East Screamer. The Dr. still insists that Coolidge is 'alive and kicking;' and has taken a number of Depositions to prove that the body taken from the S. Prison is not that of Valorus P. Coolidge - among the depositions is one from Coolidge's father who states that the body does not resemble that of his son. The article in reference to Coolidge is very lengthy, and as it would be of no particular interest to our subscribers, we deem it inexpedient to transfer it to our columns.

By the way - we perceive that the Dr.'s paper is pretty well filled up with the Patent nostrums of the day; we thought the Dr. was dead set against them - but in this No. it seems he has called in to his assistance Dr. Pratt, of the Free Press, who in such CASES is always ready to lend a HAND.

Trial of Dr. Valorus P. Coolidge

Lewiston Falls Journal September 1, 1849
[From the Skowhegan Press]
THE COOLIDGE AFFAIR

We have been requested by several of our subscribers to inform them of the substance of Dr. Mann's statements in relation to the Coolidge affair. Below we give two affidavits touching the matter, which the Dr. says "is only a foretaste of what he is prepared to show." Some of the warden's friends in this region, are looking to him urging his attention to it.

Deposition of Alexander Alden, Jr. · I, Alexander Alden, of Canton, county of Oxford, hereby certify, that I live on the adjoining farm to that of Joseph Coolidge, the father of Valorus P. Coolidge; my farm being nearest on the road one way, and John McCallister's the other way. I was living on the same place when Valorus P. College was born, and went for a physician myself, to attend at the time he was born. I was well acquainted with Valorus P. Coolidge from that time till he left home at the age of about twenty years, and have seen him since, I conclude, every time he has been at his father's since that time. I attended both examinations. At the first examination the corpse had not changed much, and the features were all distinct, and the complexion not changed more than is usual for a corpse that had been dead thirty-six or forty-eight hours. I examined the body carefully to see if the body was that of Valorous P. Coolidge, and could not find any features that appeared to me to be those of Coolidge. The whole frame was much too large for Dr. Coolidge, the hands, the feet and legs were too large, with thick, black hair upon the legs, which could not have been the legs of Dr. Coolidge.

Dr. Coolidge was quite a feminine man in appearance, with a very light beard. The beard of this corpse was very heavy, and the eyebrows near together, with heavy brows, very different from those of Coolidge. The face was much too large and wide, the nose too much Roman to be Coolidge's · At the second examination the corpse was very much changed, and turned very dark-colored, so that I could not from that examination, form much opinion as to the identity of the body. At the first examination, most of those present gave it as their opinion that it was not the body of V. P. Coolidge, and I heard no other opinion expressed by any one. There was a very distinct and large scar upon the cheek, about three-fourths of an inch long, and half an inch wide. There was no beard standing upon the scar, but beard standing all around the scar, and on the edge of it.

When the body was taken up containing the coffin, we found it thoroughly nailed, so much so that we were obliged to use wedges to get it open, and then almost every nail drawed through the lid. There was no appearance upon the box or coffin of its having been opened before, since it was nailed up. · We could not open it without marring the box considerably. I found by the appearance of the

240

corpse, that there had been an examination made by the physicians upon the body. On the first examination I examined the hands and found them not swollen, but if anything a little wrinkled or shrunk. The skin was then a little wrinkled or shrunk, the bones and muscles being distinct. The hands upon this body were much too large for Coolidge's, and the hair was too black to be Coolidge's. And upon the whole examination of the body, I am fully confident that it was not the body of Valorus P. Coolidge.

> Alexander Alden, Jr.
> Canton, July 27, 1849
> Oxford, SS. July 27, 1849

The personally appeared the above named Alexander Alden, Jr., and made oath to the truth of the above certificate by him subscribed before me.

> ISAAC RANDALL, Justice of the Peace.

Deposition of Joseph Coolidge, Father of Dr. V. P. Coolidge. · I, Joseph Coolidge, hereby certify that my son, Dr. V. P. Coolidge, was born with one of his thumbs shorter than the other, and one of his thumb-nails was shorter than the other, and that said thumb and nail remained shorter as long as he lived at home. It appears as if the end joint of one of his thumbs was wanting. When he and his sisters were children, and playing together, I have heard them talk about one his thumb being shorter than the other. My son, V. P. Coolidge, had a very small, narrow, delicate hand; was thin favored, and narrow between and across the eyes. · Never knew of his having a scar on his face or legs, but he had a scar on one of his thumbs, caused by a cut with a sickle when reaping.

My wife said that Valorus told her when she was knitting him a pair of mittens, that she must knit one of the thumbs shorter than the other. When the supposed body of my son was first disinterred, I heard several of the bystanders say that they, on measuring the thumbs, could discover no difference in the length. I did not measure them myself. It appeared to me that the corpse said to be that of my son, was wider between and across the eyes, than that of Valorus. And he always has appeared so to me. I could not discover any scar upon the thumbs of the corpse. The corpse appeared very different from what I should suppose the corpse of my son would look. JOSEPH COOLIDGE.

> Canton, July 27, 1849
> Sworn to before me,
> C. W. Walton, Justice of the Peace.

The statement of Coolidge's father that the body was not that of his son, with the specifics of the missing portion of thumb, and the scar on the cheek, convinced Dr. Drew of the Gospel Banner that the body buried in Canton was not Coolidge's. But he still held that the body that had *been* buried at Thomaston had been Coolidge's.

Portland Advertiser Sept 4, 1849
DR. COOLIDGE. – From the certificates published by Dr Mann in his Down East Screamer, we think there may be reason to suspect that the body in the grave of Dr Coolidge in Canton, is not the body of said man; but the evidence is still stronger that Coolidge was dead in the State Prison and buried in Thomaston. Who changed the bodies after internment at Canton, or for what purpose, we do not know, though it is not difficult to guess. [Gospel Banner]

By the end of October, Dr Mann had offered a large reward for some of the obvious missing pieces of the puzzle.

Portland Advertiser October 30, 1849
Dr Mann offers $500 reward to any one who will produce the man on whose person was found the ridiculous papers disclosing the awful scheme to murder Flint. Also the man that was to accomplish the dreadful deed. The original documents in Coolidge's handwriting. Also that train of cats that carried Coolidge off.

A physician who had graduated from the medical school in Brunswick in the same class as Dr. Rose made a severe criticism of the autopsy on Coolidge's body at the prison, and seems to imply that the results were distorted to make it Coolidge's sudden death look plausible. See the end of Appendix IV for a more detailed report of the autopsy by Dr. Rose. Dr. Buxton, who was also involved in the post mortem, later became president of the Maine Medical Association.

Portland Advertiser November 13, 1849
THE COOLIDGE AFFAIR. · Dr. Seavey[3] of Stetson publishes a communication in the Bangor Whig and Courier, in which he says that he is now "confirmed in the opinion which he has entertained ever since the announcement of Dr. Coolidge's death, that he is *not*

---

[3] Dr. Calvin Seavey (1809-1886), founder of the Calvin Seavey Anatomical Museum at Bowdoin College's medical school. Both he and Daniel Rose were members of the Bowdoin College Medical Class of 1837.

dead, but has been in some mysterious manner set at liberty contrary to the laws of this State, and is now enjoying privileges equal to those of the most honest and upright" - and he calls for an examination.

It will be remembered that the report of the post mortem impressed the idea upon the public mind that there was something unusual about Coolidge's heart - that it was very small and out of shape - so much so that it was "*astonishing* how such an organ could perform its necessary functions." As sudden deaths occur from diseases of the heart, it was very natural for the unlearned to suppose, the such a heart might have suddenly ceased to perform its necessary functions, and thus caused the sudden death. This part of the report was not long afterwards criticized by Dr. Mann in a manner substantially the same as does Dr. Seavey in the following extract from his communication in the Bangor paper: -

Dr Rose, who conducted and made report of the post mortem examination of Coolidge's corpse was an old friend and class-mate of mine in Brunswick medical school, and at that time, he stood very well in my estimation as a man and as a scholar. Consequently, I am not a little surprised, as well as sorry, to see such egregious blunders as were made by him in that report. For it shows upon its very face, that he is sadly deficient in the knowledge of anatomy, physiology and pathology. It appears that he is destitute of the knowledge which he formerly possessed. In speaking of the heart; he says: "it was excessively small, weighing only nine and a quarter ounces; and two thirds of which weight was appropriated in the left ventricle, the wall of the right ventricle being only about one sixteenth of an inch in thickness; and that the auricles were so very small as to render it *astonishing how such an organ could perform its necessary functions!*" Now there is nothing wonderful in all this. The description which he gives of the heart aside from the weight, is very near in keeping with that of the mot correct and substantial writers on physiology.

Let us compare. Cruveilheir estimates the mean weight at six or seven ounces, Buillaud and Lobstein weight the hearts of thirteen subjects, in whom, from the general habit previous state of health, and mode of death, there was every reason to believe they were in the natural state. The mean weight was eight ounces and three drachms. From all their data, they are led to fix the mean weight of a human heart in the adult, from the 25th to the 60th year, at from eight to nine ounces. Again, after carefully measuring the heart these renowned authors found the result to be as follows: Length from base to apex, 5 inches 6 lines; breadth at base, 3 inches; thickness of walls of right ventricle 2 1/4 lines; at apex, 1-2 lines; thickness of right auricle, 1 line; thickness of left auricle, 1-2 line. Now it appears according to the above, that the heart of which Dr. Rose makes mentioning his report, was an exceeding *large* and though in every respect, a sound and healthy organ, The size of the cavities and the thickness of their walls were just what any man having a correct knowledge of the organization of the human being, might have expected to have found. Yet the Doctor seems to be 'astonished* of find two thirds of the weight appropriated to the eft ventricle! If according to Buillaud, the thickness of the walls of the ventricles, be as 7 to 2, of course the weight will be in the same ratio.

In the same issue, the Advertiser prints a long article summarizing the controversy to date, and repeats the depositions from the officials at the state prison. The end of their article expresses the opinion that the body at Canton is the same as the body interred overnight at Thomaston, and that it is not Coolidge.

Portland Advertiser Nov 13, 1849.
1st. The deposition of the Warden is strong to the point, that there was no clandestine change of bodies between the time of the internment and disinterment at Thomaston. The same body, of which there had been a post mortem examination as that of Coolidge, was delivered up to the brother.

2d The letter of Dr Holland renders it highly improbable that there had been any change at Canton · and that the body *there* examined was the same body, of which there was a post mortem examination at Thomaston.

These points being settled, it becomes still more difficult to reconcile the contradictory testimony, and explain the mystery which hangs over the matter. The evidence which was put forth, relative to the examination at Canton, was most conclusive, that the body was not that of Coolidge. So strong was this evidence, that Mr. Drew and several other editors, who had treated the matter merely as a humbug, immediately retracted, and said that *that* body certainly could not be that of Coolidge. But they at once threw out the suggestion that there had been a clandestine change after internment. · This evidence came from the *father* and *neighbors* who had known Coolidge long. It was not confined to mere opinion, but had reference to marks which could hardly admin of deception. There appeared to have been a full and careful examination, and the result of that examination was the general opinion that the body was not that of Coolidge. That evidence was certainly of too grave a character to be set entirely aside by the mere summary suggestion in Dr. Holland's letter to Mr. Drew.

Of the witnesses at Thomaston, but *one* (the Deputy Warden) pretends to have been present at the death of Coolidge. The witnesses at Canton think it was not Coolidge's. Here seems to be the issue. We cannot see why it is not even more reasonable to suppose that some the witnesses at Thomason, who looked upon the corpse merely cursory, with no definite object and without suspicion, should be deceived or taken than those at Canton, who made examination after suspicions had been excited, and for the very purpose of settling the question. In a mere matter of opinion as to identity such are the changes sometimes wrought by death that any one might be liable to be mistaken, unless there were some known marks to guide his judgement,

Piscataquis Observer Nov 8, 1849

DR. COOLIDGE. A question in the last Gardiner Fountain, we think is entitled to some attention. It will be recollected that the officers of the State's Prison said the body of Dr. Coolidge was opened, the stomach examined; also that his heart was opened and the brains taken out. In all the testimony given by the committee and neighbors who examined the body in Canton after its disinterment, we see no mention made of any other marks on the body or head, than an old scar on the face. The question is - did the body in Canton show evidences of having been dissected for a postmortem examination? [Augusta Banner]

Piscataquis Observer Nov 15 1849

THE BODY OF DR. COOLIDGE. In reply to an inquiry made by the editor of the Augusta Banner - he has received the following letter from Dr. Holland of Canton.

Canton, Nov 5, 1849

Br. Drew: In the Banner of last week, I noticed an inquiry whether the body disinterred at Canton, (as the body of Dr. Coolidge,) bore the marks of a post mortem examination. I was a well acquainted with Dr. Coolidge and was present at the second disinterment; saw the incision in the stomach: and noticed that the skull had been removed. The position of the skull (as it was pressed forward) made him look wide across the forehead; and this is the reason, that many supposed it was not the body of Dr. Coolidge. When the head was raised, so as to let the removed part of the skull take its original position, then, it looked like Dr. V. P. Coolidge.

As the first examination I presume the head was not moved, hence, the conclusion of some of the spectators.

I write this that the public may rest satisfied in this matter.,

With much respect,

Cornelius M. Holland.

Trial of Dr. Valorus P. Coolidge

It turned out that the above letter was not from *Doctor* Cornelius Holland, but rather his son, Cornelius M. Holland, aged 27 and a farmer at the 1850 census.

Portland Advertiser Nov 27, 1849
The following communication from a physician of known respectability, will be read with interest at this time, when the public mind is agitated on the question of Dr. Coolidge's death. As we have before said, we are bound to keep the public informed of all developments in regard to this important question, until the matter is satisfactorily "put to rest" - Hallowell Gazette

Dr Coolidge Again

Messrs. Editors: - I noticed in your paper of the 10th its, a letter published originally in the Banner and signed Cornelius M. Holland, in which an opinion is expressed that the dead body of Valorous P. Coolidge was buried in Canton. Whether that opinion be correct, I cannot say, as I was not present at either of the disinternments. Had I been there at the *first*, I think it must have been very easy for me to have decided the question, to the satisfaction of my *own* mind, at least. But the *letter*, I notice, is copied into all the papers, and is acquiring an undue importance from the statement, or rather misstatement of Mr. Drew, that it was written by *Dr. Holland.* I have conversed with the Dr. on the subject, and learned from him that he did not see the body at all. The explanation is, that the letter was written by Cornelius M., the son, instead of Cornelius the father.

So I think the question is not "put to rest," as the opinion expressed in the letter is contrary to that of a great many individuals as well qualified to judge, perhaps, as the writer, not designing to detract in the least from the intelligence or honesty of Mr. Holland. On the contrary, he is distinguished for both. I feel none of the aspirations for notoriety attributed to Dr. Mann in connection with this subject, and am far from wishing to agitate unnecessarily. But I *do* think it is one in which the public interest is deeply involved, and ought to be investigated.

The question of burying at Canton, would be, it is true, *comparatively* "unimportant" where the question of dying "put to rest". But it is not. Thousands do not believe that Coolidge is dead, and never will without more light. And I hope somebody will keep the subject before the people till an investigation is had, and the question "put to rest.". W. B. S.[4]

E. Livermore, Nov. 19, 1847.

---

[4] Perhaps Dr. William B. Small. See *Notes, Historical, Descriptive and Personal, of Livermore* (1874) by Israel Washburn, p. 85.

246

Is Coolidge Dead?

Dr. Mann continued publishing depositions, and also a supporting letter from another physician who criticizes Dr. Rose's autopsy.

Piscataquis Observer Dec 27th 1849
THAT EVERLASTING COOLIDGE CASE. Dr. Mann's "Down East Screamer" which is issued *semi-occasionally*, contains its wonted supply of testimony in relation to the pretended death of V. P. Coolidge. He introduces the depositions of E. Blaisdell, G. D. Stevens, William Childs, Calvin Simmons, Alexander Alden, Jr., Joseph Coolidge and Samuel Bean to prove that the body buried at Canton, was not the body of V. P. Coolidge. - He also publishes a letter from Calvin Blake, M.D., of Hartford, who, in the closing paragraph of his letter says:

"It has fallen in my province to conduct Post Mortem examinations, in several instances where death was occasioned by arsenic, Delirium tremens, and many other diseases or causalities of a similar nature, and from my own observation and knowledge of anatomy, medicine &c., I am free to say that that the report of the Prison Physicians is most bungling, untenable, and disgraceful; and from it and the other circumstances attending the affair, we have a right to conclude that Coolidge has escaped and a trick played upon the people."

The following story was widely copied in newspapers throughout the state, but not taken seriously.

Piscataquis Observer May 21 1851
THE QUESTION SETTLED. A correspondent of the Boston Traveller, who has lately visited Rockland and Thomaston, in speaking of the Maine State Prison, says: "I went into the cell where the celebrated Dr. Coolidge was confined. The officers told me that he was undoubtedly hung, and is a dead man but some Maine people think otherwise." - That part of the story which represents that Coolidge was hung, will doubtless be news to the most of our readers.

Coolidge is Seen

Reports of Coolidge being sighted occurred sporadically for decades to come, and often were picked up and reprinted by newspapers across the country.

The earliest report of an actual sighting of Coolidge was in October of 1849. Unlike later reports, this one does not seem to have been picked up by other newspapers.

The Maine Cultivator and Hallowell Gazette October 27, 1849
A gentleman stepped into our office yesterday and told us that he had been credibly informed, by a person of unimpeached veracity, that he had seen Dr. Coolidge a few days since in the vicinity of Livermore.
Dr. Mann passed through this place on Tuesday in hot haste. He might have been on the track.

The most widely disseminated report was a brief notice that he had been seen in California; this is a logical place for a sighting, since there was a very large migration to California at the time, and all the Maine newspapers were full of stories about Maine residents' adventures travelling to California, the gold diggings, and so on.

The Daily Spy (Worcester). Tuesday November 20. 1849.
DR. COOLIDGE, THE MURDERER, IN CALIFORNIA. The editor of the American Union received, by the Empire City, a letter written by a former resident of Maine, and dated ''Short Bar, 30 miles from Coloma, Sept. 3d.' addressed to a gentleman in Boston, in which he finds the following extraordinary paragraph. The writer says he was well acquainted with Coolidge at Waterville, and cannot be mistaken in his statement.
"Yesterday morning, there came up here three strangers from Sacramento City, one of whom I recognized as the notorious Dr. Valorus P. Coolidge, formerly of Waterville, Me. – the alleged murderer of Mathews! Could I be mistaken? How came he here? Has he escaped hanging? I knew Coolidge well, at Waterville – and if this is not him, then I never saw the man, His beard was very thin and scattered over his thin narrow face, but it had grown out two or three inches in length. He passed here by the name of Wilkes, or Wilkins. His eye I could not mistake. He appeared well, but in no other way

altered, save that he was meanly dressed, and looked a little harder than usual. I told my believe to W., and the next morning, Coolidge was gone. Where he has wandered, I cannot guess – but I feel sure that it was him. – If you ever write, tell me what this can mean. – Or, am I deceived?

In 1874 Coolidge is declared to be the leader of a gang of train robbers. With the passage of 25 years, some of the facts of the case have "evolved".

New York Dispatch. January 11, 1874.
THE IOWA TRAIN ROBBERS.
THEIR LEADER RECOGNIZED AS AN ESCAPE MURDER FROM MAINE –
A STRANGE STORY.
(Correspondence of the St. Louis Dispatch,)

The following document was given to me by a man now living in Missouri, who is a native of Maine, who was perfectly familiar with the circumstances of the murder therein detailed, who was a gallant Federal officer in a Maine regiment during the war, and who, since the war, removed to Western Missouri and engaged in a profitable and extensive business:

"More than twenty years ago, V. P. Coolidge, a young physician of excellent standing in the city of Augusta, Me., murdered Edward Mathews, a rich cattle drover, by enticing him along into his office to take a drink of brandy, which he had mixed with prussic acid, and then, to make sure work of the man who had befriended him on many occasions, he beat him on the head with a hatchet until life was extinct. The body was discovered, and Coolidge was arrested on suspicion, and, after a long and exciting trial, and upon the direct evidence of a young student of his by name of Flint, he was convicted and sentenced to a year's solitary confinement, and then to be hung. During his confinement his sister, a young and beautiful girl, was permitted to visit him, but his health gradually gave way, and before the year expired his death was announced; he was buried.

"Not long after the gold excitement opened in California, a gentleman who was conversant with the case, and who had followed others to the gold regions, sent back his deposition that he had seen and conversed with V. P. Coolidge. This caused considerable excitement, and the body supposed to be his was exhumed, and his own father testified that it was not his son. Officers were at once put upon his track by Mathews's friends, but were unsuccessful, and until a few days nothing has ever been heard of the murderer. Recently, a party travelling through the State met a gentleman who knew the early history of the matter, and was at the trial, and he stated that he had met Coolidge frequently within the past two years, travelling under an assumed name; that he recognized him at sight, and charged him with being the man; that he at first denied it, but finally acknowledged his identify, and informed him of all the important facts connected with the escape, as follows: He ate very sparingly, feigned sickness, and finally a body was procured from Portland, and interred as his remains, and he was furnished with money and started for New Orleans, where he remained but a short time and left, and since that time has been traveling almost constantly, never stopping long in any one place; and the gentleman referred to as having met him in the northern part of this State gave it as his positive belief that, from the description of the leader of the Iowa train robbers, it was no other than the escaped murderer, V. P. Coolidge.

I will note, as a curiosity, that Coolidge's sister, Jane (born 1818, married to Flavel Sabin in 1841, and aged 31 in 1849), a resident of Missouri, did come to Maine and spent the winter of 1848-1849 there, where she was a regular visitor at the State Prison. She is reported to have died in New Orleans in 1850.

Another variation was published in 1892.

Portland Daily Press, March 26, 1892. Also the Ellsworth American march 31ˢᵗ.; from the Tuolumne Independent.
AFTER MANY YEARS.
MYSTERY OF A FAMOUS WATERVILLE MURDER CASE EXPLAINED.
The Guilty Man Escaped from Prison by Feigning Death.

He was a Young Physician who was convicted of killing his friend many years ago – now, a story told in California by a woman who knew him there, confirms suspicions that the Murderer Escaped.
[Special to the Press]
Waterville, March 26. – An article published in an obscure California weekly, and copied into a local paper, has occasioned much gossip here concerning a murder committed some forty-four years ago. Along in 1841, V. P Coolidge, M.D., came into Waterville and hung out his shingle. He was a nice appearing young man of twenty-three, or thereabout, and as he seemed a gentleman and to have a thorough knowledge of medicine he soon took a high place in the then small village.

Among one of the leading families of this city, almost from its founding has been the Mathews family. Mr. Edward Mathews at that time was about the same age as Doctor Coolidge, and engaged in buying cattle for the Brighton market. He also took a leading position among the young men of the community. Of course the two social leaders met, and a strong friendship developed itself.

Along in '48, Coolidge lost considerable money gambling, and applied to his friend for a loan, at the same time swearing him to secrecy, as such a report could hurt his practice.

Mathews agreed to lend his friend $2000 and keep absolutely quiet about it. But as his money was at that time almost all invested, he was obliged to get part of it from his uncle, Mr. John Mathews, and he told his uncle that he was going to lend the money to Coolidge and take his book accounts as security.

The night after John Mathews gave this money to his nephew, there was

A Dance at the Balkum Tavern,

Now the Wheeler House, on Silver street. It came out afterwards that Mathews told Coolidge he had the money, and the doctor replied that during the intermission they would go up to his office, settle the matter, and sample some of his brandy. During the intermission, as planned, they went up to the office, located over the store now occupied by O. S. Emerson. Coolidge poured out some brandy, Mathews drank it, and then fell dead. Just then in walked Tom Flint, of Anson, then studying medicine with Coolidge. Coolidge, on threat of proclaiming him the murderer, swore him to secrecy and made him help dispose of Mathews, who, Flint saw, had been poisoned by drinking prussic acid. They lugged him out, and placed him at the bottom of the cellar rollway, where it might look as if when drunk he had fallen and broken his neck.

The utter absence of any bruises, such as would accompany a fall proved that supposition wrong. Although last seen with Coolidge, so high was the latter's reputation that no suspicion was directed to him, until to his great astonishment John Mathews told about the loan.

The doctor then was tried and on Flint's evidence sent to state prison for life. His sister, a beautiful girl, at once moved down to Thomaston to comfort her brother as much as possible. The business of both men gave them a statewide reputation, and the murder made a great sensation, which had hardly died away when a report came that Coolidge has been

Found Dead in His Cell

Some of his acquaintances went over to the prison, and upon seeing the corpse declared up and down that it was not the body of the medical murderer. Soon a report came from California that Coolidge had been seen there, working under an assumed name. Numerous corroborations of this report followed. Then the announcement of the marriage of Miss Coolidge and the prison warden confirmed the belief that V. P. Coolidge had escaped.

The last number of the Tuloumne Independent tells the story of a meeting between Mrs. Richard Parker, formerly of Maine, and Coolidge, on the street in Columbia. This meeting took place many years ago, shortly after Coolidge's escape. He tried to deny his identify, but could not deceive Mrs. Parker, and finally confessed. Mrs. Parker became a friend to Coolidge and nursed him through a case of small pox in 1852. Finally, the culprit died a natural death, and was buried in Springfield, Cal. Mrs. Parker lately revealed the secret, which for the first time was given to the public though the columns of the Independent.

This story was widely reprinted, and generated a series of interesting letters in the Rockland Courier-Gazette. That paper was a descendant of the Lime Rock Gazette.

Rockland Courier-Gazette April 12, 1892
DID DR. V. P. COOLIDGE ESCAPE?
TWO OPPOSING OPINIONS ON THIS MOOTED QUESTION
A Well Known Warren Resident and C.-G. Correspondent
Thinks He Escaped - A Former "Gazette" Editor Writes a Strong
Denial

V. P. Coolidge's alleged escape from the Maine State Prison still excites attention. We print below two letters on the subject, the writers of each are well known to our people.

"At the time of the report of Coolidge's death I was engaged in remodeling the upper story of the Lincoln Court-house into a private hall, one of the inspectors of the Maine State Prison[1] being chairman of the remodeling committee. Early in the forenoon I was with the prison inspector in James Bracket's store, selecting hardware for the hall, when a person came to the door and called the inspector aside. As the topic seemed to be an exciting one, I asked, on the return of the inspector, what was wanted. He replied, 'Coolidge is dead.' I inquired: 'Do you suppose it is so?' 'Do I suppose it is so? yes. What the devil did they send up for me for, if he isn't?'

The peculiar emphasis given to the reply awakened a suspicion that Coolidge was not dead. So when the inspector came to the hall after his return, I made definite inquiries about the circumstance, the answer to which served to strengthen my morning suspicions. But I have kept these and more important facts from the public until the present time, having spoken of them privately to but a few individuals. I have always shrunk from notoriety, but will now give the Courier-Gazette, which has opened the Coolidge topic afresh, a few points that I endorse as reliable.

"After the Coolidge excitement had died down and Dr. Mann had ceased to investigate the case, I was engaged finishing the outside

---

[1] In April 1849 the three inspectors of the Maine State Prison were Dr. Benjamin F. Buxton, George A. Starr and Stephen Barrows.

of the Baptist Church in Bath. Among the inside crew was a man from the town and school-district of Dr. Coolidge, a school-mate of his. The following is his statement to me, which I fully rely on:

"Says the gentleman: 'I was a schoolmate of Dr. Coolidge, knew him well, knew he had a birth-mark which I had frequently seen. A piece, too, had been cut from the end of one thumb. I knew I could identify his body by these marks. When his body was to be taken up, I was one of the committee, and started for the grave with no other thought than that of finding Coolidge, but when we came to the family burying yard neatly fenced in from a pasture we were shown a grave on the pasture side as the Doctor's grave. This excited my suspicion, and when we had examined the body I found no birthmark, but two perfect thumbs.' "

I. J. Burton.

Warren, Mar, 31, 1892.

"Mr. Editor - I was surprised to find in your issue of March 29 a revival, without contradiction, of the old story that V. P. Coolidge, the Waterville murderer, escaped from the State Prison at Thomaston and was afterwards recognized in California, where he lived some time and subsequently died.

"Now there is not a fact in history more fully and certainly established, by direct, cumulative and irrefragable evidence, than the fact that Dr. V. P. Coolidge actually died in the Maine State Prison at the time stated, and that his body was identified by persons who had seen him daily in the prison and who testified to seeing it buried.

"If Coolidge escaped it was by the contrivance and assistance of the prison authorities. It was a most difficult undertaking, for not only was Coolidge to be smuggled out of the prison, but it was also necessary to find and smuggle in a corpse so marvelously like Coolidge as to deceive men who had seen him every day or week for months preceding his death. There was not once chance in a thousand that this latter fact could be accomplished without detection. Besides, there was never a scintilla of evidence produced that the prison officials, or any of them, were guilty of the offense implied, nor any just suspicion that they were capable of it. The only foundation for such a conclusion was a baseless rumor that Coolidge had been mysteriously released, and the only evidence to support it the fact that after Coolidge's body had been removed from its place of burial at Thomaston, by a relative, and interred in a distant part of the state, it was exhumed some time later and its identity then disputed - being denied by some and affirmed by others.

"The reason why the C-G. expressed no doubts or denial of this story of the Tuolunme, Cal., Independent is sufficiently accounted for by the fact that the present editor was not contemporary with the earlier facts, nor familiar with their re-statement some fifteen or twenty years go. But if you will look back at the files of the Rockland Gazette of the period when this Coolidge canard was first started, you will find a complete statement of the facts of Coolidge's death and burial, with affidavits from men of undoubted integrity, who saw the body and fully identified it before and at the time of the burial. And many years later (perhaps in the early 70's · cannot now recall the date) when this story of Coolidge in California was again revived and going the rounds of the Maine papers, the writer (then editor of the Gazette) endeavored to give it tis quietus by a careful resume of the case from the data and evidence in the Gazette's earlier files. This re-statement may be found in the editorial columns of the paper of the date in question.

"There is no better evidence that George Washington died in 1799 or that Napoleon ended his life in St. Helena, or that President Garfield died at Elberon, N.J., on the 20th of September, 1881, then that Valorus P. Coolidge was found dead in his prison cell at Thomaston at the time stated, but despite this fact, established a certain as any fact can be established by human testimony, I have no doubt that the sensational rumors of his subsequent appearance in California will continue to be revived and believed, while the sober evidence of disinterested and truthful men who saw him in his cell at Thomaston will be discredited."

Z. Pope Vose
Minneapolis, April 2, 1892

The first letter contains the only notice I have seen that the grave exhumed in Canton was outside the borders of the family graveyard.   Vose's letter generated a strong response from another local.

The Courier-Gazette, April 19, 1892
THE FAMOUS COOLIDGE CASE
A ROCKLAND CITIZEN IS POSITIVE THAT COOLIDGE ESCAPED
He Analyzes the Testimony · Stomps the "Dead in His Cell"
Theory as Absurd · A Belief Rife in California · Why he Was Not
Apprehended.

EDITOR COURIER GAZETTE. Having been contemporary with the trial of Dr. V. P. Coolidge for the murder at Waterville of Edward Mathews, and of the escape of the former from the prison at Thomaston I desire to present some facts bearing upon the case not all of which have heretofore been given to the public. At the outset I must deny most emphatically the statement of your correspondent Mr. Vose that there is no better evidence of the death of Washington, Napoleon, et als. than of Coolidge in his cell. There may be proof that a dead body was found in the morning where a young and robust man had been left at night, but proof they were one and the same has never been advanced against the proof that they were not the same.

The theories advanced relating to Coolidge's death are weak and absurd, and if true, show almost as great culpability on the part of those in authority at the prison as an open acknowledgement of their connivance at his escape. If, as was claimed, he died from poison, who provided the poison? It was not necessary to end his days in that way to avert hanging, and it is by no means likely that his friends provided a deadly drug and caused it to be conveyed to him. Any official who would have procured it for him would as readily · for a consideration · have assisted in his escape. A life prisoner always hopes to escape, and every one conversant with the case knows that Coolidge was constantly on the alert for that purpose. The theory that he died from poison is scarcely less preposterous than that first advanced, that he died of a broken heart!

The testimony of those who examined the resurrected body, including at least two members of Coolidge's family, not only failed to identify it as him, but positively declared that it was not his remains. In the presence of these well known and undisputed facts how can any candid person assert that the place and date of his death are as certain as events which have never been questioned. Such assertions are nonsense. If only the facts already given were at our command to substantiate the belief that Coolidge escaped, that belief would be regarded as well founded; but other proof is not wanting.

Thirty five years ago, in California, the belief was universal among Maine people that Dr. V. P. Coolidge was then living in that state. If reliable testimony is to be accepted, he was repeatedly seen and recognized. The writer of this article has met many men on the Pacific coast who not only believed, but were able to offer reasonable proof that the famous Maine homicide was a denizen of that country; one, a most candid man, had heard from the lips of an acquaintance (a Kennebec man) the most positive assertion that he had met and recognized Coolidge. For years every traveler from California brought similar accounts.

It may be asked, if these statements are true, why Coolidge was never apprehended and made to suffer the punishment he so richly merited? To those who are familiar with early times in California, no answer or explanation is necessary. To those who're not, it may be said that people were too busy minding their own business, too engrossed in the pursuit of gold to attempt the arrest of any one who was not known to be guilty of a crime in the immediate vicinity. No man was molested for what he did in another state. No officer was sent from this state to attempt his capture, and if any had gone, the object of his quest, often changing his name and residence, couldn't easily have been found.

To the foregoing may be added the statements lately published, of a lady who nursed the subject of this controversy through a severe sickness, and had personal knowledge of his whereabouts for years. It seems likely that it can be ascertained whether she is a myth or a reality.

It has been, and still is, the custom of those who deny Coolidge's escape, to browbeat the witnesses and set naked assertion against a striking array of positive and circumstantial evidence.

The statements made in this communication have come to the writer [?] He believes that much more evidence bearing on the question can be found for the seeking.

D. C. Perkins.
Rockland April 13, 1892.

Z. Pope Vose published other subsequent articles in the *Courier-Gazette* debunking the notion that Coolidge had escaped. There were another series of articles in that paper in 1897 including an original contribution by the paper: interviews with two men who were, as youths, employed at the prison at the time of Coolidge's supposed death.

The Courier-Gazette, July 6, 1897
Interviews With the Two Surviving Prison Officials - Clear
Testimony

The revival of the old Coolidge murder mystery, whether profitable or not, at least has resulted in provoking much interest and discussion, The two young men who were officials at the time of Coolidge's death - Hon. E. K. O'Brien and Col. S. H. Allen - yet reside in Thomaston. They are the only ones living so far as known who can give personal recollections of the events connected with Coolidge's death. A representative of the Courier-Gazette called on these gentlemen last week.

Mr. O'Brien laughed at the suggestion that Coolidge ever got away from prison or that the body of the man who was buried was other than that of Coolidge. Mr. O'Brien said:

"I was a guard at the prison at the time and although I was but 16 years old I recollect the event of this man's death very vividly. I was given the position of guard by Warden Carr, thinking I would like it, but was glad to sever my connection with the institution after a few months service.

"I saw Coolidge very often. He was a good looking young man, 27 years old, pleasant and agreeable, and what ladies would call a very attractive man. He had charge of one wing of the prison and was well behaved. With the exception of a man from Virginia, who was serving time for forgery, Coolidge was the only educated man in the prison. I remember once he was in solitary confinement but do not know for what reason, probably because it was customary at the time to make life prisoners serve a certain time in solitary.

"I recollect the night Coolidge died. Col. Allen was on duty and I saw him pass Coolidge a bowl of steaming porridge and saw Coolidge eat the contents. Coolidge had been complaining that day of not feeling well. The next day he died, undoubtedly of taking poison with the porridge.

"I was present at the post mortem examination and saw Coolidge's head cut open and his heart examined. The body was seen by me three times and there is not a question of doubt but that the body buried in the prison yard was that of the same man who lived in the prison cell in the person of Coolidge. I heard him ask before his death if relatives were allowed to take away the body of a prisoner after death. It is all bosh to think for a moment that Coolidge did not die in prison."

Col. Allen was seen by our representative and he spoke very freely concerning Coolidge.

"I was an overseer at the time of Coolidge's death," said Col. Allen, "and I remember very distinctly the circumstances, I was with Coolidge the night he died. He had not been feeling very well that day and asked for some hot gruel; he was very anxious to know what would become of his body, should he die. He seemed to have a fear that he would be buried in the prison yard, but I assured him that his relatives or friends could claim the body and bury it where they desired.

"Coolidge took the bowl of hot gruel which I gave him and almost immediately commenced to vomit. He soon lost consciousness from which he never recovered, dying the next day, He undoubtedly took poison in his gruel, but how he got the poison I do not know. I was not present at the post mortem examination but I helped lay the body out, also helped carry the body to the prison cemetery and bury it. There was never any question of doubt in my mind but what the body was that of Coolidge.

"It was but a short time afterwards when the body was exhumed and taken away. Coolidge never said a word to me about dying until that night. He was a model prisoner and served as a waiter. On account of his education he was much feared and respected by the other prisoners.

"I remember that he wrote several letters and gave them to a prisoner named Brown who was soon to be liberated. Some of the letters were instructions to Brown while one was in the nature of a confession. Brown, who had in his profession accidentally killed two persons, had but little regard for human life. Coolidge's instructions to him were to find a suitable person, hit him on the back of the head in such a manner as not to leave a plain wound, then force some prussic acid down the unfortunate victim's throat and leave the empty bottle by his side. This confession, written by Coolidge, was to be found in a pocket. All this to give the impression that the man had confessed to killing Mathews for which crime Coolidge himself was serving sentence, and that he (the victim) had committed suicide from remorse. Coolidge, of course, would then be set free. It was a diabolical scheme and worthy of the fertile mind of Coolidge.

"One day Brown complained of being sick, but I had my doubts, and instead of allowing him to go to the hospital I put him in confinement. He made a confession and delivered over to me the letters written and given him by Coolidge. A few days after this Coolidge died.

Coolidge died in prison, of this there can be no doubt, and it is rank nonsense to think otherwise."

"Coolidge's prison number was 927 and the prison records state that he was 27 years old, born in Canton, Me., residence Waterville, was 5 feet 8 3/4 inches tall, had black hair and dark complexion.

It is interesting that these two men both consider it certain that Coolidge was poisoned. There were two prisoners at Thomaston of the name Brown, as of April 30, 1849, as reported in the 1850 Warden's report.

- Henry Brown, age 18, convicted of larceny, sentence 2 years, committed Oct 21, 1847.
- George Brown, age 28, convicted of adultery, sentence 1 year, committed December 12, 1848.

Neither one seems a likely candidate for Coolidge's proposed confederate, based on the combination of age and crime, and their presumed release date. Both are, as would be expected, absent from the list of April 30, 1850.

There are other discrepancies with the original story- that spoke of the letters being turned in by a young prisoner, not Coolidge's confederate, and the supposed confederate had not been charged because at that time there was not sufficient proof.

258

Appendices

Appendix I: Case of Internal Strangulation of the Ileum

The following article, written by Coolidge, was published in The Boston Medical and Surgical Journal - precursor to The New England Journal of Medicine - about 5 months before the death of Mathews, and describes a case where Coolidge, along with Dr. Stephen Thayer, was called on to consult on a difficult case by Dr. Samuel Plaisted, the attending physician. After the patient's death, there was a necropsy, performed by Coolidge. Plaisted, Thayer and Coolidge were the same three physicians that performed the autopsy on Mathews, and both the procedure described in the article below and Mathews's autopsy were attended by Prof. Loomis, Dr. Boutelle and "a medical student." This helps to establish Coolidge's professional standing in the community.

"Case of Internal Strangulation of the Ileum." *The Boston Medical and Surgical Journal.* Vol XXXVI, No 17, May 26, 1847, pp 339-341.

Mrs. G., aet. 29, of medium stature; naturally of a delicate constitution; never was in gestation; for several years past has had occasional attacks of vomiting, dizziness, and pain in the abdomen, which were generally relieved in a few hours by mild cathartics and carminatives; habitually costive; was never dyspeptic, but her food produced an uneasy sensation in her bowels.

On Sunday, April 18, 11 o'clock P.M., I was called in consultation upon her case. Arriving at the house I met Dr. Thayer, who had been called at the same time, and Dr. Plaisted in attendance. I there learned that on Saturday previous she was attacked with similar symptoms as on former occasions; Dr. Plaisted being immediately called, ordered a dose of ol. ricini and an enema of fol. sennae, mag. sulph. and pulv. jalapae. The injection produced a slight evacuation. Sunday morn, the symptoms having increased in severity, Dr. P. ordered a dose of calomel, the enema to be repeated, a warm bath, and fomentations with poultices to the feet and abdomen.

I found the patient tossing about the bed, with intense pain in the back and bowels; pain not increased by pressure, nor influenced by position; pulse a little accelerated; skin moist; some thirst; occasional vomiting of substances taken into the stomach; had had no alvine evacuation for the past twenty-four hours. Prescribed, hyd. chlo. mit., j.; fomentations to be continued; an enema of soap and warm water, and one sixth of a grain of sulphate of morphia every hour or two, until the pain should be relieved.

Dr, Thayer and myself remained with her most of the time until five o'clock Monday morning when we left her, with vomiting unchecked; but coming gradually under the influence of the morphia, which was continued until 9 o'clock, A.M., when she became quiet.

From between 8 and 9 o'clock, Monday A.M., until 8 P.M., she was under unprofessional treatment, and I did not see her. At 8 o'clock, however, Drs. T., P., and myself were again called. Found her sinking; pulse 165; no evacuation from the bowels; without pain; some distention of the lower part of the abdomen; extremities cool; countenance anxious. Nothing was ordered, believing her case hopeless.

Saw her again Tuesday, 4 o'clock, A.M. Was then pulseless at the wrist; extremities cold; countenance Hippocratic. She gradually sunk, and expired between 11 and 12 o'clock, A.M., retaining her mental faculties to the last.

Permission for an examination being granted, I was requested to take charge of it.

Necropsy, 23 hours after death. Present, Prof. Loomis, Dr. Thayer, Dr. Boutelle, H.A. Smith, Esq., and a medical student. Abdomen a little distended with flatus; cavity opened by a crucial incision; beneath the integument was a deposit of fat three or four lines thick; the peritoneum contained a small quantity of bloody serum. Bowels, examined in situ, were congested; a portion of the lower part of the ileum was a very dark color, approaching gangrene; found extensive adhesions of the right hypochondriac and lumbar regions, the bowels being agglutinated and confined to the abdominal parietes, throughout nearly the whole of those divisions, by an organized adventitious deposit. No other unnatural appearances being observed, the viscera were removed for a more careful examination.

The sanguineous vessels of the stomach were injected and arborescent; a small patch of the greater curvature, softened, and of an ash color; the mucous membrane generally, throughout the whole alimentary canal, was erythematous. About three inches from the ilio-caecal valve, a portion of the ileum, twenty-eight inches long, was found strangulated by an abnormal band thrown across a convolution of that intestine, so as to strangulate it at each end of the coil, originating near the attachment of the ileum to the mesentery, and passing entirely round, with few minor adhesions, to the place of its origin; forming a ring around the neck of the strangulated part. That part of the ring opposite to its attachment, was round like a cord, and about the size of a pack threat, strong and somewhat elastic. The intercepted part was in a state of incipient gangrene, full of faecal matter, and portions of it thickened and indurated. A little above the last, unconnected with other adhesions, was another adventitious band, about an inch long, and three lined wide, lying on the ileum, parallel to the mesenteric attachment and about half an inch from it, under which the thumb could be readily passed. The examination was not carried farther, V. P. Coolidge, M.D.

Waterville, Me., May 10, 1847

The journal made several subsequent notices of Coolidge's trial and conviction.

Dr. Coolidge, of Waterville, Me., is accused, and now under arrest for the murder of a Mr. Mathews, with prussic acid, in his office. Dr. C. has been a physician in reputable standing. An interesting case of strangulation of the ileum, reported by him, may be found in the last volume of this Journal. Vol 37, 1848 p 267.

And another, published after conviction, looks like jealousy on the part of some other physician in Waterville - the journal could hardly have gotten this information in any other way. The description of his appearance is curiously detailed.

Dr. Coolidge, who was convicted of murder, in Maine is about 27 years of age, of very genteel form, dark hair, rather pleasant countenance, small dark eyes, somewhat sunken and very restless, no whiskers, and scarcely any beard, forehead not high, and temples pinched in; mouth decently well formed, nose rather thin, but finely chiselled, face narrow, and expression mild, denoting rather sweetness of temper than depravity of heart. He has not the look of a murderer, neither has he the appearance of much genius or talent. His face and form look as if he might have been a ladies' man. And this quality, no doubt, carried him along in his profession more successfully than any deep science or great skill. Vol 38, 1848, p 208.

Appendices

Appendix II: Dartmouth Medical School

Coolidge is listed as a senior in the *Catalogue of the Officers and Students of Dartmouth College, for the Academical Year 1843-44.* A description of the courses and requirements for graduation are given below.

The annual course of MEDICAL LECTURES begins one week after Commencement, and continues three months. Four Lectures are delivered daily; a part of the time, five. The fees of the course are fifty dollars. The matriculating fee is three dollars. The Library fee, for those who take books, is fifty cents. Surgical operations are performed gratuitously before the Medical Class, during the lecture term.

GRADUATION

Each candidate for the degree of M.D. Must be twenty-one years of age; must possess a good moral character, an acquaintance with natural and experimental Philosophy, and knowledge of the principles and construction of the Latin language; must have studied medicine three full years, with some regular practitioner; must have attended two courses of public Lectures in all the branches of the profession, at a regularly organized Medical Institution, one of which courses shall have been attended at the Institution; must have passed a successful private examination before the Medical Faculty; and must have read and defended, in their presence, an acceptable dissertation on some medical subject.

The graduating expenses are eighteen dollars.

Coolidge's listing as a junior gave his home as Buckfield, Maine, and shows he has studied with C. H. Coolidge, M.D. In his senior year a second instructor was added, O.P. Hubbard, M.D. Oliver Payson Hubbard was Professor of Chemistry and Pharmacy at the medical school. There were a total of 24 seniors in this class.

Appendix III: A Medical View of Prussic Acid from 1842

The article below provides considerable information on prussic acid as a poison, and on its uses as a medicine.

Extracted from:
Andrew, Thomas, M.D., Etc. *A Cyclopedia of Domestic medicine and Surgery; being an Alphabetical Account of the various Diseases incident to the Human Frame;* [...] Glasgow: Blackie and Son, 1842. Pages 270 - 273.

HYDROCYANIC, or PRUSSIC ACID.

This acid is one of the most powerful poisons derived from the vegetable kingdom with which we have yet become acquainted. It is limpid and colourless, resembling pure water in appearance, but having a pungent odour highly irritating to the nostrils, with a peculiar sensation extending down the windpipe, and if inhaled incautiously and in large quantity producing giddiness or faintness. Its taste is peculiar, resembling bitter almonds or laurel leaves, but great caution is necessary in applying the undiluted acid to the tongue, as the operation is attended with great danger, and the taste will be discovered when diluted with eight or ten times its quantity of water.

The ancients were well acquainted with the poisonous nature of many of those plants which yield this acid, for the noxious quality of the oil of bitter almonds is noticed by Xenophon and Dioscorides, and the poisonous quality of laurel leaves by Strabo. It was not, however, until about the middle of the last century that chemists had learned to extract the poisonous or other peculiar qualities from either animal, mineral, or vegetable substances, a vast number of the latter having this acid in their composition. In 1772, Scheile, a celebrated chemist, whose name we shall have often a reason to mention, discovered this acid in a dilute or mixed form, and since that another continental chemist, Gay Lussac, in its pure state. This acid, as has lately been ascertained, is not a relative but a universal poison. It is noxious to the higher animals in various degrees, according to strength and size and the nature of their food. For example, a drop or two injected into the vein of a feeble and carnivorous dog will produce as fatal and distressing effects as half an ounce in the powerful and herbivorous horse. The experiments of Coullon, Emmeret, and others, prove that it is not less deadly to fishes, insects, and worms; and still later experimenters have extended the wide domain of this poison, and shown its power over the vegetable kingdom, over those very plants that have been for ages past harbouring and nursing it in their roots and stalks, and among their leaves, flowers, and fruit; for the cherry, laurel, and bitter almond tree are not less the victims of its poisonous action than others. Nay, unlike its sister oxalic acid, which is said to promote germination, and resuscitate decayed or old seeds, it destroys the power of germination.

This acid exists in varions natural forms, and in varied proportions, in bitter almonds, and in the kernels of the cherry, the apricot, and different sorts of plums, the peach leaves and flower, the nectarine, and cherry, laurel trees, the bark of the bird cherry-tree. The *prunus padus*, or bird cherry-tree, and the *prunus spinosus*, or black thorn-tree, are indigenous to the three kingdoms. Prussic acid is likewise met with in various artificial mixtures, such as the distilled water of the cherry and laurel, the essential oil of bitter almonds, *kirschen wasser*, and cherry brandy; and to procure this, the makers of cherry brandy bruise the stones and kernel that the liquors may have the advantage of the flavour and taste imparted by the prussic acid in the kernel. Ratafla, macaroons, and other cordials and confections have the odour and taste of bitter almonds. Of all those forms the operation is essentially the same as is the noxious element, varied only by the dose, state of combination, and other incidental circumstances, especially the state of the stomach; for were those who indulge in cherry brandy and other liquors and confections often highly impregnated with this acid on an empty stomach in place of doing so after dinner, we should hear more of their deleterious effects than we now do. Many voyagers to India and other foreign parts, procuring cherry brandy free of duty, and ignorant of the very poisonous substance from which its fine flavour is derived, too frequently, we fear, indulge in the fascinating compound. On the continent, laurel water and other preparations are in common use. The symptoms produced in man are described by Dr Coullon whom we have already alluded to, and who experimented on himself by taking excessive doses, but not those necessarily perilous to life, are a quick pulse, anxiety, ptyalism, nausea, headache. When he took, says Dr Christison, from twenty to eighty-six drops of the diluted, he was attacked for a few minutes with nausea, salivation, hurried pulse, weight and pain in the head succeeded by a feeling of anxiety which lasted six hours. Such symptoms may be induced when this acid is pushed too far in treating disease. Professor Christison is of opinion that is is probable that very large doses occasion death in a few seconds, and at all events a few minutes will suffice to extinguish life when the dose is considerable, but if the individual survive thirty or forty minutes he will very generally recover. To sum up in a few words the symptoms produced by an improper use of prussic acid. When the dose is large, death is the immediate result; but if the dose do not exceed from ten to twenty drops, it is succeeded by stupor and weight in the head, nausea, faintness, and vertigo, with loss of sight, followed by difficulty of respiration, dilated pupils, a small vibrating pulse, and gaining, which terminates in death, if no curative means be employed.

The treatment, which observation and experience have proved most successful, is to administer diffusible stimuli, such as the carbonate of ammonia, or what is vulgarly called smelling salts, in solution, in such quantities as the patient can swallow, or liquid ammonia, such as the water of ammonia diluted with water and hot brandy and water. A tea spoonful of oil of juniper, or oil of turpentine, may be rubbed up in a mortar with half an ounce of lump sugar, and half a pint of brandy, run or whisky, and with an addition, an equal portion to water, the patient being compelled to swallow it in large wine glassfuls as quickly as possible. The aromatic spirit of ammonia is likewise an excellent diffusible stimulant, and a teaspoonful should be taken in every dose or wine glassful of the strong punch. Where the ammoniacal salt, or the liquid ammonia, or what are called hartshorn drops, or the aromatic spirit of ammonia, are not within reach, oil of turpentine and strong punch may be persevered in with some hope of success.

With respect to the tests commonly employed for the detection of prussic acid or any other poison, it were perhaps a work of supererogation to enter into details. We have, however, under the head of *Tests*, given an enumeration of those tests by which the most common poisons are discovered. For when any question arises before a court of law respecting the cause of the death of an individual, and that individual is supposed to have been poisoned, the most eminent physicians and chemists are summoned to examine the state and contents of the stomach, and satisfy the judge and jury on the subject. There will, however, be as much information found in our work, if attentively studied, as will enable any intelligent juryman to put an appropriate, and it may be a life-saving question even to a medical witness. Suffice it to state that the most common tests employed for the detection of prussic acid are the smell, the taste, and the reaction of the suspected substance, on the addition of certain saline solutions, viz., the solution of nitrate of silver, or lunar caustic, the sulphate of copper, or blue vitriol, both of which are cheap and easily procured. Or if a solution of common copperas is dropped into the prussic acid, it will produce a beautiful blue precipitate or Prussian blue. But the best in conjunction with this last, the most just and unequivocal, is the smell of the odour exhaled from the body. With respect to the modus operandi of this acid, there are many curious speculations, from a detail of which the general reader would derive little profit, although they might prove interesting to the curious inquirer. It may, however, not be without its use, even in a popular work of this kind, to allude to the morbid appearances discovered after death in the bodies of those who have died in consequence of an over-dose of this acid, taken either from ignorance, mistake, or wilfully, and what has been too frequently the case, secretly mixed in the food or drink of an unsuspecting individual.

We might almost state in no case has there ever been discovered any change of structure or trace of inflammatory action; but a strong odour o(bitter almonds or of the acid, pervades every part of the body; and but for this circumstance, in connection with other tests, the assassin might lull himself in entire security from any proof of his guilt being produced by an examination of the body. If the dose has proved fatal in a few minutes the blood of the heart, lungs, and great vessels will generally yield the odour of the acid; but if the subject survive for half an hour the odour may be altogether wanting. Schubarth, who appears to have investigated this point with great diligence, says that 'this speedy disappearance depends upon the rapidity with which the acid escapes in vapour by the lungs.' In cases of more speedy dissolution, the peculiar odour of the acid remains about eighteen or twenty hours after death; but this is not invariably the case, more especially if the body be exposed to rain or a current of air. A congested state of the vessels of the brain, a turgescence of the nervous system, and the empty state of the arteries throughout the body, are all appearances generally met with. Should the examination of the blood, which is frequently destitute of fluidity, and of preternatural dark colour, be deferred for some days, there is little chance of detecting the poison by the sense of smell, or indeed by any other test, so rapid the poison may have been in its operation, owing to its subtlety and volatility in the first instance, and secondly, to fragile chemical decomposition. The eyes present an uncommon appearance after death by this acid, which is by some considered almost an infallible evidence that the poison had been swallowed. There is a peculiar glistening of the eye which refers it difficult to believe that the individual is really dead. 'After poisoning its Prussic acid,' says Mark, 'even several hours after death, the eyes are found bright and animated, though utterly devoid of irritability,' which occasioned Huffland's expression, 'the clear fiery look just in such cases excite apprehension that the victim may be consigned yet living to the grave.' But Dr Christison states that death from carbonic acid or cholera may produce the same appearance. Where the sour of this acid is smelt exhaling from a dead body, an immediate examination should take place, as were it deferred to the usual period after death it were difficult, nay, impossible, to insure the ends of justice by a late examination, and the assassin might thus escape.

Medical effects of hydrocyanic acid. Strange as it may appear to those who are not versant with the laws of animal economy and effects of certain agents on the animal system, yet true it is, that this most virulent poison, in the hands of a skillful physician, may be the means of catching many a victim from an untimely grave. There is now happily a more simple and certain process discovered for its preparation than formerly, so that there is not that uncertainty as to the dose that then existed. For the simplest, and perhaps the best mode of preparing the acid, we are indebted to Dr Clark, formerly of Glasgow, now professor of chemistry in the university of Aberdeen. Cherry laurel water, emulsions of bitter almonds, and other vegetable substances and their preparations containing the acid, had, especially in Italy, been supposed to possess the power to moderate the action of the heart and lungs, and to oppose the invasion of fever and inflammation. These preparations were therefore strongly recommended in acute and chronic inflammations of the legs and heart, and especially in pulmonary consumption and expectoration of blood from the lungs. Since a method was discovered, or rather many years after a method was discovered, of separating the pure acid from the other vegetable principles with which it was united, the attention of the profession was directed to this acid as an almost infallible remedy for that scourge of Britain - consumption of the lungs; and Magendie, an eminent French physiologist and physician, was of opinion that it could cure consumption if given in the first stage of the disease; but this was no new idea, for the cherry laurel water had been long used in Italy, and even in Holland, as Linnaeus informs us, for the alleviation and cure of the same disease. Prussic acid indeed, shared the fate of every new remedy; volumes were published, and cases narrated in which it had performed wonders, and restored the consumptive invalid after there had been only one step between him and the grave. But it was not only in consumption the acid was recommended, but in a vast number of other affections, especially of the nervous system. Experiments were made, and because this acid could not effect all that its admirers pledged themselves it could do; in fine, because it would not do every thing, it was by many cast aside as if it could do nothing. Experience has, however, proved that although it cannot cure pulmonary consumption it may palliate and moderate the symptoms. In regulated doses in a diluted form it is still and justly recommended as a cure for some of the following diseases, and a useful palliative in others; but although we feel deep repugnance to see it in the hands of any other than a well educated and experienced physician, still we are well aware that there are even many besides who by proper directions administer this powerful remedy. In spasmodic asthma, whooping-cough, spasmodic cough, and in the numerous diseases of the heart, attended with inordinate action, in hiccough, in indigestion, to allay irritability of the stomach, heartburn, pain in the stomach, in inveterate vomiting, in simple or painter's colic, and in tic doloreux. It has been likewise employed as an external application to abate itching in many diseases of the skin attended with that troublesome sensation, and owing to its supposed specific action on mucus membranes, it has been used as a lotion or wash in cancerous affections of the womb.

There is one effect produced by this acid that we know of no other article in the material medica competent to effect, viz., checking continued vomiting, which it often does almost instantaneously; many lives were doubtless saved by it during the late prevalence of cholera, as it arrests the vomiting in that terrific disease almost as soon as it is administered; it was then administered to children in whom it proved equally efficacious as in adults, the pleasant tase and smell being inducement to swallow it. By arresting the vomiting of cholera, the further loss of the serous part of the blood is prevented; other medicines may be administered without any danger of their being rejected by the stomach, and if occasion require a due portion of nutriment may be given. The very inveterate and even prolonged cases of vomiting that occur in the first months of pregnancy, and which sometimes occasion abortion, but always debilitate, the sufferer may too be relieved by this remedy. In whooping-cough Professor Thomson designates it the physicians sheet anchor. The mode of administering the acid in the diseases in which experience has proved its utility, will be found under their respective title; but in the meantime we reiterate what we have already stated respecting this and other poisonous medicines, that they should never be administered by a domestic practitioner without the most urgent call to do so, such as distance from better advice, and the failure of other and safer remedies in a case becoming hopeless. The various forms in which the acid is administered will be found stated, but let it never be forgotten that a vial containing the acid should have a cork or stopper tied over by leather or bladder, and the vial plainly labelled - Prussic acid poison.

Appendix IV: Variations in Transcribing Testimony and Other Reports

THE CROSS-EXAMINATION OF DR. NOYES

This cross examination, near the beginning of the third day, provides a representative example of the differences between the three sources.

Boston Daily Times

Cross ex - I was once a student in Dr Coolidge's office and know that he was in the habit of keeping prussic acid on hand, a larger quantity than is usual with physicians, I should judge; Dr Thomas was a student with Dr Potter, at Waterville; Dr Coolidge maintained a good character, and I know nothing against his character for humanity, though I have heard reports prejudicial to his character, since this tragedy; do not remember, however, whether they were irrespective of this affair; I have been in practice at Waterville and about among the people there.

Portland Advertiser

Cross examined. - I was once a student in Dr. Coolidge's office in 1845, and he then kept prussic acid. He kept a larger stock of medicine than is usual with physicians. I do not know of this acid being used for experiments by students. He has had students. Dr. Boutelle was a student of his. I have known nothing but he had previously to this sustained a good character, and been humane.

Direct resumed. - I have since the affair heard reports against the character of Coolidge, but connected in some measure with this affair.

Maine Farmer

Cross-examined. - Was formerly a student of Dr. Coolidge; he kept a larger quantity than usual of prussic acid; Dr Boutelle formerly a student of Dr. Coolidge; have been acquainted with Dr. Coolidge since he came to Waterville; character good; humane in his practice.

Examination resumed. Have since the tragedy heard reports prejudicial to his character; don't remember to have heard anything against hm, irrespective of this transaction; remember none, but what are connected with this affair; have been in practice this season in Waterville.

Northern Tribune

Cross examined - Witness was a student in Dr. Coolidge's office a part of 1845 and 1846. Dr. C. kept prussic acid amongst his ordinary medicines - kept a larger assortment of medicines than physicians usually keep. Does not know that his students used the acid for experiments. Dr. C. has been in the habit of keeping students. Dr. Boutelle was a student there - afterwards Mr. Flint. Does not know that Dr. Thomas was a student there - he was with Dr. Potter. Has been acquainted with Dr. C. ever since he came to Waterville - knows nothing against his good reputation as a citizen, or as a humane physician.

Question by Mr. Morrill. Have you not heard things against the character of Dr. Coolidge at any time, aside from this transaction? This question was objected to by Mr. Evans. The Court said the inquiry must be confined to general reputation. Mr. Morrill then asked if the witness had heard reports prejudicial to the character of Dr. Coolidge. He answered that he had since this tragedy, but did not remember having any unconnected with this affair. Had been in practice in Waterville recently, and has been amongst there people in that vicinity.

Question by Attorney General. Have you heard any other charge against Dr. Coolidge, than that of murder? Objected to, and not allowed by the Court.

Among the variations in this brief cross-examination (ignoring spelling) are

The Boston Daily Times and the Maine farmer agree that Dr. Coolidge kept more prussic acid than most physicians; The Portland Advertiser reports that the doctor kept a larger stock of medicine than is usual for physicians, without singling out prussic acid. From the Bath Tribune we learn it was one of his ordinary medications.

The Boston Daily Times and the Northern Tribune record that Dr Thomas was a student of Dr. Potter's at Waterville.

The way the testimony on Dr. Coolidge's character is recorded varies in all four cases. From the Boston Daily Times, Noyes had heard things against his character since this tragedy; The Portland advertiser "had known nothing but he had previously to this sustained a good character, and been humane"; the Maine Farmer: "character good; humane in his practice." The Northern Tribune reports more questions about character, including several objected to.

THE POST MORTEM OF DR. COOLIDGE

The Lime Rock Gazette, which was local to the state prison, reports nothing substantive from the autopsy. The Advertiser has more detail from the autopsy, the nature of which caused other physicians to question the autopsy's validity.

The Portland Advertiser
(May 29th, 1849. Taken from the Boston Herald)
The next day (Saturday) a post mortem examination was had by Drs. Buxton and Rose, but without finding any lesions or indications of disease sufficiently grave to account for this death; and they entirely agreed that it was probably occasioned by the extreme mental depression and loss of energy which the sudden exposure of his schemes had occasioned. His brain was perfectly sound and healthy in every respect, and his lungs though affording some slight proof of former disease, presented no appearance worthy of notice. His heart was excessively small, weighting but nine and a quarter ounces, two thirds of which weight was appropriated by the left ventricle, the walls of the right ventricle not exceeding a sixteenth of an inch in thickness, and the auricles being so small as to render it astonishing how such an organ could perform its necessary functions. The stomach was almost empty, containing nothing but a little fuel,

and the walls were very much corrugated or thickened midway between the cardiac and pyleric orifices. Internally it was throughout of a uniform bright scarlet color, presenting no indications of active inflammation; neither were the vessels belonging to it in any degree turgid.

Lime Rock Gazette
(May 24, 1849)

A post mortem examination was held on Saturday morning and Dr's Rose and Buxton inform us that no signs of poison was discovered in his stomach; his lungs were slightly effected, but not sufficiently to cause death; his brain was perfectly sound and healthy; his heart was very small, weighing only 9 1/4 ounces. It is the general opinion that he died in a fit, brought on by extreme mental depression, and the general prostration of the whole nervous system, caused by the sudden frustration of his long fostered hope.

Appendix V: The Career of Dr. Thomas Flint

The following description of Thomas Flint's life subsequent to the Coolidge trial is taken from Barrows and Ingersoll - A Memorial and Biographical History of the Coast Counties of Central California, published in 1893. An introductory section with genealogical information is omitted. The details in this account, particularly of his early years, are so complete that it can only have come from Flint himself in consultation with his journals (see Sources for more information on his journals).

Dr. Thomas Flint, with whose name this sketch commences, received his literary education in the high schools and academies of Anson, Skowhegan and North Yarmouth, Maine. At the age of twenty-one, he began the study of medicine with Dr. V. P. Coolidge, at Waterville, and later attended the Jefferson Medical College, Philadelphia, where he was graduated in 1849. While in attendance at the Jefferson Medical College, his thoughts were seriously turned toward California, but circumstances intervened to delay his departure until a later time. Leaving college, he returned to Anson, Maine, where he remained until 1851. His brother Benjamin had gone to California in the early days of the gold excitement, and the consummation of the Doctor's intention to do so had only been deferred by the fact that parties who were to accompany him on the journey had been delayed. Meantime, he practiced medicine causally [*sic*], but in May, 1851, he went to New York to begin the sea voyage to California. He secured passage on the steamer "Crescent City, " which left New York harbor on May 28, arriving at Chagres on June 6. On the following day an incident occurred, which seriously threatened to mar the pleasure of the journey. Captain Jewett of the Chagres river steamboat, in violation of the terms of the contract, attempted to transfer the passengers to small boats with native boatmen, to continue to trip to Gorgona. The passengers rebelled, and soon a collision was imminent, weapons being drawn on both sides. The interference of General Hitchcock of the United States Army, however, was the means of bringing out an understanding, and as a result their Captain took them to Gorgona by steamer. Small boats manned by naked natives with long poles, conveyed them to Cruces, and from there they proceeded by foot, sending their baggage on by express. Two days, the 8th and 9th of June, were consumed in the foot journey to Panama, at which port they remained until the 15th, when they boarded the steamer "Northerner," on which the journey was to be completed. She sailed on June 16, and reached San Francisco by river steamer, and thence proceeded to Volcano (now Amador county), where he mined a little. On August 8, he started for Coloma, where he remained until January 9, 1852, engaged in mining to some extent and in the cattle and beef business. He returned from Coloma to Volcano, and there soon found himself incidentally attending to quite an extensive medical practice. The residents of Volcano at that time will recall the 3d of November, when Rod Stowell shot and stabbed Frank Kerns nearly to death at Fort John, near that place. "Old Rod" as he was called had established his reputation as a "tough customer" from his having shot and killed an Indian, and having pinned a gambling companion to the floor with his bowie knife sticking through his head. It was expected that Frank's wounds would soon prove fatal, so a vigilance committee was organized which had "Old Rod" arrested and held under guard for a lynch trial. Frank recovered, which circumstance kept "Old Rod's" neck from being stretched, and brought Dr. Flint fame as a skillful surgeon.

On Christmas day, 1852, he started on his return East, making the journey via Panama, and visited his old friends and relatives in the State of Maine. In the spring of 1853, he started again for California, this time overland, as had been his intention on coming East. He went to Terre haute, Indiana, the most westerly point which could then be reached by rail, and there was formed the firm of Flint, Bixby & Company, which afterward became so widely known through its extensive operations in California, composed of Dr. Thomas Flint, his brother Benjamin, and Llewellyn Bixby, his cousin.

At Quincy, Illinois, they purchased sheep, and then started in earnest on their westward journey, crossing the Mississippi river at Keokuk, with 2,400 head of sheep, a team of fifteen yoke of oxen, some saddle horses and other stock. From Keokuk, those in charge of the stock proceeded across the State of Iowa to Council Bluffs, where they crossed the Missouri river on the ferry. Dr. Flint, however, went to St. Louis, purchased the remainder of the outfit, and took it by steamer to Council Bluffs, where the expedition was met. From the Missouri, they proceeded up the North Platte, by the old trail, and through the

South Pass and Echo Canon to Salt Lake. Considerable trouble was had with Indians, and on the Platte river they lost one man, killed by the savages. While encamped one night some Indians crept in at midnight, cut the horses loose and when a man was aroused by the noise, he was shot by the Indians, who then fled. At Salt Lake, 100 head of cattle were purchased and added to the outfit. They arrived at the Morman capital too late, however, to take the northern route across the mountains, and they consequently turned to the southward, taking what was known as Fremont's trail. At Provo, Utah, they fell in with Colonel Hollister, with whom were Messrs. Woodworth and William Perry, who afterward made their mark in California, and the two trains traveled more or less in company from Mountain Meadows, at which point they overtook Colonel Hollister's company.

They moved along leisurely, remaining some time at places where they found favorite camping grounds, and arrived at the Mission San Gabriel January 7, 1854, having passed the winter quite comfortably on the road. They remained in the vicinity of the mission until March, and then started northward along the coast and stopped at what is now Coyote Station, in the Santa Clara valley. In July, 1855, they came down to the San Juan valley, and in October following purchased the San Justo ranch of Francisco Perez Pacheco, who boasted of being an Aztec Indian, and also made the same claim for his wife, although she may have been part Spanish. Pacheco had purchased the land from General Jose Castro, to whom it had been granted by the Mexican Government. From this point, the firm of Flint, Bixby & Co. carried on their extensive operations, which made them a power in the State. No change has ever been made in its membership since its organization at Terre Haute, except by the death of Benjamin Flint, October 3, 1881, and since that time, the remaining partners have carried on the business. They were at first engaged principally in sheep-raising, but from time to time other interests were added. In 1858, the firm disposed of half the San Justo ranch to Mrs. Lucy A. Brown, sister of Colonel Hollister, from whom the property passed to Colonel Hollister, the deed of partition being made in 1861, and the land formally divided at that time, Dr. Flint making the choice of the portion of the ranch retained by his firm, this portion consisting of 14,000 acres. This land is varied as to its topography and productive character, but is all valuable. Its capabilities in some directions, and the progress made therein, are mentioned elsewhere.

In 1858, the firm of Flint, Bixby & Company, engaged the business of staging, and became the owners of the line between San Jose and Los Angeles. Later, this line was extended to San Diego, and for four years they transacted the passenger and express-carrying business, and carried the United States mail between those remote points, the enterprise being one of vast magnitude. Seven hundred head of horses were required as stock for carrying on this business, and three days were consumed on the trip between the terminal points. Stations were established throughout the entire line, at intervals of about twelve miles, and a schedule of six miles an hour was maintained throughout, including stops.

The firm conducted this line for twelve years, but when the extension of the railroad from the north began, the length of the line was gradually lessened. Their superintendent was William Buckley, and, in connection with him, they ran the Panamint stage line for two years, the run being at first from Caliente to Panamint, and later from Mojave to Panamint. They sold out their interests to William Hamilton.

In 1872, Flint, Bixby & Co. embarked in the beet sugar manufacturing business, as stockholders in the California Beet Sugar Company, being among the pioneers in this line on the Pacific coast. They built a large factory at Alvarado, importing the special machinery from Germany, and established a plant, having the capacity of fifty tons of sugar per day. This plant was moved from Alvarado to Soquel Santa Cruz County. During their experience in this industry, they manufactured large quantities of sugar, but the methods then in vogue were considerably more expensive than those of the present time; and when the market price of sugar fell below what it cost them to produce it, on account of the admission duty free of Sandwich Island sugars, they withdrew from the business.

During this time, they were also engaged in working the Cerro Bonita quicksilver mine in this county, which, though not now in operation, is still their property, as also the Monterey quicksilver mine. About the same time, Dr. Flint became interesting in the wool-shipping and commission business. in the firms of Perkins, Flint & Co., and B. P. Flint & Co., of San Francisco. Flint, Bixby & Co. have all along been interested in mining, both in this State and in Nevada, and so continue to the present. They also took part in the original organization of the Southern Pacific Railroad Company, and were the active workers in securing for the company the franchise and grant of land in San Francisco, and the preliminary work generally, and were represented in the directorate of the road; Benjamin Flint, of their firm, was the first vice-president of the Southern Pacific Company. Dr. Flint is now largely interested, by himself, through Flint, Bixby & Co., and through other partnerships, in land and stock, banking and other interests, and in their operations his firms have handled and owned vast tracts, part of which have since been disposed of. The firm of Irvine, Flint & Co., in which he was a partner, owned the San Joaquin ranch, and in that and the Lomas de Santiago and Santa Ana ranches, together, they had about 100,000 acres. At about the same time, Flint, Bixby & Co. owned the Huer-Huer ranch, in San Luis Obispo county, containing about 46,000 acres. As a member of the firm of J. Bixby & Co., he is an owner in 9,000 acres of the Cerritos ranch, 16,000 acres in the Palos Verdes ranch, and over 7,000 acres in the Alamitos ranch. Flint, Bixby & Co. also have other and smaller tracts in this and other counties and in the State of Washington, as well as real estate in San Francisco. Their stock interests are now principally in the line of cattle, of which they have something like 7,000 head of Durham and Holstein and their crosses. They still retain sheep interests, though not nearly so extensively as formerly. They were among the first on the coast to import Merino sheep from Vermont and New York, and were the first to pay such a price as $1,000 for a Merino ram, which price they paid to Hammond, of Vermont. It was considered at the time a foolish act on their part, but was a signally successful stroke of enterprise, and helped them gain the fame they achieved in connection with the sheep interest. They have sent sheep from their flocks on orders from Panama, from the Sandwich Islands, from Nevada, and other remote points. All of their sheep are either full blood or high grades.

Dr. Flint, besides his main business interests, is connected in various ways with a multiplicity of financial and other institutions. His interests in the old Los Angeles County Bank (now the Bank of America) are represented in the directorate through Bixby, Llewellyn & Jotham; he is a director in the Grangers' Business Association, of San Francisco; a director since organization in the Bank of Hollister; and in its allied savings bank department; president and director of the

Grangers' Union, at Hollister, director of the Somerset railroad, in Maine. He has also served as director of several mining companies with which he has been identified. Fraternally, he is one of the most prominent Masons in the State of California. He is Past Master of Texas Lodge, No. 46, F. & A. M., San Juan; is High Priest and Past High Priest of Hollister Chapter, No. 68, R. A. M.; Past Commander of Watsonville Commander, No. 22, Knights Templar; member of Islam Temple, Nobles of the Mystic Shrine, San Francisco; member of the San Francisco Council, No. 2, R. & S. M.; member of the High Priesthood; and is Grand Captain of the Host of the Grand Chapter, Royal Arch Masons; in the order of the Eastern Star, he is Past Grand Patron. He also belongs to Hollister Grange, Patrons of Husbandry. In political life, Dr. Flint has been prominently identified with the Republican party since its organization in the State, and has taken an active part in the councils of the party. He served old Monterey county as a member of the Board of Supervisors, and San Benito county in the same capacity after the division. In 1876 he was elected to the State Senate, and in that body represented for four years the counties of Monterey, San Benito and Santa Cruz. He is now a member of the State Central Committee of the Republican party, and has previously served a number of years thereon, and has been chairman of the Central Committee of this Congressional District. As a delegate from the State of California to the National Republican Convention he helped to nominate Blaine at Chicago, in 1884.

Dr. Flint was married at Woodstock, Vermont, on May 20, 1857, to Miss Mary A. Mitchell [*more genealogical details, and information on his family omitted.*]

In concluding this sketch of Dr. Flint, a brief mention of his personality is necessary. Through his life has been from boyhood an active one, and though his interests have been so vast and far reaching for so many years, requiring an almost inestimable amount of thought and attention, he is in manner one of the most quiet and unassuming of men, a quality, however, generally to be found in connection with real strength and stability of character. In all respects, Dr. Flint stands today, as he has for many years, one of the foremost citizens of California.

Photo of Flint sometime after 1860. Courtesy of the California Historical Society and University of Southern California. Libraries

Sources

Primary Sources

[No author.] Trial of Dr. Valorous P. Coolidge for the Murder of Edward Mathews, at Waterville, Maine" (As Reported for and published in the Boston Daily Times.). [No place, no date.]
Carelessly proofed, with misspellings and occasionally garbled sentences. The transcriber often had to guess at witness names. And the name of the defendant himself is misspelled, but that was very common. Sometimes transcript, sometimes paraphrase.

[No author]. Trial of Dr. V. P. Coolidge, for the Murder of Edward Mathews. Before the Supreme Judicial Court at Augusta, March 14, 1848. [Bath: Northern Tribune, 1848].
Detailed and well printed. The most complete account of testimony.

The Portland Advertiser. Portland, Maine. [Weekly Newspaper]. March 22, 1848 reports on days 1 though 5, Tuesday through Saturday. March 29, 1848 covers the remainder of the trial.
Level of detail varies, but contains more description than the Boston Daily Times.

Vose, R. H. "Dr. Coolidge's Trial". The Maine Farmer. Various dates,(March 16, 1838; April 8, 1848, and others) and also published as essentially an undated special issue of the newspaper covering four newspaper pages of very small type.
R. H. Vose was a former Governor of Maine. Another very good account. Has a very good transcript of Baker's ending address to the jury.

The Lime Rock Gazette. East Thomaston, Maine.
Appears to be the original source of the documents connected with Coolidge's plot of have Flint murdered, and Coolidge's subsequent death.

Sources

The Eastern Mail. Waterville Maine
The reporter for the mail was Edward Mitchell, a student at Waterville College and the grandson of the chief justice.

Secondary Accounts

Lawson, John D., LL.D. American State Trials. St. Louis, F. H. Thomas Law Book Company, 1915. Vol 3, pp. 732-802.
The most comprehensive collection of notable American trials, published in 17 large volumes between 1914 and 1936. Lawson mostly follows the Boston Daily Times account. He accepted that "there is very strong evidence that he made his escape with the connivance of someone in authority", but did not describe that evidence.

Marriner, Ernest. *Kennebec Yesterdays.* Waterville: Colby College Press, 1954. Pp. 238-264.
Very good and useful account, with information not printed elsewhere – for example, the actual address where the body was found (27 Main street), and the verbatim language of the appeal Evans wished to file after the sentence. Disregards the whole story of Coolidge plotting in prison against Flint, and the letters. Considers that the state prison was extremely lax; reports the story of the "young and beautiful woman" – with a large amount of gold – persuading the warden to aid Coolidge's escape. Regards the truth of Coolidge's survival as a mystery that will never be solved.

He does report several things that I believe are errors, including that William Mathews sold the Blade, rather than moving it himself to Boston; that there are no prison records of Coolidge at Thomaston (Coolidge is listed in the annual Warden's Report). Writes that Coolidge left Dartmouth without a degree but the Dartmouth College Catalogues published through the nineteenth century listed him under Doctors of Medicine for the class of 1844.

A Member of the Massachusetts Bar. *Mysteries of Crime, as Shown in Remarkable Capital Trials.* Boston: Samuel Walker & Co., 1869, with subsequent editions. See Chapter XX - "Murder of Edward Mathews.A Physician's Victim", pp. 361-372.

A summary of the case, with Flint's direct testimony in full. Many of the cases were taken from the Monthly Law Reporter. The author ends with "It was commonly believed that he escaped, under a pretense of death". This volume also contains an account of the previous Maine case of conviction for murder in the first degree, "The Wilson and Thorn Case."

Spalding, Dr. James A. "The Case of Dr. Coolidge, of Waterville, Me., 1847-1849." The Journal of the Maine Medical Association, Vol VIII, No, 8, March 1928. p. 217-240.

An excellent summary of the trial, with particular attention to the controversies on the death of Coolidge. He did not believe that Coolidge escaped from prison.

Other Sources and Materials for Background

A Catalogue of the Officers and Students of Dartmouth College, for the Academical Year 1843-44. Hanover: Dartmouth Press, 1843.

Listings for Coolidge in the medical school; requirements to be awarded an M.D. Degree. At some point in editions of the latter party of their nineteenth century, Dartmouth began spelling his name "Valorous".

Barrows, Henry D. And Ingersoll, Luther A. *A Memorial and Biographical History of the Coast Counties of Central California.* Chicago: The Lewis Publishing Company, 1893.

Includes a biographical sketch of Thomas Flint, and other incidental mentions.

Bond, Henry, M.D. *Early Settlers of Watertown, Massachusetts, including Waltham and Weston; to Which is Appended the Early History of the Town. Vol. I. Genealogies.* Boston: Little, Brown & Company, 1855.

Coolidge family background.

Coolidge, V. P., M.D. "Case of Internal Strangulation of the Ileum." *The Boston Medical and Surgical Journal,* 1847, Vol.36 (17), p.339-341.

An article written by Coolidge , and dated by him May 10, 1847, about a patient he attended with Drs. Thayer and Plaisted, and upon whom he performed an autopsy to determine the causes of death. The autopsy was attended by Prof. Loomis, Dr. Thayer, Dr. Boutelle, H.A. Smith, Esq and a medical student - a familiar cast of characters. He mentions the patient being for a time "under unprofessional treatment". Printed in full in Appendix I.

Downer, Alan S. "The Down East Screamer". The New England Quarterly,, Vol. 42, No. 2, June, 1969, pp. 181-200. JSTOR URL : https://www.jstor.org/stable/363664.
An account of the career of Amos Mann, the promoter of the controversy of Coolidge's escape from the state prison in Thomaston. An opponent of the medical establishment, a hostility returned seventy years later by Dr. James Spalding in the pages of the Maine Medical Journal cited in the secondary accounts.

Griffin, Joseph. History of the Press of Maine. Brunswick, 1879.
Not complete, but useful for tracing the histories of Maine newspapers in the mid-nineteenth century

Schriver, Edward. "Reluctant Hangman: the State of Maine and Capital Punishment, 1820-1887." The New England Quarterly, Vol. 63 No. 2, June, 1990, pp 271-287, JSTOR URL: https://www.jstor.org/stable/365802.
Schriver writes, in error, that the governor of Maine did not commute Coolidge's sentence. A very interesting survey of the sentiment for and against capital punishment in Maine during the mid-nineteenth century.

Westergaard, Waldemar (editor). "Diary of Thomas Flint: California to Maine and Return, 1851-1855." Annual Publications of the Historical Society of California Vol 12, No 3 (1923), pp. 53-127. Reprinted, 2021, Waterville Maine: pagesofpages.com. ISBN: 979-8709343993.
Flint's diary of his travels between Maine and California.

Annual Report of the Warden of the State Prison. Volumes for 1848, 1849, 1850, all part of the *Documents Printed by Order of the State Legislature of Maine.*

In 1848 Coolidge is listed as sentenced to handing; in 1849 his sentence is reported commuted to imprisonment for life. In 1850 there is a new warden.

Index

Names of persons from the jury pool, and testifying, are listed separately under the headings of "Jurors" and "Testimony".